The Prose Works of Jonathan Swift, Vol. VI; The Drapier's Letters

Jonathan Swift

[ZHINGOORA BOOKS]

This edition is published by
Zhingoora Books.

The Cover is Designed by Pallav Sethiya.

Apart from any fair dealing for the purposes of research or private study, or criti-cism or review, this publication may only be reproduced, stored or transmitted, in any form or by any means, with the prior permission in writing of the publishers. All disputes are subject to exclusive jurisdiction of Mandsaur Courts only. For any suggestions and feedback or book on new concept/domain, please contact us at the email given below.

zhingoora_books@yahoo.com

INTRODUCTION

In 1714 Swift left England for Ireland, disappointed, distressed, and worn out with anxiety in the service of the Harley Ministry. On his installation as Dean of St. Patrick's he had been received in Dublin with jeering and derision. He had even been mocked at in his walks abroad. In 1720, however, he entered for the second time the field of active political polemics, and began with renewed energy the series of writings which not only placed him at the head and front of the political writers of the day, but secured for him a place in the affections of the people of Ireland—a place which has been kept sacred to him even to the present time. A visitor to the city of Dublin desirous of finding his way to St. Patrick's Cathedral need but to ask for the Dean's Church, and he will be understood. There is only one Dean, and he wrote the "Drapier's Letters." The joy of the people of Dublin on the withdrawal of Wood's Patent found such permanent expression, that it has descended as oral tradition, and what was omitted from the records of Parliament and the proceedings of Clubs and Associations founded in the Drapier's honour, has been embalmed in the hearts of the people, whose love he won, and whose homage it was ever his pride to accept.

The spirit of Swift which Grattan invoked had, even in Grattan's time, power to stir hearts to patriotic enthusiasm. That spirit has not died out yet, and the Irish people still find it seasonable and refreshing to be awakened by it to a true sense of the dignity and majesty of Ireland's place in the British Empire.

A dispassionate student of the condition of Ireland between the years of Swift's birth and death—between, say, 1667 and 1745—could rise from that study in no unprejudiced mood. It would be difficult for him to avoid the conclusion that the government of

Ireland by England had not only degraded the people of the vassal nation, but had proved a disgrace and a stigma on the ruling nation. It was a government of the masses by the classes, for no other than selfish ends. It ended, as all such governments must inevitably end, in impoverishing the people, in wholesale emigration, in starvation and even death, in revolt, and in fostering among those who remained, and among those whom circumstances exiled, the dangerous spirit of resentment and rebellion which is the outcome of the sense of injustice. It has also served, even to this day, to give vitality to those associations that have from time to time arisen in Ireland for the object of realizing that country's self-government.

It may be argued that the people of Ireland of that time justified Swift's petition when he prayed to be removed from "this land of slaves, where all are fools and all are knaves"; but that is no justification for the injustice. The injustice from which Ireland suffered was a fact. Its existence was resented with all the indignation with which an emotional and spiritual people will always resent material obstructions to the free play of what they feel to be their best powers.

There were no leaders at the time who could see this, and seeing it, enforce its truth on the dull English mind to move it to saner methods of dealing with this people. Nor were there any who could order the resentment into battalions of fighting men to give point to the demands for equal rights with their English fellow-subjects.

Had Swift been an Irishman by nature as he was by birth, it might have been otherwise; but Swift was an Irishman by accident, and only became an Irish patriot by reason of the humanity in him which found indignant and permanent expression against oppression. Swift's indignation against the selfish hypocrisy of his fellow-men was the cry from the pain which the sight of man's inhumanity to man inflicted on his sensitive and truth-loving nature. The folly and baseness of his fellow-creatures stung him, as he once wrote to Pope, "to perfect rage and resentment." Turn where he would, he found either the knave as the slave driver, or the slave as a fool, and the latter became even a willing sacrifice. His indignation at the one was hardly greater than his contempt for the other, and his different feelings found trenchant expression in such writings as the "Drapier's Letters," the "Modest Proposal," and "Gulliver's Travels."

It has been argued that the *saeva indignatio* which lacerated his heart was the passion of a mad man. To argue thus seems to us to misunderstand entirely the peculiar qualities of Swift's nature. It was not the mad man that made the passion; it was rather the passion that made the man mad. As we understand him, it seems to us that Swift's was an eminently majestic spirit, moved by the tenderest of human sympathies, and capable of ennobling love—a creature born to rule and to command, but with all the noble qualities which go to make a ruler loved. It happened that circumstances placed him early in his career into poverty and servitude. He extricated himself from both in time; but his liberation was due to an assertion of his best powers, and not to a dissimulation of them. Had he been less honest, he might have risen to a position of great power, but it would have been at the price of those very qualities which made him the great man he was. That assertion cost him his natural vocation, and Swift lived on to rage in the narrow confines of a Dublin Deanery House. He might have flourished as the greatest of English statesmen—he became instead a monster, a master-scourger of men, pitiless to them as they had been blind to him. But monster and master-scourger as he proved himself, he always took the side of the oppressed as against the oppressor. The impulse which sent him abroad collecting guineas for "poor Harrison" was the same impulse which moved him in his study at the Deanery to write as "M.B. Drapier." On this latter occasion, however, he also had an opportunity to lay bare the secret springs of oppression, an opportunity which he was not the man to let go by.

No doubt Swift was not quite disinterested in the motives which prompted him to enter the political arena for the second time. He hated the Walpole Ministry in power; he resented his exile in a country whose people he despised; and he scorned the men who, while they feared him, had yet had the power to prevent his advancement. But, allowing for these personal incentives, there was in Swift such a large sympathy for the degraded condition of the Irish people, such a tender solicitude for their best welfare, and such a deep-seated zeal for their betterment, that, in measuring to him his share in the title of patriot, we cannot but admit that what we may call his public spirit far outweighed his private spleen. Above all things Swift loved liberty, integrity, sincerity and justice; and if it be that it was his love for these, rather than his love for the country, which inspired him to patriotic efforts, who shall say that he does not still deserve well of us. If a patriot be a man who nobly teaches a people to become aware of its highest functions as a nation, then was Swift a great patriot, and he better deserves that title than many who have been accorded it.

The matter of Wood's Halfpence was a trivial one in itself; but it was just that kind of a matter which Swift must instantly have appreciated as the happiest for his purpose. It was a matter which appealed to the commonest news-boy on the street, and its meaning once made plain, the principle which gave vitality to the meaning was ready for enunciation and was assured of intelligent acceptance. In writing the "Drapier's Letters," he had, to use his own words, seasonably raised a spirit among the Irish people, and that spirit he continued to refresh, until when he told them in his Fourth Letter, "by the Laws of God, of Nature, of Nations, and of your Country, you are, and ought to be, as free a people as your brethren in England," the country rose as one man to the appeal. Neither the suavities of Carteret nor the intrigues of Walpole had any chance against the set opposition which met them. The question to be settled was taken away from the consideration of ministers, and out of the seclusion of Cabinets into the hands of the People, and before the public eye. There was but one way in which it could be settled—the way of the people's will—and it went that way. It does not at all matter that Walpole finally had his way—that the King's mistress pocketed her *douceur*, and that Wood retired satisfied with the ample compensation allowed him. What does matter is that, for the first time in Irish History, a spirit of national life was breathed into an almost denationalized people. Beneath the lean and starved ribs of death Swift planted a soul; it is for this that Irishmen will ever revere his memory.

In the composition of the "Letters" Swift had set himself a task peculiarly fitting to his genius. Those qualities of mind which enabled him to enter into the habits of the lives of footmen, servants, and lackeys found an even more congenial freedom of play here. His knowledge of human nature was so profound that he instinctively touched the right keys, playing on the passions of the common people with a deftness far surpassing in effect the acquired skill of the mere master of oratory. He ordered his arguments and framed their language, so that his readers responded with almost passionate enthusiasm to the call he made upon them. Allied to his gift of intellectual sympathy with his kind was a consummate ability in expression, into which he imparted the fullest value of the intended meaning. His thought lost nothing in its statement. Writing as he did from the point of view of a tradesman, to the shopkeepers, farmers, and common people of Ireland, his business was to speak with them as if he were one of them. He had already laid bare their grievances caused by the selfish legislation of the English Parliament, which had ruined Irish manufactures; he had written grimly of the iniquitous laws which had destroyed the woollen trade of the country; he had not forgotten the condition of the people as he saw it on his journeys from Dublin to Cork—a condition which he was later to reveal in the most terrible of his satirical tracts—and he realized with almost personal anguish the degradation of the people brought about by the rapacity and selfishness of a class which governed with no thought of ultimate consequences, and with no apparent understanding of what justice implied. It was left for him to precipitate his private opinion and public spirit in such form as would arouse the nation to a sense of self-respect, if not to a pitch of resentment. The "Drapier's Letters" was the reagent that accomplished both.

* * * * *

The editor takes this opportunity to express his thanks and obligations to Mr. G.R. Dennis, to Mr. W. Spencer Jackson, to the late Colonel F.R. Grant, to Mr. C. Litton Falkiner of Killiney, and to Mr. O'Donoghue of Dublin. His acknowledgment is here also made to Mr. Strickland, of the National Gallery of Ireland, to whose kindness and learning he is greatly indebted.

TEMPLE SCOTT.

NEW YORK, *March*, 1903.

CONTENTS

LETTER I. TO THE SHOPKEEPERS, TRADESMEN, FARMERS, AND COMMON-PEOPLE OF IRELAND

LETTER II. TO MR. HARDING THE PRINTER

THE REPORT OF THE COMMITTEE OF THE LORDS OF HIS MAJESTY'S MOST HONOURABLE PRIVY-COUNCIL, IN RELATION TO MR. WOOD'S HALFPENCE AND FARTHINGS, ETC.

LETTER III. TO THE NOBILITY AND GENTRY OF THE KINGDOM OF IRELAND

LETTER IV. TO THE WHOLE PEOPLE OF IRELAND

SEASONABLE ADVICE TO THE GRAND JURY, CONCERNING THE BILL PREPARING AGAINST THE PRINTER OF THE DRAPIER'S FOURTH LETTER

LETTER V. TO THE LORD CHANCELLOR MIDDLETON

LETTER VI. TO THE RIGHT HONOURABLE THE LORD VISCOUNT MOLESWORTH

LETTER VII. AN HUMBLE ADDRESS TO BOTH HOUSES OF PARLIAMENT

APPENDIXES

I. ADDRESSES TO THE KING

II. REPORT OF THE ASSAY ON WOOD'S COINAGE, MADE BY SIR ISAAC NEWTON, EDWARD SOUTHWELL, ESQ., AND THOMAS SCROOPE, ESQ.

III. TOM PUNSIBI'S DREAM

IV. A LETTER FROM A FRIEND TO THE RIGHT HONOURABLE ——

A SECOND LETTER FROM A FRIEND TO THE RIGHT HONOURABLE ——

V. THE PRESENTMENT OF THE GRAND JURY OF THE COUNTY OF THE CITY OF DUBLIN

VI. PROCLAMATION AGAINST THE DRAPIER

VII. REPORT OF THE IRISH PRIVY COUNCIL ON WOOD'S COINAGE

VIII. THE PATENTEE'S COMPUTATION OF IRELAND, IN A LETTER FROM THE AUTHOR OF THE "WHITEHALL EVENING POST" CONCERNING THE MAKING OF COPPER COIN

IX. DESCRIPTIONS OF THE VARIOUS SPECIMENS OF WOOD'S COINS

PLATES.

JONATHAN SWIFT. From a painting in the National Gallery of Ireland, ascribed to Francis Bindon

HALFPENCE AND FARTHINGS coined by William Wood, 1722 and 1723

[Illustration: *Half-pence & farthings coined by William Wood, 1722 & 1723*]

LETTER I.

TO THE SHOP-KEEPERS, TRADESMEN, FARMERS, AND COMMON-PEOPLE OF IRELAND.

NOTE

About the year 1720 it was generally acknowledged in Ireland that there was a want there of the small change, necessary in the transaction of petty dealings with shopkeepers and tradesmen. It has been indignantly denied by contemporary writers that this small change meant copper coins. They asserted that there was no lack of copper money, but that there was a great want of small silver. Be that as it may, the report that small change was wanting was sufficiently substantiated to the English government to warrant it to proceed to satisfy the want. In its dealings with Ireland, however, English governments appear to have consistently assumed that attitude which would most likely cause friction and arouse disturbance. In England coins for currency proceeded from a mint established under government supervision. In Scotland such a mint was specially provided for in the Act of Union. But in Ireland, the government acted otherwise.

The Irish people had again and again begged that they should be permitted to establish a mint in which coins could be issued of the same standard and intrinsic value as those used in England. English parliaments, however, invariably disregarded these petitions. Instead of the mint the King gave grants or patents by which a private individual obtained the right to mint coins for the use of the inhabitants. The right was most often given for a handsome consideration, and held for a term of years. In 1660 Charles II. granted such a patent to Sir Thomas Armstrong, permitting him to coin farthings for twenty years. It appears, however, that Armstrong never actually coined the farthings, although he had gone to the expense of establishing a costly plant for the purpose.

Small copper coins becoming scarce, several individuals, without permission, issued tokens; but the practice was stopped. In 1680 Sir William Armstrong, son of Sir Thomas, with Colonel George Legg (afterwards Lord Dartmouth), obtained a patent for twenty-one years, granting them the right to issue copper halfpence. Coins were actually struck and circulated, but the patent itself was sold to John Knox in the very year of its issue. Knox, however, had his patent specially renewed, but his coinage was interrupted when James II. issued his debased money during the Revolution (see Monck Mason, p. 334, and the notes on this matter to the Drapier's Third Letter, in present edition).

Knox sold his patent to Colonel Roger Moore, who overstocked the country with his coins to such an extent that the currency became undervalued. When, in 1705, Moore endeavoured to obtain a renewal of his patent, his application was refused. By 1722, owing either to Moore's bad coinage, or to the importation of debased coins from other countries, the copper money had degraded considerably. In a pamphlet[1] issued by George Ewing in Dublin

(1724), it is stated that in that year, W. Trench presented a memorial to the Lords of the Treasury, complaining of the condition of the copper coinage, and pointing out that the evil results had been brought about by the system of grants to private individuals. Notwithstanding this memorial, it was attempted to overcome the difficulty by a continuance of the old methods. A new patent was issued to an English iron merchant, William Wood by name, who, according to Coxe, submitted proposal with many others, for the amelioration of the grievance. Wood's proposals, say this same authority, were accepted "as beneficial to Ireland." The letters patent bear the date July 12th, 1722, and were prepared in accordance with the King's instructions to the Attorney and Solicitor General sent in a letter from Kensington on June 16th, 1722. The letter commanded "that a bill should be prepared for his royal signature, containing and importing an indenture, whereof one part was to pass the Great Seal of Great Britain." This indenture, notes Monck Mason,[2] between His Majesty of the one part, "and William Wood, of Wolverhampton, in the County of Stafford, Esq.," of the other, signifies that His Majesty

"has received information that, in his kingdom of Ireland, there was a great want of small money for making small payments, and that retailers and others did suffer by reason of such want."

[Footnote 1: "A Defence of the Conduct of the People of Ireland in their unanimous refusal of Mr. Wood's Copper Money," pp. 22-23.]

[Footnote 2: "History of St. Patrick's Cathedral," note v, pp. 326-327.]

By virtue, therefore, of his prerogative royal, and in consideration of the rents, covenants, and agreements therein expressed, His Majesty granted to William Wood, his executors, assigns, etc., "full, free, sole, and absolute power, privilege, licence, and authority," during fourteen years, from the annunciation of the Blessed Virgin, 1722, to coin halfpence and farthings of copper, to be uttered and disposed of in Ireland, and not elsewhere. It was provided that the whole quantity coined should not exceed 360 tons of copper, whereof 100 tons only were to be coined in the first year, and 20 tons in each of the last thirteen, said farthings and halfpence to be of good, pure, and merchantable copper, and of such size and bigness, that one avoirdupois pound weight of copper should not be converted into more farthings and halfpence than would make thirty pence by tale; all the said farthings and halfpence to be of equal weight in themselves, or as near thereunto as might be, allowing a remedy not exceeding two farthings over or under in each pound. The same "to pass and to be received as current money, by such as shall or will, voluntarily and willingly, and not otherwise, receive the same, within the said kingdom of Ireland, and not elsewhere." Wood also covenanted to pay to the King's clerk or comptroller of the coinage, £200 yearly, and £100 per annum into his Majesty's treasury.

Most of the accounts of this transaction and its consequent agitation in Ireland, particularly those given by Sir W. Scott and Earl Stanhope, are taken from Coxe's "Life of Walpole." Monck Mason, however, in his various notes appended to his life of Swift, has once and for all placed Coxe's narrative in its true light, and exposed the specious special pleading on behalf of his hero, Walpole. But even Coxe cannot hide the fact that the granting of the patent and the circumstances under which it was granted, amounted to a disgraceful job, by which an opportunity was seized to benefit a "noble person" in England at the expense of Ireland. The patent was really granted to the King's mistress, the Duchess of Kendal, who sold it to William Wood for the sum of £10,000, and (as it was reported with, probably, much truth) for a share in the profits of the coining. The job was alluded to by Swift when he wrote:

> "When late a feminine magician,
> Join'd with a brazen politician,
> Expos'd, to blind a nation's eyes,
> A parchment of prodigious size."

Coxe endeavors to exonerate Walpole from the disgrace attached to this business, by expatiating on Carteret's opposition to Walpole, an opposition which went so far as to attempt to injure the financial minister's reputation by fomenting jealousies and using the Wood patent agitation to arouse against him the popular indignation; but this does not explain away the fact itself. He lays some blame for the agitation on Wood's indiscretion in flaunting his rights and publicly boasting of what the great minister would do for him. At the same time he takes care to censure the government for its misconduct in not consulting with the Lord Lieutenant and his Privy Council before granting the patent. His censure, however, is founded on the consideration that this want of attention was injudicious and was the cause of the spread of exaggerated rumours of the patent's evil tendency. He has nothing to say of the rights and liberties of a people which had thereby been infringed and ignored.

The English parliament had rarely shown much consideration for Irish feelings or Irish rights. Its attitude towards the Irish Houses of Legislation had been high-handed and even dictatorial; so that constitutional struggles were not at all infrequent towards the end of the seventeenth and during the first quarter of the eighteenth century. The efforts of Sir Constantine Phipps towards a non-parliamentary government,[3] and the reversal by the English

House of Lords of the decision given by the Irish House of Lords in the famous Annesley case, had prepared the Irish people for a revolt against any further attempts to dictate to its properly elected representatives assembled in parliament. Moreover, the wretched material condition of the people, as it largely had been brought about by a selfish, persecuting legislation that practically isolated Ireland commercially in prohibiting the exportation of its industrial products, was a danger and a menace to the governing country. The two nations were facing each other threateningly. When, therefore, Wood began to import his coin, suspicion was immediately aroused.

[Footnote 3: See Lecky's "History of Ireland," vol. i., p. 446, etc.]

The masses took little notice of it at first; but the commissioners of revenue in Dublin took action in a letter they addressed to the Right Hon. Edward Hopkins, secretary to the Lord Lieutenant. This letter, dated August 7th, 1722, began by expressing surprise at the patent granted to Mr. Wood, and asked the secretary "to lay before the Lord Lieutenant a memorial, presented by their agent to the Lords of the Treasury, concerning this patent, and also a report of some former Commissioners of the revenue on the like occasion, and to acquaint his Grace, that they concurred in all the objections in those papers, and were of opinion, that such a patent would be highly prejudicial to the trade, and welfare of this kingdom, and more particularly to his Majesty's revenue, which they had formerly found to have suffered very much, by too great a quantity of such base coin."[4] No reply was received to this letter.

[Footnote 4: "A Defence of the Conduct of the People of Ireland," etc., p. 6.]

Fears began to be generally felt, and the early murmurs of an agitation to be heard when, on September 19th, 1722, the Commissioners addressed a second letter, this time to the Lords Commissioners of His Majesty's Treasury. The letter assured their Lordships "that they had been applied to by many persons of rank and fortune, and by the merchants and traders in Ireland, to represent the ill effects of Mr. Wood's patent, and that they could from former experience assure their Lordships, it would be particularly detrimental to his Majesty's revenue. They represented that this matter had made a great noise here, and that there did not appear the *least want of such small species of coin for change*, and hoped that the importance of the occasion would excuse their making this representation of a matter that had not been referred to them."[5]

[Footnote 5: *Ibid*, pp. 6-7.]

To this letter also no reply was vouchsafed. In the meantime, Wood kept sending in his coins, landing them at most of the ports of the kingdom.

"Then everyone that was not interested in the success of this coinage," writes the author of the pamphlet already quoted, "by having contracted for a great quantity of his halfpence at a large discount, or biassed by the hopes of immoderate gain to be made out of the ruins of their country, expressed their apprehensions of the pernicious consequences of this copper money; and resolved to make use of the *right they had by law to refuse the same*".[6]

[Footnote 6: *Ibid*, p. 7.]

The Lord Lieutenant, the Duke of Grafton, had arrived in August, 1723, and parliament sat early in September. Its first attention was paid to the Wood patent. After the early excitement had subsided, they resolved to appeal to the King. During the early stages of the discussion, however, the Commons addressed the Lord Lieutenant, asking that a copy of the patent and other papers relating to it, be laid before them. This was on September 13th. On the following day Mr. Hopkins informed the House that the Lord Lieutenant had no such copy, nor any papers. The House then unanimously resolved to inquire into the matter on its own account, and issued orders for several persons to appear before it to give evidence, fixing the day for examination for September 16th. On that day, however, Mr. Hopkins appeared before the members with a copy of the patent, and informed them that the Lord Lieutenant had received it since his last communication with them. This incident served but to arouse further ridicule. A broadside, published at the time with the title "A Creed of an Irish Commoner," amusingly reveals the lameness of the excuse for this non-production of the exemplification. Coxe says that the cause for the delay was due to the fact that the copy of the patent had been delivered to the Lord Lieutenant's servant, instead of to his private secretary; but this excuse is probably no more happily founded than the one offered.

On Friday, September 20th, the House resolved itself into a committee "to take into consideration the state of the nation, particularly in relation to the importing and uttering of copper halfpence and farthings in this kingdom." After three days' debate, and after examining competent witnesses under oath, it passed resolutions to the following effect

(1) That Wood's patent is highly prejudicial to his Majesty's revenue, and is destructive of trade and commerce, and most dangerous to the rights and properties of the subject.

(2) That for the purpose of obtaining the patent Wood had notoriously misrepresented the state of the nation.

(3) That great quantities of the coin had been imported of different impressions and of much less weight than the patent called for.

(4) That the loss to the nation by the uttering of this coin would amount to 150 per cent.

(5) That in coining the halfpence Wood was guilty of a notorious fraud.

(6) "That it is the opinion of this Committee, that it hath been always highly prejudicial to this kingdom to grant the power or privilege of coining money to private persons; and that it will, at all times, be of dangerous consequence to grant any such power to any body politic, or corporate, or any private person or persons whatsoever."[7]

[Footnote 7: "Comm. Journals," vol. iii., pp. 317-325.]

Addresses to his Majesty in conformity with these resolutions were voted on September 27th.

The House of Lords passed similar resolutions on September 26th, and voted addresses embodying them on September 28th.[8]

[Footnote 8: "Lords' Journals," vol. ii., pp. 745-751.]

These Addresses received a better attention than did the letters from the revenue commissioners. The Houses were courteously informed that their communications would receive His Majesty's careful consideration. Walpole kept his promise, but not before he had fought hard to maintain the English prerogative, as he might have called it. The "secret" history as narrated in Coxe's lively manner, throws some light on the situation. Coxe really finds his hero's conduct not marked with "his usual caution." The Lord Lieutenant was permitted to go to Ireland without proper instructions; the information on which Walpole acted was not reliable; and he did not sufficiently appreciate the influence of Chancellor Midleton and his family. "He bitterly accused Lord Midleton of treachery and low cunning, of having made, in his speeches, distinction between the King and his ministers, of caballing with Carteret, Cadogan, and Roxburgh, and of pursuing that line of conduct, because he was of opinion the opposite party would gain the ascendency in the cabinet. He did not believe the disturbances to be so serious as they were represented, nor was he satisfied with the Duke of Grafton's conduct, as being solely directed by Conolly, but declared that the part acted by Conolly, almost excused what the Brodricks had done." Carteret complained to the King and proved to him that Walpole's policy was a dangerous one. The King became irritated and Walpole "ashamed." He even became "uneasy," and it is to be supposed, took a more "cautious" course; for he managed to conciliate the Brodricks and the powers in Dublin. But the devil was not ill long. The cabinet crisis resulted in the triumph of Townshend and Walpole, and the devil got well again. Carteret must be removed and the patent promoted. But Midleton and the Brodricks must be kept friendly. So Carteret went to Ireland as Lord Lieutenant, Midleton remained Chancellor, and constituted a lord justice, and St. John Brodrick was nominated a member of the Privy Council. Still farther on his "cautious" way, Ireland must be given some consideration; hence the Committee of the Privy Council, specially called to inquire into the grievances complained of by the Irish Houses of Parliament in their loyal addresses.

The Committee sat for several weeks, and the report it issued forms the subject of Swift's animadversions in the Drapier's third letter. But the time spent by the Committee in London was being utilized in quite a different fashion by Swift in Ireland. "Cautious" as was Walpole, he had not reckoned with the champion of his political opponents of Queen Anne's days. Swift had little humour for court intrigues and cabinet cabals. He came out into the open to fight the good fight of the people to whom courts and cabinets should be servants and not self-seeking masters. Whatever doubts the people of Ireland may have had about the legal validity of their resentment towards Wood and his coins, were quickly dissipated when they read "A Letter to the Shop Keepers, Tradesmen, Farmers, and Common People of Ireland, concerning the Brass Half-pence coined by Mr. Wood," and signed, "M.B. Drapier." The letter, as Lord Orrery remarked, acted like the sound of a trumpet. At that sound "a spirit arose among the people, that in the eastern phrase, was *like unto a trumpet in the day of the whirlwind*. Every person of every rank, party, and denomination was convinced, that the admission of Wood's copper must prove fatal to the Commonwealth. The papist, the fanatic, the Tory, the Whig, all listed themselves volunteers under the banners of M.B. Drapier, and were all equally zealous to serve the Common cause."

The present text of the first of the Drapier's letters is based on that given by Sir W. Scott, carefully collated with two copies of the first edition which differed from each other in many particulars. One belonged to the late Colonel F. Grant, and the other is in the British Museum. It has also been read with the collection of the Drapier's Letters issued by the Drapier Club in 1725, with the title, "Fraud Detected"; with the London edition of "The Hibernian Patriot" (1730), and with Faulkner's text issued in his collected edition of Swift's Works in 1735.

[T.S.]

A
LETTER
TO THE
Shop-Keepers, Tradesmen, Farmers
and *Common-People* of
IRELAND,

Concerning the
Brass Half-pence
Coined by

Mr. Woods,

WITH
A *Design* to have them *Pass* in this
KINGDOM.

Wherein is shewn the Power of the said PATENT, the Value of the HALF-PENCE, and how far every Person may be oblig'd to take the same in Payments, and how to behave in Case such an Attempt shou'd be made by WOODS or any other Person.

[Very Proper to be kept in every FAMILY.]

By M.B. *Drapier*.

DUBLIN: Printed by *J. Harding* in *Molesworth's-Court.*]

LETTER I.

TO THE TRADESMEN, SHOP-KEEPERS, FARMERS, AND COMMON-PEOPLE IN GENERAL OF IRELAND.

BRETHREN, FRIENDS, COUNTRYMEN AND FELLOW-SUBJECTS,

What I intend now to say to you, is, next to your duty to God, and the care of your salvation, of the greatest concern to yourselves, and your children, your bread and clothing, and every common necessary of life entirely depend upon it. Therefore I do most earnestly exhort you as men, as Christians, as parents, and as lovers of your country, to read this paper with the utmost attention, or get it read to you by others; which that you may do at the less expense, I have ordered the printer to sell it at the lowest rate.

It is a great fault among you, that when a person writes with no other intention than to do you good, you will not be at the pains to read his advices: One copy of this paper may serve a dozen of you, which will be less than a farthing a-piece. It is your folly that you have no common or general interest in your view, not even the wisest among you, neither do you know or enquire, or care who are your friends, or who are your enemies.

About three[9] years ago, a little book was written, to advise all people to wear the manufactures of this our own dear country:[10] It had no other design, said nothing against the King or Parliament, or any man, yet the POOR PRINTER was prosecuted two years, with the utmost violence, and even some WEAVERS themselves, for whose sake it was written, being upon the JURY, FOUND HIM GUILTY. This would be enough to discourage any man from endeavouring to do you good, when you will either neglect him or fly in his face for his pains, and when he must expect only danger to himself and loss of money, perhaps to his ruin.[11]

[Footnote 9: In his reprint of the Drapier's Letters, issued in 1725 with the title, "Fraud Detected; or the Hibernian Patriot," Faulkner prints "four" instead of "three"; but this, of course, is a correction made to agree with the date of the publication of this reprint. The "Proposal" was published in 1720. [T.S.]]

[Footnote 10: The "little book" was "A Proposal for the Universal Use of Irish Manufactures." See vol. vii. [T.S.]]

[Footnote 11: Instead of the words "loss of money," Faulkner in the reprint of 1725 has "to be fined and imprisoned." [T.S.]]

However I cannot but warn you once more of the manifest destruction before your eyes, if you do not behave yourselves as you ought.

I will therefore first tell you the plain story of the fact; and then I will lay before you how you ought to act in common prudence, and according to the laws of your country.

The fact is thus: It having been many years since COPPER HALFPENCE OR FARTHINGS were last coined in this kingdom, they have been for some time very scarce,[12] and many counterfeits passed about under the name of *raps*, several applications were made to England, that we might have liberty to coin new ones, as in former times we did; but they did not succeed. At last one Mr. Wood,[13] a mean ordinary man, a hardware dealer, procured a patent[14] under his Majesty's broad seal to coin fourscore and ten thousand pounds[15] in copper for this kingdom, which patent however did not oblige any one here to take them, unless they pleased. Now you must know, that the halfpence and farthings in England pass for very little more than they are worth. And if you should beat them to pieces, and sell them to the brazier you would not lose above a penny in a shilling. But Mr. Wood made his halfpence of such base metal, and so much smaller than the English ones, that the brazier would not give you above a penny of good money for a shilling of his; so that this sum of fourscore and ten thousand pounds in good gold and silver, must be given for trash that will not be worth above eight or nine thousand pounds real value. But this is not the worst, for Mr. Wood when he pleases may by stealth send over another and another fourscore and ten thousand pounds, and buy all our goods for eleven parts in twelve, under the value. For example, if a hatter sells a dozen of hats for five shillings a-piece, which amounts to three pounds, and receives the payment in Mr. Wood's coin, he really receives only the value of five shillings.

[Footnote 12: They had become scarce because they had been undervalued, and therefore sent out of the country in payment of goods bought. See Prior's "Observations on Coin," issued in 1729, where it is stated that this scarcity had occurred only within the last twenty years. [T.S.]]

[Footnote 13: William Wood (1671-1730) was an ironmaster of Wolverhampton. In addition to the patent for coining copper halfpence which he obtained for Ireland, and to which full reference is made in the introductory note to this first Drapier's Letter, Wood also obtained a patent, in 1722, for coining halfpence, pence and twopence for the English colonies in America. This latter patent fared no better than the Irish one. The coins introduced in America bear the dates 1722 and 1723, and are now much sought after by collectors. They are known as the Rosa American coinage. A list of the poems and pamphlets on Wood, during the excitement in Dublin, attending on the Drapier's Letters, will be found in the bibliography of Swift's works to be given in vol. xi. of this edition. See also Monck Mason's "History of St. Patrick's Cathedral." In the original edition of the Letter, Wood's name is mis-spelt Woods. [T. S.]]

[Footnote 14: See the introductory note for the manner in which this patent was obtained. [T.S.]]

[Footnote 15: This is how the amount is named in the first edition; but the amount in reality was £100,800 (the value of 360 tons of copper, as stated by the patent). Sir W. Scott prints this as £108,000. Coxe, in his "Memoirs of Sir Robert Walpole" gives the amount as £100,000. Lecky states it as £108,000. [T.S.]]

Perhaps you will wonder how such an ordinary fellow as this Mr. Wood could have so much interest as to get His Majesty's broad seal for so great a sum of bad money, to be sent to this poor country, and that all the nobility and gentry here could not obtain the same favour, and let us make our own halfpence, as we used to do. Now I will make that matter very plain. We are at a great distance from the King's court, and have nobody there to solicit for us, although a great number of lords and squires, whose estates are here, and are our countrymen, spending all their lives and fortunes there. But this same Mr. Wood was able to attend constantly for his own interest; he is an Englishman and had great friends, and it seems knew very well where to give money, to those that would speak to others that could speak to the King and could tell a fair story. And His Majesty, and perhaps the great lord or lords who advised him, might think it was for our country's good; and so, as the lawyers express it, "the King was deceived in his grant," which often happens in all reigns. And I am sure if His Majesty knew that such a patent, if it should take effect according to the desire of Mr. Wood, would utterly ruin this kingdom, which hath given such great proofs of its loyalty, he would immediately recall it, and perhaps shew his displeasure to somebody or other. But "a word to the wise is enough." Most of you must have heard, with what anger our honourable House of Commons received an account of this Wood's patent.[16] There were several fine speeches made upon it, and plain proofs that it was all A WICKED CHEAT from the bottom to the top, and several smart votes were printed, which that same Wood had the assurance to answer likewise in print, and in so confident a way, as if he were a better man than our whole Parliament put together.[17]

[Footnote 16: The Irish House of Commons reported that the loss to the country, even if the patent were carried out as required, would amount to about 150 per cent.; and both Irish Houses of Parliament voted addresses against the coinage, and accused the patentee of fraud and deceit. They asserted that the terms of the patent had not been fulfilled and "that the circulation of the halfpence would be highly prejudicial to the revenue, destructive of the commerce, and of most dangerous consequences to the rights and properties of the subjects." See introductory note. [T.S.]]

[Footnote 17: Wood's indiscreet retort was published in the "Flying Post" October 8th, 1723. Later he boasted that he would, with Walpole's assistance, "pour the coin down the throats of the people." [T.S.]]

This Wood, as soon as his patent was passed, or soon after, sends over a great many barrels of these halfpence, to Cork and other seaport towns,[18] and to get them off offered an hundred pounds in his coin for seventy or eighty in silver. But the collectors of the King's customs very honestly refused to take them, and so did almost everybody else. And since the Parliament hath condemned them, and desired the King that they might be stopped, all the kingdom do abominate them.

[Footnote 18: At Dublin, Cork, Waterford and other ports, the merchants refused to accept the copper coins. Monck Mason notes that "in the 'Dublin Gazette,' No. 2562, we meet with resolutions by the merchants of Cork, dated the 25th of Aug., 1724, and like resolutions by those of Waterford, dated 22d Aug. wherein they declare, that, 'they will never receive or utter in any payment, the halfpence or farthings coined by William Wood; as they conceive the importing and uttering the same, to be highly prejudicial to His Majesty's revenue, and to the trade of the kingdom': these resolutions are declared to be conformable to those of the Trinity Guild, of merchants, of the city of Dublin, voted at their guild-hall, on the 18th day of the same month" (Hist. St. Patrick's, p. 346, note r). See also Appendix No. IX. [T.S.]]

But Wood is still working underhand to force his halfpence upon us, and if he can by help of his friends in England prevail so far as to get an order that the commissioners and collectors of the King's money shall receive them, and that the army is to be paid with them, then he thinks his work shall be done. And this is the difficulty you will be under in such a case. For the common soldier when he goes to the market or alehouse will offer this money, and if it be refused, perhaps he will swagger and hector, and threaten to beat the butcher or alewife, or take the goods by force, and throw them the bad halfpence. In this and the like cases, the shopkeeper or victualler, or any other tradesman has no more to do, than to demand ten times the price of his goods, if it is to be paid in Wood's money; for example, twenty-pence of that money for a quart of ale, and so in all things else, and not part with his goods till he gets the money.

For suppose you go to an alehouse with that base money, and the landlord gives you a quart for four of these halfpence, what must the victualler do? His brewer will not be paid in that coin, or if the brewer should be such a fool, the farmers will not take it from them for their bere,[19] because they are bound by their leases to pay their rents in good and lawful money of England, which this is not, nor of Ireland neither, and the 'squire their landlord will never be so bewitched to take such trash for his land, so that it must certainly stop somewhere or other, and wherever it stops it is the same thing, and we are all undone.

[Footnote 19: Bere = barley. Cf. A.S. *baerlic*, Icelandic, *barr*, meaning barley, the grain used for making malt for the preparation of beer. [T.S.]]

The common weight of these halfpence is between four and five to an ounce, suppose five, then three shillings and fourpence will weigh a pound, and consequently twenty shillings will weigh six pound butter weight. Now there are many hundred farmers who pay two hundred pound a year rent. Therefore when one of these farmers comes with his half-year's rent, which is one hundred pound, it will be at least six hundred pound weight, which is three horse load.

If a 'squire has a mind to come to town to buy clothes and wine and spices for himself and family, or perhaps to pass the winter here; he must bring with him five or six horses loaden with sacks as the farmers bring their corn; and when his lady comes in her coach to our shops, it must be followed by a car loaden with Mr. Wood's money. And I hope we shall have the grace to take it for no more than it is worth.

They say 'Squire Conolly[20] has sixteen thousand pounds a year, now if he sends for his rent to town, as it is likely he does, he must have two hundred and forty horses to bring up his half-year's rent, and two or three great cellars in his house for stowage. But what the bankers will do I cannot tell. For I am assured, that some great bankers keep by them forty thousand pounds in ready cash to answer all payments, which sum, in Mr. Wood's money, would require twelve hundred horses to carry it.

[Footnote 20: William Conolly (d. 1729) was chosen Speaker of the Irish House of Commons on November 12th, 1715. He held this office until October 12th, 1729. Swift elsewhere says that Wharton sold Conolly the office of Chief Commissioner of the Irish Revenue for £3,000. Between the years 1706 and 1729 Conolly was ten times selected for the office of a Lord Justice of Ireland. The remark in the text as to Conolly's income is repeated by Boulter ("Letters," vol. i., p. 334), though the Primate writes of £17,000 a year. The reference to Conolly is of set purpose, because Conolly had advocated the patent as against Midleton's condemnation of it. [T.S.]]

For my own part, I am already resolved what to do; I have a pretty good shop of Irish stuffs and silks, and instead of taking Mr. Wood's bad copper, I intend to truck with my neighbours the butchers, and bakers, and brewers, and the rest, goods for goods, and the little gold and silver I have, I will keep by me like my heart's blood till better times, or till I am just ready to starve, and then I will buy Mr. Wood's money as my father did the brass money in K. James's time,[21] who could buy ten pound of it with a guinea, and I hope to get as much for a pistole, and so purchase bread from those who will be such fools as to sell it me.

[Footnote 21: James II., during his unsuccessful campaign in Ireland, debased the coinage in order to make his funds meet the demands of his soldiery. Archbishop King, in his work on the "State of the Protestants in Ireland," describes the evil effects which this proceeding had: "King James's council used not to stick at the formalities of law or reason, and therefore vast quantities of brass money were coined, and made current by a proclamation, dated 18th June, 1689, under severe penalties. The metal of which this money was made was the worst kind of brass; old guns, and the refuse of metals were melted down to make it; workmen rated it at threepence or a groat a pound, which being coined into sixpences, shillings, or half-crowns, one pound weight made about £5. And by another proclamation, dated 1690, the half-crowns were called in, and being stamped anew, were made to pass for crowns; so that then, three pence or four pence worth of metal made £10. There was coined in all, from the first setting up of the mint, to the rout at the Boyne, being about twelve months, £965,375. In this coin King James paid all his appointments, and all that received the king's pay being generally papists, they forced the protestants to part with the goods out of their shops for this money, and to receive their debts in it; so that the loss by the brass money did, in a manner, entirely fall on the protestants, being defrauded (for I can call it no better) of about, £60,000 per month by this stratagem, which must, in a few months, have utterly exhausted them. When the papists had gotten most of their saleable goods from their protestant neighbours, and yet great quantities of brass money remained in their hands, they began to consider how many of them, who had estates, had engaged them to protestants by judgments, statutes staple, and mortgages; and to take this likewise from them they procured a proclamation, dated 4 Feb. 1689, to make brass money current in all payments whatsoever." A proclamation of William III., dated July 10th, 1690, ordered that these crown pieces of James should pass as of equal value with one penny each. [T.S.]]

These halfpence, if they once pass, will soon be counterfeit, because it may be cheaply done, the stuff is so base. The Dutch likewise will probably do the same thing, and send them over to us to pay for our goods.[22] And Mr. Wood will never be at rest but coin on: So that in some years we shall have at least five times fourscore and ten thousand pounds of this lumber. Now the current money of this kingdom is not reckoned to be above four hundred thousand pounds in all, and while there is a silver sixpence left these blood-suckers will never be quiet.

[Footnote 22: The Dutch had previously counterfeited the debased coinage of Ireland and sent them over in payment for Irish manufactures. [T. S.]]

When once the kingdom is reduced to such a condition, I will tell you what must be the end: The gentlemen of estates will all turn off their tenants for want of payment, because as I told you before, the tenants are obliged by their leases to pay sterling which is lawful current money of England; then they will turn their own farmers, as too many of them do already, run all into sheep where they can, keeping only such other cattle as are necessary, then they will be their own merchants and send their wool and butter and hides and linen beyond sea for ready money and wine and spices and silks. They will keep only a few miserable cottiers.[23] The farmers must rob or beg, or leave their country. The shopkeepers in this and every other town, must break and starve: For it is the landed man that maintains the merchant, and shopkeeper, and handicraftsman.

[Footnote 23: "Unlike the peasant proprietor," says Lecky, "and also unlike the mediaeval serf, the cottier had no permanent interest in the soil, and no security for his future position. Unlike the English farmer, he was no capitalist, who selects land as one of the many forms of profitable investment that are open to him. He was a man destitute of all knowledge and of all capital, who found the land the only thing that remained between himself and starvation. Rents in the lower grades of tenancies were regulated by competition, but it was competition between a half-starving population, who had no other resources except the soil, and were therefore prepared to promise anything rather than be deprived of it. The landlord did nothing for them. They built their own mud hovels, planted their hedges, dug their ditches. They were half naked, half starved, utterly destitute of all providence and of all education, liable at any time to be turned adrift from their holdings, ground to the dust by three great burdens—rack-rents, paid not to the landlord but to the middleman; tithes, paid to the clergy—often the absentee clergy—of the church to which they did not belong; and dues, paid to their own priests" ("Hist, of Ireland," vol. i., pp. 214-215, ed. 1892). [T.S.]]

But when the 'squire turns farmer and merchant himself, all the good money he gets from abroad, he will hoard up or send for England, and keep some poor tailor or weaver and the like in his own house, who will be glad to get bread at any rate.

I should never have done if I were to tell you all the miseries that we shall undergo if we be so foolish and wicked as to take this CURSED COIN. It would be very hard if all Ireland should be put into one scale, and this sorry fellow Wood into the other, that Mr. Wood should weigh down this whole kingdom, by which England gets above a million of good money every year clear into their pockets, and that is more than the English do by all the world besides.

But your great comfort is, that as His Majesty's patent does not oblige you to take this money, so the laws have not given the crown a power of forcing the subjects to take what money the King pleases: For then by the same reason we might be bound to take pebble-stones or cockle-shells or stamped leather for current coin, if ever we should happen to live under an ill prince, who might likewise by the same power make a guinea pass for ten pounds, a shilling for twenty shillings, and so on, by which he would in a short time get all the silver and gold of the kingdom into his own hands, and leave us nothing but brass or leather or what he pleased. Neither is anything reckoned more cruel or oppressive in the French government than their common practice of calling in all their money after they have sunk it very low, and then coining it anew at a much higher value, which however is not the thousandth part so wicked as this abominable project of Mr. Wood. For the French give their subjects silver for silver and gold for gold, but this fellow will not so much as give us good brass or copper for our gold and silver, nor even a twelfth part of their worth.

Having said thus much, I will now go on to tell you the judgments of some great lawyers in this matter, whom I fee'd on purpose for your sakes, and got their opinions under their hands, that I might be sure I went upon good grounds.

A famous law-book, called "The Mirror of Justice,"[24] discoursing of the articles (or laws) ordained by our ancient kings declares the law to be as follows: "It was ordained that no king of this realm should change, impair or amend the money or make any other money than of gold or silver without the assent of all the counties," that is, as my Lord Coke says,[25] without the assent of Parliament.

[Footnote 24: This was an important legal treatise often quoted by Coke. Its full title is: "The Booke called, The Mirrour of Justices: Made by Andrew Home. With the book, called, The Diversity of Courts, And Their Jurisdictions ... London ... 1646." The French edition was printed in 1642 with the title, "La somme appelle Mirroir des Justices: vel speculum Justiciariorum, Factum per Andream Home." Coke quotes it from a manuscript, as he died before it was printed. [T.S.]]

[Footnote 25: 2 Inst. 576. [ORIG. ED.]]

This book is very ancient, and of great authority for the time in which it was wrote, and with that character is often quoted by that great lawyer my Lord Coke.[26] By the law of England, the several metals are divided into lawful or true metal and unlawful or false metal, the former comprehends silver or gold; the latter all baser metals: That the former is only to pass in payments appears by an act of Parliament[27] made the twentieth year of Edward the First, called the "Statute concerning the Passing of Pence," which I give you here as I got it translated into English, for some of our laws at that time, were, as I am told writ in Latin: "Whoever in buying or selling presumeth to refuse an halfpenny or farthing of lawful money, bearing the stamp which it ought to have, let him be seized on as a contemner of the King's majesty, and cast into prison."

[Footnote 26: 2 Inst. 576-577. [ORIG. ED.]]

[Footnote 27: 2 Inst. 577. [ORIG. ED.]]

By this statute, no person is to be reckoned a contemner of the King's majesty, and for that crime to be committed to prison; but he who refuses to accept the King's coin made of lawful metal, by which, as I observed before, silver and gold only are intended.

That this is the true construction of the act, appears not only from the plain meaning of the words, but from my Lord Coke's observation upon it. "By this act" (says he) "it appears, that no subject can be forced to take in buying or selling or other payments, any money made but of lawful metal; that is, of silver or gold."[28]

[Footnote 28: 2 Inst. 577. [ORIG. ED.]]

The law of England gives the King all mines of gold and silver, but not the mines of other metals, the reason of which prerogative or power, as it is given by my Lord Coke[29] is, because money can be made of gold and silver, but not of other metals.

[Footnote 29: 2 Inst. 577. [ORIG. ED.]]

Pursuant to this opinion halfpence and farthings were anciently made of silver, which is most evident from the act of Parliament of Henry the 4th. chap. 4.[30] by which it is enacted as follows: "Item, for the great scarcity that is at present within the realm of England of halfpence and farthings of silver, it is ordained and established that the third part of all the money of silver plate which shall be brought to the bullion, shall be made in halfpence and farthings." This shews that by the word "halfpenny" and "farthing" of lawful money in that statute concerning the passing of pence, are meant a small coin in halfpence and farthings of silver.

[Footnote 30: Swift makes an incorrect reference here. The act was 4
Henry IV., cap. 10. [T.S.]]

This is further manifest from the statute of the ninth year of Edward the 3d. chap. 3. which enacts, "That no sterling halfpenny or farthing be molten for to make vessel, nor any other thing by the goldsmiths, nor others, upon forfeiture of the money so molten" (or melted).

By another act in this King's reign[31] black money was not to be current in England, and by an act made in the eleventh year of his reign chap. 5. galley halfpence were not to pass, what kind of coin these were I do not know, but I presume they were made of base metal, and that these acts were no new laws, but farther declarations of the old laws relating to the coin.

[Footnote 31: The act against black money was passed in Henry IV.'s reign not Edward III.'s. The "galley halfpence" were dealt with by 9 Hen. IV., cap. 4. [T.S.]]

Thus the law stands in relation to coin, nor is there any example to the contrary, except one in Davis's Reports,[32] who tells us that in the time of Tyrone's rebellion Queen Elizabeth ordered money of mixed metal to be coined in the Tower of London, and sent over hither for payment of the army, obliging all people to receive it and commanding that all silver money should be taken only as bullion, that is, for as much as it weighed. Davis tells us several particulars in this matter too long here to trouble you with, and that the privy-council of this kingdom obliged a merchant in England to receive this mixed money for goods transmitted hither.[33]

[Footnote 32: This refers to Sir John Davies's "Abridgement of Sir Edward Coke's Reports," first published in 1651. Davies was Attorney-General for Ireland and a poet. His works have been collected
and edited by Dr. A.B. Grosart in the Fuller Worthies Library. [T.S.]]

[Footnote 33: Charles I., during the Civil War, paid his forces with debased coin struck by him. [T.S.]]

But this proceeding is rejected by all the best lawyers as contrary to law, the Privy-council here having no such power. And besides it is to be considered, that the Queen was then under great difficulties by a rebellion in this kingdom assisted from Spain, and whatever is done in great exigences and dangerous times should never be an example to proceed by in seasons of peace and quietness.

I will now, my dear friends to save you the trouble, set before you in short, what the law obliges you to do, and what it does not oblige you to.

First, You are obliged to take all money in payments which is coined by the King and is of the English standard or weight, provided it be of gold or silver.

Secondly, You are not obliged to take any money which is not of gold or silver, no not the halfpence, or farthings of England, or of any other country, and it is only for convenience, or ease, that you are content to take them, because the custom of coining silver halfpence and farthings hath long been left off, I will suppose on account of their being subject to be lost.

Thirdly, Much less are you obliged to take those vile halfpence of that same Wood, by which you must lose almost eleven-pence in every shilling.

Therefore my friends, stand to it one and all, refuse this filthy trash. It is no treason to rebel against Mr. Wood. His Majesty in his patent obliges nobody to take these halfpence,[34] our gracious prince hath no so ill advisers about him; or if he had, yet you see the laws have not left it in the King's power, to force us to take any coin but what is lawful, of right standard gold and silver, therefore you have nothing to fear.

[Footnote 34: The words of the patent are "to pass and to be received as current money; by such as shall or will, voluntarily and wittingly, and not otherwise, receive the same" (the halfpence and farthings). [T.S.]]

And let me in the next place apply myself particularly to you who are the poor sort of tradesmen, perhaps you may think you will not be so great losers as the rich, if these halfpence should pass, because you seldom see any silver, and your customers come to your shops or stalls with nothing but brass, which you likewise find hard to be got, but you may take my word, whenever this money gains footing among you, you will be utterly undone; if you carry these halfpence to a shop for tobacco or brandy, or any other thing you want, the shopkeeper will advance his goods accordingly, or else he must break, and leave the key under the door. Do you think I will sell you a yard of tenpenny stuff for twenty of Mr. Wood's halfpence? No, not under two hundred at least, neither will I be at the trouble of counting, but weigh them in a lump; I will tell you one thing further, that if Mr. Wood's project should take, it will ruin even our beggars; For when I give a beggar an halfpenny, it will quench his thirst, or go a good way to fill his belly, but the twelfth part of a halfpenny will do him no more service than if I should give him three pins out of my sleeve.

In short these halfpence are like "the accursed thing, which" as the Scripture tells us, "the children of Israel were forbidden to touch," they will run about like the plague and destroy every one who lays his hands upon them. I have heard scholars talk of a man who told a king that he had invented a way to torment people by putting them into a bull of brass with fire under it, but the prince put the projector first into his own brazen bull to make the experiment;[35] this very much resembles the project of Mr. Wood, and the like of this may possibly be Mr. Wood's fate, that the brass he contrived to torment this kingdom with, may prove his own torment, and his destruction at last.

[Footnote 35: It is curious to find Swift so referring to Phalaris, of whom he had heard so much in the days of the "Battle of the Books." [SIR H. CRAIK.]]

N.B. The author of this paper is informed by persons who have made it their business to be exact in their observations on the true value of these halfpence, that any person may expect to get a quart of twopenny ale for thirty-six of them.

I desire all persons may keep this paper carefully by them to refresh their memories whenever they shall have farther notice of Mr. Wood's halfpence, or any other the like imposture.

LETTER II.

TO MR. HARDING THE PRINTER.

NOTE.

Towards the beginning of the August of 1724, the Committee of Inquiry had finished their report on Wood's patent. Somehow, an advance notice of the contents of the report found its way, probably directed by Walpole himself, into the pages of a London journal, from whence it was reprinted in Dublin, in Harding's Newspaper on the 1st of August. The notice stated that the Committee had recommended a reduction in the amount of coin Wood was to issue to £40,000. It informed the public that the report notified that Wood was willing to take goods in exchange for his coins, if enough silver were not to be had, and he agreed to restrict the amount of each payment to 5-1/2_d_. But a pretty broad hint was given that a refusal to accept the compromise offered might possibly provoke the higher powers to an assertion of the prerogative.

Walpole also had already endeavoured to calm the situation by consenting to a minute examination of the coins themselves at the London Mint. The Lords Commissioners had instructed Sir Isaac Newton, the Master of the Mint, Edward Southwell, and Thomas Scroope, to make an assay of Wood's money. The report of the assayists was issued on April 27th, 1724;[1] and certified that the coins submitted had been tested and found to be correct both as to weight and quality. In addition to this evidence of good faith, Walpole had nominated Carteret in place of the Duke of Grafton to the Lord-Lieutenancy. Carteret was a favourite with the best men in Ireland, and a man of culture as well as ability. It was hoped that his influence would smooth down the members of the opposition by an acceptance of the altered measure. He was in the way in London, and he might be of great service in Dublin; so to Dublin he went.

[Footnote 1: A full reprint of this report is given in Appendix II.]

But Walpole had not reckoned with the Drapier. In the paragraph in Harding's sheet, Swift saw a diplomatist's move to win the game by diplomatic methods. Compromise was the one result Swift was determined to render impossible; and the Drapier's second letter, "To Mr. Harding the Printer," renews the conflict with yet stronger passion and with even more satirical force. It is evident Swift was bent now on raising a deeper question than merely this of the acceptance or refusal of Wood's halfpence and farthings. There was a principle here that had to be insisted and a right to be safeguarded. Mr. Churton Collins ably expresses Swift's attitude at this juncture when he says:[2] "Nothing can be more certain than that it was Swift's design from the very beginning to make the controversy with Wood the basis of far more extensive operations. It had furnished him with the means of waking Ireland from long lethargy into fiery life. He looked to it to furnish him with the means of elevating her from servitude to independence, from ignominy to honour. His only fear was lest the spirit which he had kindled should burn itself out or be prematurely quenched. And of this he must have felt that there was some danger, when it was announced that England had given way much more than it was expected she would give way, and much more than she had ever given way before."

[Footnote 2: "Jonathan Swift," pp. 179-180.]

This letter to Harding was but the preliminary leading up to the famous fourth letter "to the whole people of Ireland." It was also an introduction to, and preparation of the public mind for, the drastic criticism of the Privy Council's Report, the arrival of which was expected shortly.

The present text of this second letter is that given by Sir W. Scott, collated with the copies of the original edition in the possession of the late Colonel F. Grant and in the British Museum. It has also been compared with Faulkner's issue of 1725, in "Fraud Detected."

[T.S.]

LETTER
TO
Mr. *Harding* the Printer,
Upon Occasion of a

PARAGRAPH
IN HIS
News-Paper
of *Aug.* 1st.

Relating to Mr. *Wood's* Half-pence.

By M.B. *Drapier*.
AUTHOR of the LETTER to the
SHOP-KEEPERS, &c.

DUBLIN: Printed by *J. Harding*
in *Molesworth's-Court*.
]

LETTER II.

TO MR. HARDING THE PRINTER.

Sir, In your Newsletter of the 1st. instant there is a paragraph dated from London, July 25th. relating to Wood's halfpence; whereby it is plain what I foretold in my "Letter to the Shopkeepers, &c." that this vile fellow would never be at rest, and that the danger of our ruin approaches nearer, and therefore the kingdom requires NEW and FRESH WARNING; however I take that paragraph to be, in a great measure, an imposition upon the public, at least I hope so, because I am informed that Wood is generally his own newswriter. I cannot but observe from that paragraph that this public enemy of ours, not satisfied to ruin us with his trash, takes every occasion to treat this kingdom with the utmost contempt. He represents "several of our merchants and traders upon examination before a committee of council, agreeing that there was the utmost necessity of copper money here, before his patent, so that several gentlemen have been forced to tally with their workmen and give them bits of cards sealed and subscribed with their names." What then? If a physician prescribes to a patient a dram of physic, shall a rascal apothecary cram him with a pound, and mix it up with poison? And is not a landlord's hand and seal to his own labourers a better security for five or ten shillings, than Wood's brass seven times below the real value, can be to the kingdom, for an hundred and four thousand pounds?[3]

[Footnote 3: Thus in original edition. £108,000 is the amount generally given. See note on p. 15. [T.S.]]

But who are these merchants and traders of Ireland that make this report of "the utmost necessity we are under of copper money"? They are only a few betrayers of their country, confederates with

Wood, from whom they are to purchase a great quantity of his coin, perhaps at half value, and vend it among us to the ruin of the public, and their own private advantage. Are not these excellent witnesses, upon whose integrity the fate of a kingdom must depend, who are evidences in their own cause, and sharers in this work of iniquity?

If we could have deserved the liberty of coining for ourselves, as we formerly did, and why we have not *is everybody's wonder as well as mine*,[4] ten thousand pounds might have been coined here in Dublin of only one-fifth below the intrinsic value, and this sum, with the stock of halfpence we then had, would have been sufficient:[5] But Wood by his emissaries, enemies to God and this kingdom, hath taken care to buy up as many of our old halfpence as he could, and from thence the present want of change arises; to remove which, by Mr. Wood's remedy, would be, to cure a scratch on the finger by cutting off the arm. But supposing there were not one farthing of change in the whole nation, I will maintain, that five and twenty thousand pounds would be a sum fully sufficient to answer all our occasions. I am no inconsiderable shopkeeper in this town, I have discoursed with several of my own and other trades, with many gentlemen both of city and country, and also with great numbers of farmers, cottagers, and labourers, who all agree that two shillings in change for every family would be more than necessary in all dealings. Now by the largest computation (even before that grievous discouragement of agriculture, which hath so much lessened our numbers [6]) the souls in this kingdom are computed to be one million and a half, which, allowing but six to a family, makes two hundred and fifty thousand families, and consequently two shillings to each family will amount only to five and twenty thousand pounds, whereas this honest liberal hardwareman Wood would impose upon us above four times that sum.

[Footnote 4: Time and again Ireland had petitioned the King of England for the establishment of a mint in Dublin. Both Houses of Parliament addressed King Charles I. in 1634, begging for a mint which should coin money in Ireland of the same standard and values as those of England, and allowing the profits to the government. Wentworth supported the address; but it was refused (Carte's "Ormond," vol. i., pp. 79-80). When Lord Cornwallis's petition for a renewal of his patent for minting coins was presented in 1700, it was referred to a committee of the Lords Justices. In their report the Lords Justices condemned the system in vogue, and urged the establishment of a mint, in which the coining of money should be in the hands of the government and in those of a subject. No notice was taken of this advice. See Lecky's "Ireland," vol. i., p. 448 (ed 1892) [T.S.]]

[Footnote 5: Boulter stated that £10,000 or £15,000 would have amply fulfilled the demand ("Letters," vol. i., pp. 4, 11). [T.S.]]

[Footnote 6: It was not alone the direct discouragement of agriculture which lessened the population. This result was also largely brought about by the anti-Catholic legislation of Queen Anne's reign, which "reduced the Roman Catholics to a state of depression," and caused thousands of them to go elsewhere for the means of living. See Crawford's "Ireland," vol. ii., pp. 264-267. [T.S.]]

Your paragraph relates further, that Sir Isaac Newton reported an assay taken at the Tower of Wood's metal, by which it appears, that Wood had in all respects performed his contract[7]. His contract! With whom? Was it with the parliament or people of Ireland? Are not they to be the purchasers? But they detest, abhor, and reject it, as corrupt, fraudulent, mingled with dirt and trash. Upon which he grows angry, goes to law, and will impose his goods upon us by force.

[Footnote 7: For the full text of Newton's report see Appendix, No. II.
[T.S.]]

But your Newsletter says that an assay was made of the coin. How impudent and insupportable is this? Wood takes care to coin a dozen or two halfpence of good metal, sends them to the Tower and they are approved, and these must answer all that he hath already coined or shall coin for the future. It is true indeed, that a gentleman often sends to my shop for a pattern of stuff, I cut it fairly off, and if he likes it, he comes or sends and compares the pattern with the whole piece, and probably we come to a bargain. But if I were to buy an hundred sheep, and the grazier should bring me one single wether fat and well fleeced by way of pattern, and expect the same price round for the whole hundred, without suffering me to see them before he was paid, or giving me good security to restore my money for those that were lean or shorn or scabby, I would be none of his customer. I have heard of a man who had a mind to sell his house, and therefore carried a piece of brick in his pocket, which he shewed as a pattern to encourage purchasers: And this is directly the case in point with Mr. Wood's assay.[8]

[Footnote 8: Monck Mason remarks on this assay that "the assay-masters do not report that Mr. Wood's coinage was superior to that of former kings, but only to those specimens of such coinages as were exhibited by Mr. Wood, which, it is admitted were much worn. Whether the money coined in the preceding reign was good or bad is in fact nothing to the purpose." "'What argument,'" quotes

Monck Mason from the tract issued in 1724 entitled, "A Defence of the Conduct of the People of Ireland, in their unanimous refusal of Mr. Wood's Copper Money," "'can be drawn from the badness of our former coinages but this, that because we have formerly been cheated by our coiners, we ought to suffer Mr. Wood to cheat us over again? Whereas, one reason for our so vigorously opposing Mr. Wood's coinage, is, because we have always been imposed upon in our copper money, and we find he is treading exactly in the steps of his predecessors, and thinks he has a right to cheat us because he can shew a precedent for it.' In truth, there was a vast number of counterfeits of those coins, which had been imported, chiefly from Scotland, as appears from a proclamation prohibiting the Importation of them in 1697" ("History St. Patrick's Cathedral," p, 340, note d.) [T.S.]]

The next part of the paragraph contains Mr. Wood's voluntary proposals for "preventing any future objections or apprehensions."

His first proposal is, that "whereas he hath already coined seventeen thousand pounds, and has copper prepared to make it up forty thousand pounds, he will be content to coin no more, unless the EXIGENCES OF TRADE REQUIRE IT, though his patent empowers him to coin a far greater quantity."

To which if I were to answer it should be thus: "Let Mr. Wood and his crew of founders and tinkers coin on till there is not an old kettle left in the kingdom: let them coin old leather, tobacco-pipe clay or the dirt in the streets, and call their trumpery by what name they please from a guinea to a farthing, we are not under any concern to know how he and his tribe or accomplices think fit to employ themselves." But I hope and trust, that we are all to a man fully determined to have nothing to do with him or his ware.

The King has given him a patent to coin halfpence, but hath not obliged us to take them, and I have already shewn in my "Letter to the Shopkeepers, &c." that the law hath not left it in the power of the prerogative to compel the subject to take any money, beside gold and silver of the right sterling and standard.

Wood further proposes, (if I understand him right, for his expressions are dubious) that "he will not coin above forty thousand pounds, unless the exigences of trade require it." First, I observe that this sum of forty thousand pounds is almost double to what I proved to be sufficient for the whole kingdom, although we had not one of our old halfpence left. Again I ask, who is to be judge when the exigences of trade require it? Without doubt he means himself, for as to us of this poor kingdom, who must be utterly ruined if his project should succeed, we were never once consulted till the matter was over, and he will judge of our exigences by his own; neither will these be ever at an end till he and his accomplices will think they have enough: And it now appears that he will not be content with all our gold and silver, but intends to buy up our goods and manufactures with the same coin.

I shall not enter into examination of the prices for which he now proposes to sell his halfpence, or what he calls his copper, by the pound; I have said enough of it in my former letter, and it hath likewise been considered by others. It is certain that by his own first computation, we were to pay three shillings for what was intrinsically worth but one,[9] although it had been of the true weight and standard for which he pretended to have contracted; but there is so great a difference both in weight and badness in several of his coins that some of them have been nine in ten below the intrinsic value, and most of them six or seven.[10]

[Footnote 9: The report of the Committee of the Privy Council which sat on Wood's coinage, stated that copper ready for minting cost eighteen pence per pound before it was brought into the Mint at the Tower of London. See the Report prefixed to Letter III. and Appendix II., in which it is also stated that Wood's copper was worth thirteen pence per pound. [T.S.]]

[Footnote 10: Newton's assay report says that Wood's pieces were of unequal weight. [T.S.]]

His last proposal being of a peculiar strain and nature, deserves to be very particularly considered, both on account of the matter and the style. It is as follows.

"Lastly, in consideration of the direful apprehensions which prevail in Ireland, that Mr. Wood will by such coinage drain them of their gold and silver, he proposes to take their manufactures in exchange, and that no person be obliged to receive more than fivepence halfpenny at one payment."

First, Observe this little impudent hardwareman turning into ridicule "the direful apprehensions of a whole kingdom," priding himself as the cause of them, and daring to prescribe what no King of England ever attempted, how far a whole nation shall be obliged to take his brass coin. And he has reason to insult; for sure there was never an example in history, of a great kingdom kept in awe for above a year in daily dread of utter destruction, not by a powerful invader at the head of twenty thousand men, not by a plague or a famine, not by a tyrannical prince (for we never had one more gracious) or a corrupt administration, but by one single, diminutive, insignificant, mechanic.

But to go on. To remove our "direful apprehensions that he will drain us of our gold and silver by his coinage:" This little arbitrary mock-monarch most graciously offers to "take our manufactures in exchange." Are our Irish understandings indeed so low in his opinion? Is not this the very misery we complain of? That his cursed project will put us under the necessity of selling our goods for what is equal to nothing. How would such a proposal sound from France or Spain or any other country we deal with, if they should offer to deal with us only upon this condition, that we should take their money at ten times higher than the intrinsic value? Does Mr. Wood think, for instance, that we will sell him a stone of wool for a parcel of his counters not worth sixpence, when we can send it to England and receive as many shillings in gold and silver? Surely there was never heard such a compound of impudence, villainy and folly.

His proposals conclude with perfect high treason. He promises, that no person shall be *obliged* to receive more than fivepence halfpenny of his coin in one payment: By which it is plain, that he pretends to *oblige* every subject in this kingdom to take so much in every payment, if it be offered; whereas his patent obliges no man, nor can the prerogative by law claim such a power, as I have often observed; so that here Mr. Wood takes upon him the entire legislature, and an absolute dominion over the properties of the whole nation.

Good God! Who are this wretch's advisers? Who are his supporters, abettors, encouragers, or sharers? Mr. Wood will *oblige* me to take fivepence halfpenny of his brass in every payment! And I will shoot Mr. Wood and his deputies through the head, like highwaymen or housebreakers, if they dare to force one farthing of their coin upon me in the payment of an hundred pounds. It is no loss of honour to submit to the lion, but who, with the figure of a man, can think with patience of being devoured alive by a rat. He has laid a tax upon the people of Ireland of seventeen shillings at least in the pound; a tax I say, not only upon lands, but interest-money, goods, manufactures, the hire of handicraftsmen, labourers, and servants. Shopkeepers look to yourselves. Wood will *oblige* and force you to take fivepence halfpenny of his trash in every payment, and many of you receive twenty, thirty, forty payments in a day, or else you can hardly find bread: And pray consider how much that will amount to in a year: Twenty times fivepence halfpenny is nine shillings and twopence, which is above an hundred and sixty pounds a year, whereof you will be losers of at least one hundred and forty pounds by taking your payments in his money. If any of you be content to deal with Mr. Wood on such conditions they may. But for my own particular, "let his money perish with him." If the famous Mr. Hampden rather chose to go to prison, than pay a few shillings to King Charles 1st. without authority of Parliament, I will rather choose to be hanged than have all my substance taxed at seventeen shillings in the pound, at the arbitrary will and pleasure of the venerable Mr. Wood.

The paragraph concludes thus. "N.B." (that is to say *nota bene*, or *mark well*), "No evidence appeared from Ireland, or elsewhere, to prove the mischiefs complained of, or any abuses whatsoever committed in the execution of the said grant."

The impudence of this remark exceeds all that went before. First; the House of Commons in Ireland, which represents the whole people of the kingdom; and secondly the Privy-council, addressed His Majesty against these halfpence. What could be done more to express the universal sense and opinion of the nation? If his copper were diamonds, and the kingdom were entirely against it, would not that be sufficient to reject it? Must a committee of the House of

Commons, and our whole Privy-council go over to argue *pro* and *con* with Mr. Wood? To what end did the King give his patent for coining of halfpence in Ireland? Was it not, because it was represented to his sacred Majesty, that such a coinage would be of advantage to the good of this kingdom, and of all his subjects here? It is to the patentee's peril if his representation be false, and the execution of his patent be fraudulent and corrupt. Is he so wicked and foolish to think that his patent was given him to ruin a million and a half of people, that he might be a gainer of three or four score thousand pounds to himself? Before he was at the charge of passing a patent, much more of raking up so much filthy dross, and stamping it with His Majesty's "image and superscription," should he not first in common sense, in common equity, and common manners, have consulted the principal party concerned; that is to say, the people of the kingdom, the House of Lords or Commons, or the Privy-council? If any foreigner should ask us, "whose image and superscription" there is in Wood's coin, we should be ashamed to tell him, it was Caesar's. In that great want of copper halfpence, which he alleges we were, our city set up our Caesar's statue[11] in excellent copper, at an expense that is equal in value to thirty thousand pounds of his coin: And we will not receive his *image* in worse metal.

[Footnote 11: An equestrian statue of George I. at Essex Bridge, Dublin,
[F.]]

I observe many of our people putting a melancholy case on this subject. "It is true" say they, "we are all undone if Wood's halfpence must pass; but what shall we do, if His Majesty puts out a proclamation commanding us to take them?" This hath been often dinned in my ears. But I desire my countrymen to be assured that there is nothing in it. The King never issues out a proclamation but to enjoin what the law permits him. He will not issue out a proclamation against law, or if such a thing should happen by a mistake, we are no more obliged to obey it than to run our heads into the fire. Besides, His Majesty will never command us by a proclamation, what he does not offer to command us in the patent itself. There he leaves it to our discretion, so that our destruction must be entirely owing to ourselves. Therefore let no man be afraid of a proclamation, which will never be granted; and if it should, yet upon this occasion, will be of no force. The King's revenues here are near four hundred thousand pounds a year, can you think his ministers will advise him to take them in Wood's brass, which will reduce the value to fifty thousand pounds. England gets a million sterl. by this nation, which, if this project goes on, will be almost reduced to nothing: And do you think those who live in England upon Irish estates will be content to take an eighth or a tenth part, by being paid in Wood's dross?

If Wood and his confederates were not convinced of our stupidity, they never would have attempted so audacious an enterprise. He now sees a spirit hath been raised against him, and he only watches till it begins to flag, he goes about "watching" when to "devour us." He hopes we shall be weary of contending with him, and at last out of ignorance, or fear, or of being perfectly tired with opposition, we shall be forced to yield. And therefore I confess it is my chief endeavour to keep up your spirits and resentments. If I tell you there is a precipice under you, and that if you go forwards you will certainly break your necks. If I point to it before your eyes, must I be at the trouble of repeating it every morning? Are our people's "hearts waxed gross"? Are "their ears dull of hearing," and have "they closed their eyes"? I fear there are some few vipers among us, who, for ten or twenty pounds gain, would sell their souls and their country, though at last it would end in their own ruin as well as ours. Be not like "the deaf adder, who refuses to hear the voice of the charmer, charm he never so wisely."

Though my letter be directed to you, Mr. Harding, yet I intend it for all my countrymen. I have no interest in this affair but what is common to the public. I can live better than many others, I have some gold and silver by me, and a shop well furnished, and shall be able to make a shift when many of my betters are starving. But I am grieved to see the coldness and indifference of many people, with whom I discourse. Some are afraid of a proclamation, others shrug up their shoulders, and cry, "What would you have us do?" Some give out, there is no danger at all. Others are comforted that it will be a common calamity and they shall fare no worse than their neighbours. Will a man, who hears midnight robbers at his door, get out of bed, and raise his family for a common defence, and shall a whole kingdom lie in a lethargy, while Mr. Wood comes at the head of his confederates to rob them of all they have, to ruin us and our posterity for ever? If an highwayman meets you on the road, you give him your money to save your life, but, God be thanked, Mr. Wood cannot touch a hair of your heads. You have all the laws of God and man on your side. When he or his accomplices offer you his dross it is but saying no, and you are safe. If a madman should come to my shop with an handful of dirt raked out of the kennel, and offer it in payment for ten yards of stuff, I would pity or laugh at him, or, if his behaviour deserved it, kick him out of my doors. And if Mr. Wood comes to demand any gold and silver, or commodities for which I have paid my gold and silver, in exchange for his trash, can he deserve or expect better treatment?

When the evil day is come (if it must come) let us mark and observe those who presume to offer these halfpence in payment. Let their names, and trades, and places of abode be made public, that every one may be aware of them, as betrayers of their country, and confederates with Mr. Wood. Let them be watched at markets and fairs, and let the first honest discoverer give the word about, that Wood's halfpence have been offered, and caution the poor innocent people not to receive them.

Perhaps I have been too tedious; but there would never be an end, if I attempted to say all that this melancholy subject will bear. I will conclude with humbly offering one proposal, which, if it were put in practice, would blow up this destructive project at once. Let some skilful judicious pen draw up an advertisement to the following purpose.

That "Whereas one William Wood hardware-man, now or lately sojourning in the city of London, hath, by many misrepresentations, procured a patent for coining an hundred and forty thousand pounds[12] in copper halfpence for this kingdom, which is a sum five times greater than our occasions require. And whereas it is notorious that the said Wood hath coined his halfpence of such base metal and false weight, that they are, at least, six parts in seven below the real value. And whereas we have reason to apprehend, that the said Wood may, at any time hereafter, clandestinely coin as many more halfpence as he pleases. And whereas the said patent neither doth nor can *oblige* His Majesty's subjects to receive the said halfpence in any payment, but leaves it to their voluntary choice, because, by law the subject cannot be *obliged* to take any money except gold or silver. And whereas, contrary to the letter and meaning of the said patent, the said Wood hath declared that every person shall be *obliged* to take fivepence halfpenny of his coin in every payment. And whereas the House of Commons and Privy-council have severally addressed his

Most Sacred Majesty, representing the ill consequences which the said coinage may have upon this kingdom. And lastly whereas it is universally agreed, that the whole nation to a man (except Mr. Wood and his confederates) are in the utmost apprehensions of the ruinous consequences, that must follow from the said coinage. Therefore we whose names are underwritten, being persons of considerable estates in this kingdom, and residers therein, do unanimously resolve and declare that we will never receive, one farthing or halfpenny of the said Wood's coining, and that we will direct all our tenants to refuse the said coin from any person whatsoever; Of which that they may not be ignorant, we have sent them a copy of this advertisement, to be read to them by our stewards, receivers, &c."

[Footnote 12: In the first paragraph of this letter the sum was given as £104,000. [T.S.]]

I could wish, that a paper of this nature might be drawn up, and signed by two or three hundred principal gentlemen of this kingdom, and printed copies thereof sent to their several tenants; I am deceived, if anything could sooner defeat this execrable design of Wood and his accomplices. This would immediately give the alarm, and set the kingdom on their guard. This would give courage to the meanest tenant and cottager. "How long, O Lord, righteous and true."

I must tell you in particular, Mr. Harding, that you are much to blame. Several hundred persons have enquired at your house for my "Letter to the Shopkeepers, &c." and you had none to sell them. Pray keep yourself provided with that letter, and with this; you have got very well by the former, but I did not then write for your sake, any more than I do now. Pray advertise both in every newspaper, and let it not be *your* fault or *mine*, if our countrymen will not take warning. I desire you likewise to sell them as cheap as you can.

I am your servant,

M.B.

Aug. 4, 1724.

The Report of the Committee of the Lords of His Majesty's most honourable Privy-Council, in relation to Mr. Wood's Halfpence and Farthings, etc.[1]

AT THE COUNCIL CHAMBER AT WHITEHALL, THE 24TH DAY OF JULY, 1724.

In obedience to your Majesty's order of reference, upon the several resolutions and addresses of both Houses of Parliament of Ireland, during their late session, the late address of your Majesty's justices, and Privy-council of that kingdom, and the petitions of the county and city of Dublin, concerning a patent granted by your Majesty to William Wood Esq; for the coining and uttering copper halfpence and farthings in the kingdom of Ireland, to such persons as would voluntarily accept the same; and upon the petition of the said William Wood, concerning the same coinage, the Lords of the Committee have taken into their consideration the said patent, addresses, petitions, and all matters and papers relating thereto, and have heard and examined all such persons, as upon due and sufficient notice, were desirous and willing to be heard upon the subject matter under their consideration, and have agreed upon the following Report, containing a true state of the whole matter, as it appeared before them, with their humble opinion, to be laid before your Majesty for your royal consideration and determination, upon a matter of such importance.

[Footnote 1: For the story of the origin of this report see the Note prefixed to Letter III. [T.S.]]

The several addresses to your Majesty from your subjects of Ireland, contain in general terms the strongest representations of the great apprehensions they were under, from the importing and uttering copper halfpence and farthings in Ireland, by virtue of the patent granted to Mr. Wood, which they conceived would prove highly prejudicial to your Majesty's revenue, destructive of the trade and commerce of the kingdom, and of dangerous consequence to the properties of the subject. They represent, That the patent had been obtained in a clandestine and unprecedented manner, and by notorious misrepresentations of the state of Ireland; That if the terms of the patent had been complied with, this coinage would have been of infinite loss to the kingdom, but that the patentee, under colour of the powers granted to him, had imported and endeavoured to utter great quantities of different impressions, and of less weight, than required by the patent, and had been guilty of notorious frauds and deceit in coining the said copper money: And they humbly beseech your Majesty, that you would give such directions, as in your great wisdom you should think proper, to prevent the fatal effects of uttering any half pence or farthings by virtue of the said patent: And the House of Commons of Ireland, in a second address upon this subject, pray, That your Majesty would be pleased to give directions to the several officers intrusted in the receipt of your Majesty's revenue, That they do not on any pretence whatever, receive or utter any of the said copper halfpence or farthings.

In answer to the addresses of the Houses of Parliament of Ireland, your Majesty was most graciously pleased to assure them, "That if any abuses had been committed by the patentee, you would give the necessary orders for enquiring into and punishing those abuses; and that your Majesty would do everything, that was in your power, for the satisfaction of your people."

In pursuance of this your Majesty's most gracious declaration, your Majesty was pleased to take this matter into you royal consideration; and that you might be the better enabled effectually to answer the expectations of your people of Ireland, your Majesty was pleased by a letter from Lord Carteret, one of your principal secretaries of state, dated March 10, 1723-4, to signify your pleasure to your Lord Lieutenant of Ireland, "That he should give directions for sending over such papers and witnesses as should be thought proper to support the objections made against the patent, and against the patentee, in the execution of the powers given him by the patent."

Upon the receipt of these your Majesty's orders, the Lord Lieutenant, by his letter of the 20th of March, 1723-4, represented the great difficulty he found himself under, to comply with these your Majesty's orders; and by another letter of the 24th of March 1723-4, "after consulting the principal members of both Houses, who were immediately in your Majesty's service, and of the Privy Council," acquainted your Majesty, "That none of them would take upon them to advise, how any material persons or papers might be sent over on this occasion; but they all seemed apprehensive of the ill temper any miscarriage, in a trial, upon *scire facias* brought against the patentee, might occasion in both Houses, if the evidence were not laid as full before a jury, as it was before them," and did therefore, a second time, decline sending over any persons, papers or materials whatsoever, to support this charge brought against your Majesty's patent and the patentee.

As this proceeding seemed very extraordinary, that in a matter that had raised so great and universal a clamour in Ireland, no one person could be prevailed upon to come over from Ireland, in support of the united sense of both Houses of Parliament of Ireland; That no papers, no materials, no evidence whatsoever of the mischiefs arising from this patent, or of the notorious frauds and deceit committed in the execution of it, could now be had, to give your Majesty satisfaction herein; "your Majesty however, desirous to give your people of Ireland all possible satisfaction, but sensible that you cannot in any case proceed against any of the meanest of your subjects, but according to the known rules and maxims of law and justice," repeated your orders to your Lord Lieutenant of Ireland, that by persuasion, and making proper allowances for their expenses, new endeavours might be used to procure and send over such witnesses as should be thought material to make good the charge against the patent.

In answer to these orders, the Lord Lieutenant of Ireland acquaints your Majesty, by his letter of the 23d of April to one of your principal secretaries of state, "That in order to obey your Majesty's commands as far as possibly he could, at a meeting with my Lord Chancellor, the Chief Judges, your Majesty's Attorney and Solicitor-General, he had earnestly desired their advice and assistance, to enable him to send over such witnesses as might be necessary to support the charge against Mr. Wood's patent, and the execution of it. The result of this meeting was such, that the Lord Lieutenant could not reap the least advantage or assistance from it, every one being so guarded with caution, against giving any advice or opinion in this matter of state, apprehending great danger to themselves from meddling in it."

The Lords of the Committee think it very strange, that there should be such great difficulty in prevailing with persons, who had already given their evidence before the Parliament of Ireland, to come over and give the same evidence here, and especially, that the chief difficulty should arise, from a general apprehension of a miscarriage, in an enquiry before your Majesty, or in a proceeding by due course of law, in a case, where both Houses of Parliament had declared themselves so fully convinced, and satisfied upon evidence, and examinations taken in the most solemn manner.

At the same time that your Majesty sent your orders to the Lord Lieutenant of Ireland, to send over such evidences as were thought material to support the charge against the patent, that your Majesty might, without any further loss of time than was absolutely necessary, be as fully informed as was possible, and that the abuses and frauds alleged to be committed by the patentee, in executing the powers granted to him, might be fully and strictly enquired into, and examined, your Majesty was pleased to order that an assay should be made of the fineness, value, and weight of this copper money, and the goodness thereof, compared with the former coinages of copper money for Ireland, and the copper money coined in your Majesty's Mint in England; and it was accordingly referred to Sir Isaac Newton, Edward Southwell, and Thomas Scroope, Esqs. to make the said assay and trial.

By the reports made of this assay, which are hereunto annexed, it appears,[2] "That the pix of the copper moneys coined at Bristol by Mr. Wood for Ireland, containing the trial pieces, which was sealed and locked up at the time of coining, was opened at your Majesty's mint at the Tower; that the comptroller's account of the quantities of halfpence and farthings coined, agreed with Mr. Wood's account, amounting to 59 tons, 3 hundred, 1 quarter, 11 pounds, and 4 ounces; That by the specimens of this coinage, which had from time to time been taken from the several parcels coined, and sealed up in papers, and put into the pix, 60 halfpence weighed 14 ounces troy, and 18 penny-weight, which is about a quarter of an ounce above one pound weight avoirdupois; and 30 farthings weighed 3 ounces and 3 quarters of an ounce troy, and 46 grams, which is also above the weight required by the patent. It also appears, that both halfpence and farthings when heated red-hot spread thin under the hammer without cracking; that the copper of which Mr. Wood's coinage is made, is of the same goodness and value with the copper of which the copper money is coined in your Majesty's mint for England, and worth in the market about 13 pence per pound weight avoirdupois; That a pound of copper wrought into bars of fillets, and made fit for coinage, before brought into the mint at the Tower of London, is worth 18 pence per pound, and always cost as much, and is coined into 23 pence of copper money by tale, for England; It likewise appears, that the halfpence and farthings coined by Mr. Wood, when compared with the copper money coined for Ireland, in the reigns of King Charles II. King James II. and King William and Queen Mary, considerably exceeds them all in weight, very far exceeds them all in goodness, fineness, and value of the copper, none of them bearing the fire so well, not being malleable, wasting very much in the fire, and great part of them burning into a cinder of little or no value at all; Specimens of all which, as likewise of Mr. Wood's copper money, upon trials and assays made by Sir Isaac Newton, Mr. Southwell, and Mr. Scroope, were laid before this Committee for their information."

[Footnote 2: See Appendix, No. II. [T.S.]]

The Lords of the Committee beg leave upon this article of the complaint, "That notorious frauds and deceits had been committed by the patentee, in executing the powers granted him," to observe to your Majesty, That this is a fact expressly charged upon the patentee, and if it had in any manner been proved, it might have enabled your Majesty, by due course of law, to have given the satisfaction to your people of Ireland, that has been so much insisted upon; but as it is now above four months since your Majesty was pleased to send over to Ireland for such evidence, as might prove a fact alleged to be so notorious, and no evidence at all has been as yet transmitted, nor the least expectation given of any that may hereafter be obtained, and the trials and assays that have been taken of the halfpence, and farthings coined by Mr. Wood proving so unquestionably the weight, goodness and fineness of the copper money coined, rather exceeding the conditions of the patent, than being any way defective, the Lords of the Committee cannot advise your Majesty, by a writ of *scire facias*, or any other manner to endeavour vacating the said patent, when there is no probability of success in such an undertaking.

As these trials and assays fully shew that the patentee hath acted fairly according to the terms and conditions of his patent, so they evidently prove, that the care and caution made use of in this patent, by proper conditions, checks, and comptrols have effectually provided, that the copper money coined for Ireland by virtue of this patent, should far exceed the like coinages for Ireland, in the reigns of your Majesty's royal predecessors.

And that your Majesty's royal predecessors have exercised this undoubted prerogative of granting to private persons the power and privilege of coining copper halfpence and farthings for the kingdom of Ireland, was proved to this Committee by several precedents of such patents granted to private persons by King Charles II. and King James II. none of which were equally beneficial to your kingdom of Ireland, nor so well guarded with proper covenants and conditions for the due execution of the powers thereby granted, although the power and validity of those patents, and a due compliance with them, was never in any one instance, till this time, disputed or controverted.

By these former patents, the sole power of coining copper money for Ireland, was granted to the patentees for the term of 21 years, to be coined in such place as they should think convenient, and "such quantities as they could conveniently issue within the term of

21 years," without any restriction of the quantity to be coined within the whole term, or any provision of a certain quantity, only to be coined annually to prevent the ill consequences of too great a quantity to be poured in at once, at the will and pleasure of the patentees; no provision was made for the goodness and fineness of the copper, no comptroller appointed to inspect the copper in bars and fillets, before coined, and take constant assays of the money when coined, and the power of issuing not limited "to such as would voluntarily accept the same"; but by the patent granted to John Knox, the money coined by virtue of the patent, "is made and declared to be the current coin of the kingdom of Ireland," and a pound weight of copper was allowed to be coined into 2 shillings and 8 pence, and whatever quantity should be coined, a rent of 16_l_ *per annum* only was reserved to the crown, and 700 tons of copper were computed to be coined within the 21 years, without any complaint.

The term granted to Mr. Wood for coining copper money is for 14 years only, the quantity for the whole term limited to 360 tons, 100 ton only to be issued within one year, and 20 tons each year for the 13 remaining years; a comptroller is appointed by the authority of the crown to inspect, comptrol, and assay the copper, as well not coined as coined; the copper to be fine British copper, cast into bars or fillets, which when heated red hot would spread thin under the hammer; a pound weight of copper to be coined into 2 shillings and sixpence, and without any compulsion on currency enforced, to be received by such only as would voluntarily and wilfully accept the same"; a rent of 800_l_ *per annum* is reserved unto your Majesty,[3] and 200_l per annum_ to your Majesty's clerk comptroller, to be paid annually by the patentee, for the full term of the fourteen years, which for 13 years when 20 tons of copper only are coined, is not inconsiderable; these great and essential differences in the several patents, that have been granted for coining copper money for the kingdom of Ireland, seemed sufficiently to justify the care and caution that was used in granting the letters-patent to Mr. Wood.

[Footnote 3: See the extract from the patent itself, where the amount is given differently [T.S.]]

It has been further represented to your Majesty, That these letters-patent were obtained by Mr. Wood in a clandestine and unprecedent manner, and by gross misrepresentations of the state of the kingdom of Ireland. Upon enquiring into this fact it appears, That the petition of Mr. Wood for obtaining this coinage, was presented to your Majesty at the time that several other petitions and applications were made to your Majesty, for the same purpose, by sundry persons, well acquainted and conversant with the affairs of Ireland, setting forth the great want of small money and change in all the common and lower parts of traffic, and business throughout the kingdom, and the terms of Mr. Wood's petition seeming to your Majesty most reasonable, thereupon a draught of a warrant directing a grant of such coinage to be made to Mr. Wood, was referred to your Majesty's then Attorney and Solicitor-general of England, to consider and report their opinion to your Majesty; Sir Isaac Newton, as the Committee is informed was consulted in all the steps of settling and adjusting the terms and conditions of the patent; and after mature deliberation, your Majesty's warrant was signed, directing an indenture in such manner as is practised in your Majesty's mint in the Tower of London, for the coining of gold and silver moneys, to pass the Great Seal of Great Britain, which was carried through all the usual forms and offices without haste or precipitation, That the Committee cannot discover the least pretence to say, this patent was passed or obtained in a clandestine or unprecedented manner, unless it is to be understood, that your Majesty's granting a liberty of coining copper money for Ireland, under the Great Seal of Great Britain, without referring the consideration thereof to the principal officers of Ireland, is the grievance and mischief complained of. Upon this head it must be admitted, that letters-patent under the Great Seal of Great Britain for coining copper money for Ireland, are legal and obligatory, a just and reasonable exercise of your Majesty's royal prerogative, and in no manner derogatory, or invasive, of any liberties or privileges of your subjects of Ireland. When any matter or thing is transacting that concerns or may affect your kingdom of Ireland, if your Majesty has any doubts concerning the same, or sees just cause for considering your officers of Ireland, your Majesty is frequently pleased to refer such considerations to your chief governors of Ireland, but the Lords of the Committee hope it will not be asserted, that any legal orders or resolutions of your Majesty can or ought to be called in question or invalidated, because the advice or consent of your chief governors of that kingdom was not previously had upon them: The precedents are many, wherein cases of great importance to Ireland, and that immediately affected, the interests of that kingdom, warrants, orders, and directions, by the authority of your Majesty and your royal predecessors, have been issued under the royal sign manual, without any previous reference, or advice of your officers of Ireland, which have always had their due force, and have been punctually complied with and obeyed. And as it cannot be disputed but this patent might legally and properly pass under the Great Seal of Great Britain, so their Lordships cannot find any precedents of references to the officers of Ireland, of what passed under the Great Seal of England; on the contrary, there are precedents of patents passed under the Great Seal of Ireland, where in all the previous steps the references were made to the officers of England.

By the misrepresentation of the state of Ireland, in order to obtain this patent, it is presumed, is meant, That the information given to your Majesty of the great want of small money, to make small payments, was groundless, and that there is no such want of small money: The Lords of the Committee enquired very particularly into this article, and Mr. Wood produced several witnesses, that directly asserted the great want of small money for change, and the great damage that retailers and manufactures suffered for want of such copper money. Evidence was given, That considerable manufacturers have been obliged to give tallies, or tokens in cards, to their workmen for want of small money, signed upon the back, to be afterwards exchanged for larger money: That a premium was often given to obtain small money for necessary occasions: Several letters from Ireland to correspondents in England were read, complaining of the want of copper money, and expressing the great demand there was for this money.

The great want of small money was further proved by the common use of *raps*, a counterfeit coin, of such base metal, that what passes for a halfpenny, is not worth half a farthing, which raps appear to have obtained a currency, out of necessity and for want of better small money to make change with, and by the best accounts, the Lords of the Committee have reason to believe, That there can be no doubt, that there is a real want of small money in Ireland, which seems to be so far admitted on all hands, that there does not appear to have been any misrepresentation of the state of Ireland in this respect.

In the second address from the House of Commons to your Majesty, They most humbly beseech your Majesty, that you will be graciously pleased to give directions to the several officers intrusted with the receipt of your Majesty's revenue, that they do not, on any pretence whatsoever, receive or utter such halfpence or farthings, and Mr. Wood, in his petition to your Majesty, complains, that the officers of your Majesty's revenue had already given such orders to all the inferior officers not to receive any of this coin.

Your Majesty, by your patent under the Great Seal of Great Britain, wills, requires and commands your "lieutenant, deputy, or other chief governor or governors of your kingdom of Ireland, and all other officers and ministers of your Majesty, your heirs and successors in England, Ireland or elsewhere, to be aiding and assisting to the said William Wood, his executors, &c. in the execution of all or any the powers, authorities, directions, matters or things to be executed by him or them, or for his or their benefit and advantage, by virtue, and in pursuance of the said indentures, in all things as becometh, &c." And if the officers of the revenue have, upon their own authority, given any orders, directions, significations, or intimations, to hinder or obstruct the receiving and uttering the copper money coined and imported, pursuant to your Majesty's letters-patent, this cannot but be looked upon as a very extraordinary proceeding.

In another paragraph of the patent your Majesty has covenanted and granted unto the said William Wood, his executors, &c. "That upon performance of covenants, on his and their parts, he and they shall peaceably, and quietly, have, hold, and enjoy all the powers, authorities, privileges, licences, profits, advantages, and all other matters and things thereby granted, without any let, suit, trouble, molestation or denial of your Majesty, your heirs or successors, or of or by any of your or their officers or ministers, or any person or persons, &c." This being so expressly granted and covenanted by your Majesty, and there appearing no failure, non-performance, or breach of covenants, on the part of the patentee, the Lords of the Committee cannot advise your Majesty to give directions to the officers of the revenue, not to receive or utter any of the said copper halfpence or farthings as has been desired.

Mr. Wood having been heard by his counsel, produced his several witnesses, all the papers and precedents, which he thought material, having been read and considered, and having as he conceived, fully vindicated both the patent, and the execution thereof. For his further justification, and to clear himself from the imputation of attempting to make to himself any unreasonable profit or advantage, and to enrich himself at the expense of the kingdom of Ireland, by endeavouring to impose upon them, and utter a greater quantity of copper money, than the necessary occasions of the people shall require, and can easily take off, delivered a proposal in writing, signed by himself, which is hereunto annexed, and Mr. Wood having by the said letters-patent, "covenanted, granted, and promised to, and with your Majesty, your heirs and successors, that he shall and will from time to time in the making the said copper farthings and halfpence in England, and in transporting the same from time to time to Ireland, and in uttering, vending, disposing and dispersing the same there, and in all his doings and accounts concerning the same, submit himself to the inspection, examination, order and comptrol of your Majesty and your commissioners of the treasury or high-treasurer for the time being;" the Lords of the Committee are of opinion, that your Majesty upon this voluntary offer and proposal of Mr. Wood, may give proper orders and directions for the execution and due performance of such parts of the said proposal, as shall be judged most for the interest and accommodation of your subjects of Ireland: In the mean time, it not appearing to their Lordships that Mr. Wood has done or committed any act or deed, that may tend to invalidate, or make void his letters-patent, or to forfeit the privileges and advantages thereby granted to him by your Majesty; It is but just and reasonable, that your Majesty should immediately send orders to your commissioners of the revenue, and all other your officers in Ireland, to revoke all orders, directions, significations, or intimations whatsoever, that may have been given by them, or any of them, to hinder or obstruct the receiving and uttering this copper money, and that the halfpence and farthings already coined by Mr. Wood, amounting to about 17,000_l_. and such further quantity as shall make up the said 17,000_l_. to 40,000_l_. "be suffered and permitted without any let, suit, trouble, molestation, or denial of any of your Majesty's officers or ministers whatsoever, to pass, and be received as current money by such as shall be willing to receive the same." At the same time, it may be advisable for your Majesty, to give the proper orders, that Mr. Wood shall not coin, import into Ireland, utter or dispose of any more copper halfpence or farthings, than to the amount of 40,000_l_. according to his own proposal, without your Majesty's special licence or authority, to be had for that purpose; and if your Majesty shall be pleased to order, that Mr. Wood's proposal, delivered to the Lords of the Committee, shall be transmitted to your Majesty's chief governor, deputies, or other your ministers, or officers in Ireland, it will give them a proper opportunity to consider, Whether, after the reduction of 360 tons of copper, being in value 100,800_l_. to 142 tons, 17 hundred, 16 pounds being in value 40,000_l_. only, anything can be done for the further satisfaction of the people of Ireland.

LETTER III.

TO THE NOBILITY AND GENTRY OF THE KINGDOM OF IRELAND.

NOTE.

The Drapier's second letter was dated August 4th, 1724. A few days later the English Privy Council's Report, dated 24th July, 1724, arrived in Dublin, and on August 25th, Swift had issued his reply to it in this third letter.

The Report itself, which is here prefixed to the third letter, was said to have been the work of Walpole. Undoubtedly, it contains the best arguments that could then be urged in favour of Wood and the patent, and undoubtedly, also, it would have had the desired effect had it been allowed to do its work uncriticised. But Swift's opposition was fatal to Walpole's intentions. He took the report as but another attempt to foist on the people of Ireland a decree in which they had not been consulted, and no amount of yielding, short of complete abandonment of it, would palliate the thing that was hateful in itself. He resented the insult. After specific rebuttals of the various arguments urged in the report in favour of the patent, Swift suddenly turns from the comparatively petty and insignificant consideration as to the weight and quality of the coins, and deals with the broad principle of justice which the granting of the patent had ignored. Had the English Houses of Parliament and the English Privy Council, he said, addressed the King against a similar breach of the English people's rights, his Majesty would not have waited to discuss the matter, nor would his ministers have dared to advise him as they had done in this instance. "Am I a free man in England," he exclaims, "and do I become a slave in six hours in crossing the channel?"

The report, however, is interesting inasmuch as it assists us to appreciate the pathetic condition of Irish affairs at the time. The very fact that the petition of the Irish parliament could be so handled, proves how strong had been the hold over Ireland by England, and with what daring insistence the English ministers continued to efface the last strongholds of Irish independence.

Monck Mason, in reviewing the report, has devoted a very elaborate note to its details, and has fortified his criticisms with a series of remarkable letters from the Archbishop of Dublin, which he publishes for the first time.[1] I have embodied much of this note in the annotations which accompany the present reprint of this letter.

[Footnote 1: "History of St. Patrick's Cathedral," pp. lxxxvi-xcv.]

The text of this third letter is based on Sir W. Scott's, collated with the first edition and that given by Faulkner in "Fraud Detected." It has also been read with Faulkner's text given in the fourth volume of his edition of Swift's Works, published in 1735.

[T.S.]

SOME
Observations

Upon a PAPER, Call'd, The

REPORT

OF THE
COMMITTEE
OF THE
Most Honourable the *Privy-Council*
IN

ENGLAND,
Relating to WOOD's *Half-pence*.

By. M.B. *Drapier*.
AUTHOR of the LETTER to the
SHOP-KEEPERS, &c.

DUBLIN:
Printed by *John Harding* in
Molesworth's-Court in *Fishamble Street*.
]

LETTER III.

TO THE NOBILITY AND GENTRY OF THE KINGDOM OF IRELAND.

Having already written two letters to people of my own level, and condition; and having now very pressing occasion for writing a third; I thought I could not more properly address it than to your lordships and worships.

The occasion is this. A printed paper was sent to me on the 18th instant, entitled, "A Report of the Committee of the Lords of His Majesty's Most Honourable Privy-Council in England, relating to Mr. Wood's Halfpence and Farthings."[2] There is no mention made where the paper was printed, but I suppose it to have been in Dublin; and I have been told that the copy did not come over in the Gazette, but in the London Journal, or some other print of no authority or consequence; and for anything that legally appears to the contrary, it may be a contrivance to fright us, or a project of some printer, who hath a mind to make a penny by publishing something upon a subject, which now employs all our thoughts in this kingdom. Mr. Wood in publishing this paper would insinuate to the world, as if the Committee had a greater concern for his credit and private emolument, than for the honour of the Privy-council and both Houses of Parliament here, and for the quiet and welfare of this whole kingdom; For it seems intended as a vindication of Mr. Wood, not without several severe remarks on the Houses of Lords and Commons of Ireland.

[Footnote 2: The full text of this report is prefixed to this third letter of the Drapier. The report was published in the "London Journal" about the middle of August of 1724. Neither the "Gazette" nor any other ministerial organ printed it, which evidently gave Swift his cue to attack it in the merciless manner he did. Monck Mason thought it "not improbable that the minister [Walpole] adopted this method of communication, because it served his own purpose; he dared not to stake his credit upon such a document, which, in its published form, contains some gross mis-statements" ("History of St. Patrick's Cathedral," note, on p. 336). [T.S.]]

The whole is indeed written with the turn and air of a pamphlet, as if it were a dispute between William Wood on the one part, and the Lords Justices, Privy-council and both Houses of Parliament on the other; the design of it being to clear and vindicate the injured reputation of William Wood, and to charge the other side with casting rash and groundless aspersions upon him.

But if it be really what the title imports, Mr. Wood hath treated the Committee with great rudeness, by publishing an act of theirs in so unbecoming a manner, without their leave, and before it was communicated to the government and Privy-council of Ireland, to whom the Committee advised that it should be transmitted. But with all deference be it spoken, I do not conceive that a Report of a Committee of the Council in England is hitherto a law in either kingdom; and until any point is determined to be a law, it remains disputable by every subject.

This (may it please your lordships and worships) may seem a strange way of discoursing in an illiterate shopkeeper. I have endeavoured (although without the help of books) to improve that small portion of reason which God hath pleased to give me, and when reason plainly appears before me, I cannot turn away my head from it. Thus for instance, if any lawyer should tell me that such a point were law, from which many gross palpable absurdities must follow, I would not, I could not believe him. If Sir Edward Coke should positively assert (which he nowhere does, but the direct contrary) that a limited prince, could by his prerogative oblige his subjects to take half an ounce of lead, stamped with his image, for twenty shillings in gold, I should swear he was deceived or a deceiver, because a power like that, would leave the whole lives and fortunes of the people entirely at the mercy of the monarch: Yet this, in effect, is what Wood hath advanced in some of his papers, and what suspicious people may possibly apprehend from some passages in that which is called the "Report."

That paper mentions "such persons to have been examined, who were desirous and willing to be heard upon that subject." I am told, they were four in all, Coleby, Brown, Mr. Finley the banker, and one more whose name I know not. The first of these was tried for robbing the Treasury in Ireland, and although he was acquitted for want of legal proof, yet every person in the Court believed him to be guilty. The second was tried for a rape, and stands recorded in the votes of the House of Commons, for endeavouring by perjury and subornation, to take away the life of John Bingham, Esq.[3]

[Footnote 3: Referring to these persons who were examined by the Committee, Monck Mason quotes from two letters from Archbishop King to Edward Southwell, Esq. King was one of the council, and Southwell secretary of state at the time. The first of these letters remarks: "Could a greater contempt be put upon a nation, than to see such a little fellow as Wood favoured and supported against them, and such profligates as Brown and Coleby believed before a whole parliament, government, and private council." From the second letter, written on August 15th, 1724, Monck Mason gives the following extracts:

"—When I returned to Dublin I met with resolutions concerning our halfpence, founded chiefly on the testimony of two infamous persons, John Brown and Coleby: as to the first of these, you will find his character in the votes of the house of commons, last parliament. Tuesday, the 5th of November.

"'Resolved, that it appears to this Committee, that a wicked conspiracy was maliciously contrived and carried on against John Bingham, to take away his life and fortune.

"'Resolved, that it is the opinion of this Committee, that the said John Brown, of Rabens, Esq. and his accomplices, were the chief promoters and advisers of the said conspiracy.

"'Resolved, that it is the opinion of this Committee, that the said John Brown is a person not fit to serve his majesty, in any office or employment, civil or military, whatsoever.

"'Resolved, that the said John Brown has, in the course of his examination, grossly prevaricated with this Committee.

"'To all which resolutions, the question being severally put, the house did agree, *nemine contradicente*.

"'Ordered, that the said John Brown be, for his said prevarication, taken into the custody of the serjeant at arms attending this house.

"'Ordered, that his majesty's attorney-general do present the said John Brown, for conniving and maliciously carrying on the said conspiracy to take away the life of the said John Bingham, and others.'

"As to Coleby, he was turned out of the treasury for robbing it of a considerable sum of money. I was present at his trial at the King's-bench, and the evidence was such as convinced every one, in his conscience, that he was guilty; but, the proofs being presumptive, and not direct, the jury acquitted him; on which the judge (Pine, if I remember right) observed the happiness of English subjects, that, though everybody was convinced of a man's guilt, yet, if the evidence did not come up to the strict requisites of the law, he would escape" ("History of St. Patrick's Cathedral," pp. xciv-xcv.) [T.S.]]

But since I have gone so far as to mention particular persons, it may be some satisfaction to know who is this Wood himself, that has the honour to have a whole kingdom at his mercy, for almost two years together. I find he is in the patent entitled *Esq*; although he were understood to be only a hardware-man, and so I have been bold to call him in my former letters; however a *'squire* he is, not only by virtue of his patent, but by having been a collector in Shropshire, where pretending to have been robbed, and suing the county, he was cast, and for the infamy of the fact, lost his employment.

I have heard another story of this 'Squire Wood from a very honourable lady, that one Hamilton told her. He (Hamilton) was sent for six years ago by Sir Isaac Newton to try the coinage of four men, who then solicited a patent for coining halfpence for Ireland; their names were Wood, Coster, Elliston, and Parker. Parker made the fairest offer, and Wood the worst, for his coin were three halfpence in a pound less value than the other. By which it is plain with what intentions he solicited this patent, but not so plain how he obtained it.

It is alleged in the said paper, called the "Report," that upon repeated orders from a secretary of state, for sending over such papers and witnesses, as should be thought proper to support the objections made against the patent (by both Houses of Parliament) the Lord Lieutenant represented "the great difficulty he found himself in to comply with these orders. That none of the principal members of both Houses, who were in the King's service or council, would take upon them to advise how any material person or papers might be sent over on this occasion, &c." And this is often repeated and represented as "a proceeding that seems very extraordinary, and that in a matter which had raised so great a clamour in Ireland, no one person could be prevailed upon to come over from Ireland in support of the united sense of both Houses of Parliament in Ireland, especially that the chief difficulty should arise from a general apprehension of a miscarriage, in an enquiry before His Majesty, or in a proceeding by due course of law, in a case where both Houses of Parliament had declared themselves so fully convinced, and satisfied upon evidence, and examinations taken in the most solemn manner."[4]

[Footnote 4: Commenting on this Monck Mason has the following note. This learned biographer's remarks are specially important inasmuch as he has fortified them with letters from Archbishop King, unpublished at the time he wrote: "But this [referring to the extract from the Report given by Swift] will not appear so strange or inexplicable after perusing the following letter from Archbishop King ... to Edward Southwell, Esq. ...; this important state paper may, therefore, be considered as an official communication of the sentiments of the Irish Privy Council upon this matter.

"Letter from William King, Archbishop of Dublin, to Edward Southwell,
Esq., dated the 23d March, 1723.

"'I have not had any occasion of late to trouble you with my letters; but yesternight I came to the knowledge of an affair which gave me some uneasiness, and, I believe, will do so to the whole kingdom, when it becomes public. My lord lieutenant sent for several lords and commoners of the privy council, and communicated to them a letter from my Lord Carteret, writ by his majesty's command, in which was repeated the answer given to the addresses of the lords and commons, about one William Wood's farthings and halfpence; and his grace is required to send over witnesses and evidences against the patentee or patent: this has surprised most people, because we were borne in hand that that affair was dead, and that we should never hear any more of it.

"'His grace's design was, to be advised by what means and methods he might effectually comply with his majesty's commands; and, by what I could perceive, it was the sense of all, that it was not possible, in the present situation of affairs, to answer his majesty's expectations or those of the kingdom; and that, for these reasons:

"'1st, because this is a controversy between the parliament of Ireland and William Wood, and, the parliament being now prorogued, nobody either would, or durst, take on them to meddle in a business attacked by the parliament, or pretend to manage a cause which so deeply concerned the parliament, and the whole nation, without express orders. If this letter had come whilst the parliament was sitting, and had been communicated to the houses, they could have appointed certain persons to have acted for them, and raised a fund to support them, as has been done formerly in this kingdom on several occasions; but, for any, without such authority, to make himself a party for the legislature and people of Ireland, would be a bold undertaking, and, perhaps, dangerous; for, if such undertaker or undertakers should fail in producing all evidences that may be had, or any of the papers necessary to make the case evident, they must expect to be severely handled the next parliament for their officiousness, and bear the blame of the miscarriage of the cause: for these reasons, as it seemed to me, the privy councillors were unwilling to engage at all in the business, or to meddle with it.

"'But, 2dly, the thing seemed impracticable; because it would signify nothing to send over the copies of the papers that were laid before the parliament, if the design is, as it seems to be, to bring the patent to a legal trial; for such copies we were told by lawyers, could not be produced in any court as evidence; and, as to the originals, they are in the possession of the houses, and (as was conceived) could not be taken from the proper officers with whom they were trusted, but by the like order.

"'And, as to the witnesses, it was a query whether my lord lieutenant by his own power could send them; and, if he have such power, yet it will not be possible to come at the witnesses, for several in each house vouched several facts on their own knowledge, to whom the houses gave credit; my lord lieutenant can neither be apprised of the persons nor of the particulars which the members testified; whereas, if the parliament was sitting, those members would appear, and make good their assertions.

"'There were several sorts of farthings and halfpence produced to the houses, differing in weight, and there was likewise a difference in the stamp. These were sent over by William Wood to his correspondents here, and by them produced. But can it be proved, on a legal trial, that these particular halfpence were coined by him? It is easy for him to say, that they are counterfeited, as (if I remember right) he has already affirmed in the public prints, in his answer to the address of the commons.

"'But, 3dly, it was not on the illegality of the patent, nor chiefly on the abuse of it the patentee (which was not so much as mentioned by the lords), that the parliament insisted, but on the unavoidable mischief and destruction it would bring on the kingdom, and on its being obtained by most false and notorious misinformation of his majesty; it being suggested, as appears by the preamble, that the kingdom wanted such halfpence and farthings: now, if the king be misinformed, the lawyers tell us, that the grant is void. And, that his majesty was deceived in this grant by a false representation, it was said, needed no further proof than the patent itself.—William Wood by it was empowered to coin 360 tons of copper into halfpence and farthings, which would have made £90,000, about the fifth part of all the current cash of Ireland; for that is not reckoned, by those who suppose it most, to be £500,000. Now, the current cash of England is reckoned above twenty millions; in proportion, therefore, if Ireland wants £90,000 England will want four millions. It is easy to imagine what would be said to a man that would propose to his majesty such a coinage; and it is agreed, that the people of England would not be more alarmed by such a patent, than the people of Ireland are, by the prospect of turning the fifth part of their current coin into brass.

"'This, so far as I can remember, is a brief of what passed in the meeting before my lord lieutenant'" ("History of St. Patrick's Cathedral," pp. lxxxvii-lxxxviii). [T.S.]]

How shall I, a poor ignorant shopkeeper, utterly unskilled in law, be able to answer so weighty an objection. I will try what can be done by plain reason, unassisted by art, cunning or eloquence.

In my humble opinion, the committee of council, hath already prejudged the whole case, by calling the united sense of both Houses of Parliament in Ireland an "universal clamour." Here the addresses of the Lords and Commons of Ireland against a ruinous destructive project of an "obscure, single undertaker," is called a "clamour." I desire to know how such a style would be resented in England from a committee of council there to a Parliament, and how many impeachments would follow upon it. But supposing the appellation to be proper, I never heard of a wise minister who despised the universal clamour of a people, and if that clamour can be quieted by disappointing the fraudulent practice of a single person, the purchase is not exorbitant.

But in answer to this objection. First it is manifest, that if this coinage had been in Ireland, with such limitations as have been formerly specified in other patents, and granted to persons of this kingdom, or even of England, able to give sufficient security, few or no inconveniencies could have happened, which might not have been immediately remedied. As to Mr. Knox's patent mentioned in the Report, security was given into the exchequer, that the patentee should at any time receive his halfpence back, and pay gold or silver in exchange for them. And Mr. Moor (to whom I suppose that patent was made over) was in 1694 forced to leave off coining, before the end of that year, by the great crowds of people continually offering to return his coinage upon him. In 1698 he coined again, and was forced to give over for the same reason. This entirely alters the case; for there is no such condition in Wood's patent, which condition was worth a hundred times all other limitations whatsoever.[5]

[Footnote 5: It will serve to elucidate this paragraph if an account be given of the various coinage patents issued for Ireland. Monck Mason gives an account in a long note to his biography of Swift; but as he has obtained it from the very ably written tract, "A Defence of the Conduct of the People of Ireland," etc., I have gone to that pamphlet for the present *résumé*. I quote from pp. 21-24 of the Dublin edition, issued in 1724 and printed by George Ewing:

"K. Charles 2d. 1660 granted a patent for coining only farthings for the kingdom of Ireland to Coll. Armstrong: But I do not find he ever made any use of it.[A] For all our copper and brass money to the year 1680 was issued by private persons, who obtained particular licences, *on giving security to change their half-pence and farthings for gold and silver*; but some of their securities failing, others pretending the half-pence which were tendered to be changed were counterfeits, the public always suffered. Col. Armstrong's son, finding great profit was made by coining half-pence in Ireland, by virtue of particular licences recallable at pleasure, solicited and obtained a patent in the name of George Legg afterwards Lord Dartmouth, for coining half-pence for Ireland from 1680, for 21 years, *he giving security to exchange them for gold or silver on demand*.[B] In pursuance of this he coined considerable quantities of half-pence for four years; but in 1685 [John] Knox, with the consent of Armstrong, got the remaining part of this term granted by patent in his own name, he giving security as above, and got his half-pence declared the current coin of Ireland, notwithstanding two Acts of Parliament had enacted that they should not be received in the revenue. Knox was interrupted in his coinage in 1689, by King James's taking it into his own hands, to coin his famous brass money, of which he coined no less than £965,375, three penny worth of metal passing for £10 *ster*. In this money creditors were obliged to receive their debts, and by this cruel stratagem Ireland lost about £60,000 per month. This not only made our gold and silver, but even our half-pence to disappear; which obliged King William to coin pewter half-pence for the use of his army....

[Footnote A: Monck Mason, quoting Simon "On Irish Coins" (Append., No. LXV), says: "Sir Thomas [Armstrong] was never admitted to make use of this grant, nor could he obtain allowance of the chief governor of Ireland, to issue them as royal coin among the subjects of that kingdom."]

[Footnote B: "A proclamation was issued by the lord lieutenant, declaring these half-pence to be the current coin of the kingdom, but it provided that none should be enforced to take more than five shillings in the payment of one hundred pounds, and so proportionately in all greater and lesser sums.... This patent was granted, by and with, the advice of James, Duke of Ormond" (Monck Mason, "History of St. Patrick's," p. 334, note y).]

"After the Revolution, Col. Roger Moore being possessed of Knox's patent, commenced his coinage in Dublin, and at first kept several offices for changing his half-pence for gold or silver. He soon overstocked the kingdom so with copper money, that persons were obliged to receive large sums in it; for the officers of the crown were industrious dispensers of it, for which he allowed them a premium. It was common at that time for one to compound for 1/4 copper, and the collectors paid nothing else. The country being thus overcharged with a base coin, everyone tendered it to Col. Moore to be changed. This he refused, on pretence they were counterfeits.... On this he quitted coining in 1698, but left us in a miserable condition, which is lively represented in a Memorial presented by Will. Trench, Esq. to the Lords of the Treasury, on Mr. Wood's obtaining his patent, and which our Commissioners referred to.... Col. Moore finding the sweet of such a patent, applied to King William for a renewal of it; but his petition being referred to the government of Ireland, the affair was fairly represented to the king, whereby his designs were frustrated.

"In the reign of the late Queen, application was made by Robert Baird and William Harnill, Trustees for the garrison which defended Londonderry, for a patent to coin base money for Ireland ... their petition was rejected.... Since this time there have been many applications made for such patents." [T.S.]]

Put the case, that the two Houses of Lords and Commons of England, and the Privy-council there should address His Majesty to recall a patent, from whence they apprehend the most ruinous consequences to the whole kingdom: And to make it stronger if possible, that the whole nation, almost to a man, should thereupon discover the "most dismal apprehensions" (as Mr. Wood styles them) would His Majesty debate half an hour what he had to do? Would any minister dare advise him against recalling such a patent? Or would the matter be referred to the Privy-Council or to Westminster-hall, the two Houses of Parliament plaintiffs, and William Wood defendant? And is there even the smallest difference between the two cases?

Were not the people of Ireland born as free as those of England? How have they forfeited their freedom? Is not their Parliament as fair a representative of the people as that of England? And hath not their Privy-council as great or a greater share in the administration of public affairs? Are they not subjects of the same King? Does not the same sun shine on them? And have they not the same God for their protector? Am I a freeman in England, and do I become a slave in six hours by crossing the Channel? No wonder then, if the boldest persons were cautious to interpose in a matter already determined by the whole voice of the nation, or to presume to represent the representatives of the kingdom, and were justly apprehensive of meeting such a treatment as they would deserve at the next session. It would seem very extraordinary if an inferior court in

England, should take a matter out of the hands of the high court of Parliament, during a prorogation, and decide it against the opinion of both Houses.

It happens however, that, although no persons were so bold, as to go over as evidences, to prove the truth of the objections made against this patent by the high court of Parliament here, yet these objections stand good, notwithstanding the answers made by Wood and his Council.

The Report says, that "upon an assay made of the fineness, weight and value of this copper, it exceeded in every article." This is possible enough in the pieces upon which the assay was made; but Wood must have failed very much in point of dexterity, if he had not taken care to provide a sufficient quantity of such halfpence as would bear the trial; which he was well able to do, although "they were taken out of several parcels." Since it is now plain, that the bias of favour hath been wholly on his side.[6]

[Footnote 6: The report of the assayers as abstracted by the Lords of the Committee in their report is not accurately stated. Monck Mason notes that the abstract omits the following passage: "But although the copper was very good, and the money, one piece with another, was full weight, yet the single pieces were not so equally coined in the weight as they should have been." Nor is it shown that the coins assayed were of the same kind as those sent into Ireland. The Committee's report fails to see the question that must arise when it is noted that while in England a pound of copper was made into twenty-three pence, yet for Ireland Wood was permitted to make it into thirty pence, in spite of the statement that the copper used in England was worth fivepence a pound more than that used by Wood. [T.S.]]

But what need is there of disputing, when we have positive demonstration of Wood's fraudulent practices in this point? I have seen a large quantity of these halfpence weighed by a very skilful person, which were of four different kinds, three of them considerably under weight. I have now before me an exact computation of the difference of weight between these four sorts, by which it appears that the fourth sort, or the lightest, differs from the first to a degree, that, in the coinage of three hundred and sixty tons of copper, the patentee will be a gainer, only by that difference, of twenty-four thousand four hundred and ninety-four pounds, and in the whole, the public will be a loser of eighty-two thousand one hundred and sixty-eight pounds, sixteen shillings, even supposing the metal in point of goodness to answer Wood's contract and the assay that hath been made; which it infallibly doth not. For this point hath likewise been enquired into by very experienced men, who, upon several trials in many of these halfpence, have found them to be at least one fourth part below the real value (not including the raps or counterfeits that he or his accomplices have already made of his own coin, and scattered about). Now the coinage of three hundred and sixty ton of copper coined by the weight of the fourth or lightest sort of his halfpence will amount to one hundred twenty-two thousand four hundred eighty-eight pounds, sixteen shillings, and if we subtract a fourth part of the real value by the base mixture in the metal, we must add to the public loss one fourth part to be subtracted from the intrinsic value of the copper, which in three hundred and sixty tons amounts to ten thousand and eighty pounds, and this added to the former sum of eighty-two thousand one hundred sixty-eight pounds, sixteen shillings, will make in all, ninety-two thousand two hundred forty-eight pounds loss to the public; besides the raps or counterfeits that he may at any time hereafter think fit to coin. Nor do I know whether he reckons the dross exclusive or inclusive with his three hundred and sixty ton of copper; which however will make a considerable difference in the account.

You will here please to observe, that the profit allowed to Wood by the patent is twelvepence out of every pound of copper valued at *1s. 6d*. whereas *5d*. only is allowed for coinage of a pound weight for the English halfpence, and this difference is almost 25 *per cent*. which is double to the highest exchange of money, even under all the additional pressures, and obstructions to trade, that this unhappy kingdom lies at present. This one circumstance in the coinage of three hundred and sixty ton of copper makes a difference of twenty-seven thousand seven hundred and twenty pounds between English and Irish halfpence, even allowing those of Wood to be all of the heaviest sort.

It is likewise to be considered, that for every halfpenny in a pound weight exceeding the number directed by the patent, Wood will be a gainer in the coinage of three hundred and sixty ton of copper, sixteen hundred and eighty pounds profit more than the patent allows him; Out of which he may afford to make his comptrollers easy upon that article.

As to what is alleged, that "these halfpence far exceed the like coinage for Ireland in the reigns of His Majesty's predecessors;" there cannot well be a more exceptionable way of arguing: Although the fact were true, which however is altogether mistaken; not by any fault in the Committee, but by the fraud and imposition of Wood, who certainly produced the worst patterns he could find, such as were coined in small numbers by permissions to private men, as butchers' halfpence, black dogs and the like, or perhaps the small St. Patrick's coin which passes for a farthing, or at best some of the smallest raps of the latest kind. For I have now by me some halfpence coined in the year 1680 by virtue of the patent granted to my Lord Dartmouth, which was renewed to Knox, and they are heavier by a ninth part than those of Wood, and in much better metal. And the great St. Patrick's halfpenny is yet larger than either.

But what is all this to the present debate? If under the various exigencies of former times, by wars, rebellions, and insurrections, the Kings of England were sometimes forced to pay their armies here with mixed or base money, God forbid that the necessities of turbulent times should be a precedent for times of peace, and order, and settlement.

In the patent above mentioned granted to Lord Dartmouth, in the reign of King Charles 2d. and renewed to Knox, the securities given into the exchequer, obliging the patentee to receive his money back upon every demand, were an effectual remedy against all inconveniencies. And the copper was coined in our own kingdom, so that we were in no danger to purchase it with the loss of all our silver and gold carried over to another, nor to be at the trouble of going to England for the redressing of any abuse.

That the Kings of England have exercised their prerogative of coining copper for Ireland and for England is not the present question: But (to speak in the style of the Report) it would "seem a little extraordinary," supposing a King should think fit to exercise his prerogative by coining copper in Ireland, to be current in England, without referring it to his officers in that kingdom to be informed whether the grant was reasonable, and whether the people desired it or no, and without regard to the addresses of his Parliament against it. God forbid that so mean a man as I should meddle with the King's prerogative: But I have heard very wise men say, that the

King's prerogative is bounded and limited by the good and welfare of his people. I desire to know, whether it is not understood and avowed that the good of Ireland was intended by this patent. But Ireland is not consulted at all in the matter, and as soon as Ireland is informed of it, they declare against it; the two Houses of Parliament and the Privy-council addresses His Majesty upon the mischiefs apprehended by such a patent. The Privy-council in England takes the matter out of the Parliament's cognizance; the good of the kingdom is dropped, and it is now determined that Mr. Wood shall have the power of ruining a whole nation for his private advantage.

I never can suppose that such patents as these were originally granted with the view of being a job for the interest of a particular person, to the damage of the public: Whatever profit must arise to the patentee was surely meant at best but as a secondary motive, and since somebody must be a gainer, the choice of the person was made either by favour, or *something else*[7] or by the pretence of merit and honesty. This argument returns so often and strongly into my head, that I cannot forbear frequently repeating it. Surely His Majesty, when he consented to the passing of this patent, conceived he was doing an act of grace to his most loyal subjects of Ireland, without any regard to Mr. Wood, farther than as an instrument. But the people of Ireland think this patent (intended *no doubt* for their good) to be a most intolerable grievance, and therefore Mr. Wood can never succeed, without an open avowal that his profit is preferred not only before the interests, but the very safety and being of a great kingdom; and a kingdom distinguished for its loyalty, perhaps above all others upon earth. Not turned from its duty by the "jurisdiction of the House of Lords, abolished at a stroke, by the hardships of the Act of Navigation newly enforced; By all possible obstructions in trade," and by a hundred other instances, "enough to fill this paper." Nor was there ever among us the least attempt towards an insurrection in favour of the Pretender. Therefore whatever justice a free people can claim we have at least an equal title to it with our brethren in England, and whatever grace a good prince can bestow on the most loyal subjects, we have reason to expect it: Neither hath this kingdom any way deserved to be sacrificed to one "single, rapacious, obscure, ignominious projector."

[Footnote 7: A hint at the Duchess of Kendal's influence in the procuring of the patent. [T.S.]]

Among other clauses mentioned in this patent, to shew how advantageous it is to Ireland, there is one which seems to be of a singular nature, that the patentee shall be obliged, during his term, "to pay eight hundred pounds a year to the crown, and two hundred pounds a year to the comptroller."[8] I have heard indeed that the King's council do always consider, in the passing of a patent, whether it will be of advantage to the crown, but I have likewise heard that it is at the same time considered whether the passing of it may be injurious to any other persons or bodies politic. However, although the attorney and solicitor be servants to the King, and therefore bound to consult His Majesty's interest, yet I am under some doubt whether eight hundred pounds a year to the crown would be equivalent to the ruin of a kingdom. It would be far better for us to have paid eight thousand pounds a year into His Majesty's coffers, in the midst of all our taxes (which, in proportion, are greater in this kingdom than ever they were in England, even during the war) than purchase such an addition to the revenue at the price of our *utter undoing.*

[Footnote 8: By the terms of the patent, Wood covenanted to pay to the King's clerk, or comptroller of the coinage, £200 yearly, and

£100 per annum into his Majesty's exchequer, and not as Walpole's report has it, £800 and £200. [T.S.]]

But here it is plain that fourteen thousand pounds are to be paid by Wood, only as a small circumstantial charge for the purchase of his patent, what were his other visible costs I know not, and what were his latent, is variously conjectured. But he must be surely a man of some wonderful merit. Hath he saved any other kingdom at his own expense, to give him a title of reimbursing himself by the destruction of ours? Hath he discovered the longitude or the universal medicine? No. But he hath found out the philosopher's stone after a new manner, by debasing of copper, and resolving to force it upon us for gold.

When the two Houses represented to His Majesty, that this patent to Wood was obtained in a clandestine manner, surely the Committee could not think the Parliament would insinuate that it had not passed in the common forms, and run through every office where fees and perquisites were due. They knew very well that persons in places were no enemies to grants, and that the officers of the crown could not be kept in the dark. But the late Lord Lieutenant of Ireland[9] affirmed it was a secret to him (and who will doubt of his veracity, especially when he swore to a person of quality; from whom I had it, that Ireland should never be troubled with these halfpence). It was a secret to the people of Ireland, who were to be the only sufferers, and those who best knew the state of the kingdom and were most able to advise in such an affair, were wholly strangers to it.

[Footnote 9: The Duke of Grafton. Walpole called him "a fair-weather pilot, that knew not what he had to do, when the first storm arose." Charles, second Duke of Grafton (1683-1757), was the grandfather of the third duke, so virulently attacked by Junius in his famous letters. [T. S.]]

It is allowed by the Report that this patent was passed without the knowledge of the chief governor or officers of Ireland; and it is there elaborately shewn, that "former patents have passed in the same manner, and are good in law." I shall not dispute the legality of patents, but am ready to suppose it in His Majesty's power to grant a patent for stamping round bits of copper to every subject he hath. Therefore to lay aside the point of law, I would only put the question, whether in reason and justice it would not have been proper, in an affair upon which the welfare of a kingdom depends, that the said kingdom should have received timely notice, and the matter not be carried on between the patentee and the officers of the Crown, who were to be the only gainers by it.

The Parliament, who in matters of this nature are the most able and faithful counsellors, did represent this grant to be "destructive of trade, and dangerous to the properties of the people," to which the only answer is, that "the King hath a prerogative to make such a grant."

It is asserted that in the patent to Knox, his "halfpence, are made and declared the current coin of the kingdom," whereas in this to Wood, there is only a "power given to issue them to such as will receive them." The authors of the Report, I think, do not affirm that the King can by law declare *anything* to be current money by his letters-patents. I dare say they will not affirm it, and if Knox's patent contained in it powers contrary to law, why is it mentioned as a precedent in His Majesty's just and merciful reign:[10] But although that clause be not in Wood's patent, yet possibly there are others, the legality whereof may be equally doubted, and particularly that, whereby "a power is given to William Wood to break into houses in search of any coin made in imitation of his." This may perhaps be affirmed to be illegal and dangerous to the liberty of the subject. Yet this is a precedent taken from Knox's patent, where the same power is granted, and is a strong instance what uses may be sometimes made of precedents.

[Footnote 10: Knox's patent, as Monck Mason points out, did not contain the right to have his coins pass as the current coin of the realm; that was permitted by a proclamation of the lord lieutenant, and could in the same manner be withdrawn. Knox's patent differed materially from that granted to Wood, since he was obliged to take back his coins and give gold or silver for them, and no one was compelled to take more than five shillings in the payment of each £100. See note, p. 66. [T.S.]]

But although before the passing of this patent, it was not thought necessary to consult any persons of this kingdom, or make the least enquiry whether copper money were wanted among us; yet now at length, when the matter is over, when the patent hath long passed, when Wood hath already coined seventeen thousand pounds, and hath his tools and implements prepared to coin six times as much more; the Committee hath been pleased to make this affair the subject of enquiry. Wood is permitted to produce his evidences, which consist as I have already observed, of four in number, whereof Coleby, Brown and Mr. Finley the banker are three. And these were to prove that copper money was extremely wanted in Ireland. The first had been out of the kingdom almost twenty years, from the time that he was tried for robbing the treasury, and therefore his knowledge and credibility are equal. The second may be allowed a more knowing witness, because I think it is not above a year since the House of Commons ordered the Attorney-general to prosecute him, for endeavouring "to take away the life of John Bingham Esq; member of parliaments by perjury and subornation." He asserted that he was forced to tally with his labourers for want of small money (which hath often been practised in England by Sir Ambrose Crawley[11] and others) but those who knew him better give a different reason, (if there be any truth at all in the fact) that he was forced to tally with his labourers not for want of halfpence, but of more substantial money, which is highly possible, because the race of suborners, forgers, perjurers and ravishers, are usually people of no fortune, or of those who have run it out by their vices and profuseness. Mr. Finley the third witness honestly confessed, that he was ignorant whether Ireland wanted copper money or no; but all his intention was to buy a certain quantity from Wood at a large discount, and sell them as well as he could, by which he hoped to get two or three thousand pounds for himself.

[Footnote 11: Ambrose Crowley (not Crawley) was alderman and sheriff of London. He was knighted January 1st, 1706-1707, and sat in the House of Commons as member for Andover in 1713-1714. [T.S.]]

But suppose there were not one single halfpenny of copper coin in this whole kingdom (which Mr. Wood seems to intend, unless we will come to his terms, as appears by employing his emissaries to buy up our old ones at a penny in the shilling more than they pass for), it could not be any real evil to us, although it might be some inconvenience. We have many sorts of small silver coins, to which they are strangers in England, such as the French threepences, fourpence halfpennies and eightpence half-pennies, the Scotch fivepences and tenpences, besides their twenty-pences, and three-and-four-pences, by all which we are able to make change to a halfpenny of almost any piece of gold or silver, and if we are driven to Brown's expedient of a sealed card, with the little gold or silver still remaining, it will I suppose, be somewhat better than to have nothing left but Wood's adulterated copper, which he is neither obliged by his patent, nor hitherto able by his estate to make good.

The Report farther tells us, it "must be admitted that letters-patents under the Great Seal of Great Britain for coining copper money for Ireland are legal and obligatory, a just and reasonable exercise of His Majesty's royal prerogative, and in no manner derogatory or invasive of any liberty or privilege of his subjects of Ireland." First we desire to know, why His Majesty's prerogative might not have been as well asserted, by passing this patent in Ireland, and subjecting the several conditions of the contract to the inspection of those who are only concerned, as was formerly done in the only precedents for patents granted for coining for this kingdom, since the mixed money[12] in Queen Elizabeth's time, during the difficulties of a rebellion: Whereas now upon the greatest imposition that can possibly be practised, we must go to England with our complaints, where it hath been for some time the fashion to think and to affirm that "we cannot be too hardly used." Again the Report says, that "such patents are obligatory." After long thinking, I am not able to find out what can possibly be meant here by this word *obligatory*. This patent of Wood neither obligeth him to utter his coin, nor us to take it, or if it did the latter, it would be so far void, because no patent can oblige the subject against law, unless an illegal patent passed in one kingdom can bind another and not itself.

[Footnote 12: "Civill warre having set all Ireland in a combustion, the Queene [Elizabeth] more easily to subdue the rebels, did take silver coyne from the Irish, some few years before her death, and paid her army with a mixed base coyne, which, by proclamation, was commanded to be spent and received, for sterling silver money. This base mixed money had three parts of copper, and the fourth part of silver, which proportion of silver was in some part consumed by the mixture, so as the English goldsmiths valued a shilling thereof at no more than two silver pence, though they acknowledged the same to be worth two pence halfpenny." (Fynes Moryson's "Itinerary," pt. i., p. 283). [T.S.]]

Lastly, it is added that "such patents are in no manner derogatory or invasive of any liberty or privilege of the King's subjects of Ireland." If this proposition be true, as it is here laid down, without any limitation either expressed or implied, it must follow that a King of England may at any time coin copper money for Ireland, and oblige his subjects here to take a piece of copper under the value of half a farthing for half-a-crown, as was practised by the late King James, and even without that arbitrary prince's excuse, from the necessity and exigences of his affairs. If this be in no manner "derogatory nor evasive of any liberties or privileges of the subjects of Ireland," it ought to have been expressed what our liberties and privileges are, and whether we have any at all, for in specifying the word *Ireland*, instead of saying "His Majesty's subjects," it would seem to insinuate that we are not upon the same foot with our fellow-subjects in *England*; which, however the practice may have been, I hope will never be directly asserted, for I do not understand that Poining's act[13] deprived us of our liberty, but only changed the manner of passing laws here (which however was a power most indirectly obtained) by leaving the negative to the two Houses of Parliament. But, waiving all controversies relating to the legislature, no person, I believe, was ever yet so bold as to affirm that the people of Ireland have not the same title to the benefits of the common law, with the rest of His Majesty's subjects, and therefore whatever liberties or privileges the people of England enjoy by common law, we of Ireland have the same; so that in my humble opinion, the word *Ireland* standing in that proposition, was, in the mildest interpretation, *a lapse of the pen.*

[Footnote 13: It was not intended that Poyning's act should interfere with the liberty of the people, but it is undoubted that advantage was taken of this law, and an interpretation put on it far different from the intention that brought it on the statute books. It was passed by a parliament convened by Sir Edward Poyning, at Drogheda, in the tenth year of Henry VII.'s reign. Its immediate cause was the invasion of Perkin Warbeck. That pretender assumed royal authority in Ireland and had several statutes passed during his short-lived term of power. To prevent any viceroy from arrogating to himself the powers of law-making it was enacted by Poyning's parliament:

"That no parliament be holden hereafter in Ireland, but at such season as the King's lieutenant and counsaile there first do certifie the King, under the Great Seal of that land, the causes and considerations, and all such acts as them seemeth should pass in the same parliament, and such causes, considerations, and acts affirmed by the King and his counsaile to be good and expedient for that land, and his licence thereupon, as well in affirmation of the said causes and acts, as to summon the said parliament, under his Great Seal of England had and obtained; that done, a parliament to be had and holden as afore rehearsed" ("Irish Statutes," vol. i., p. 44).

Two statutes, one, the Act of 3 and 4 Phil., and Mary, cap. 4, and the other of II Eliz. Ses. 3, cap. 8, explain this act further, and the latter points out the reason for the original enactment, namely, that "before this statute, when liberty was given to the governors to call parliaments at their pleasure, acts passed as well to the dishonour of the prince, as to the hindrance of their subjects" ("Irish Statutes," vol. i., p. 346).

"By Poyning's Law," says Lecky, "a great part of the independence of the Irish Parliament had indeed been surrendered; but even the servile Parliament which passed it, though extending by its own authority to Ireland laws previously enacted in England, never admitted the right of the English Parliament to make laws for Ireland." ("Hist. Ireland," vol. ii., p. 154; 1892 ed). [T.S.]]

The Report farther asserts, that "the precedents are many, wherein cases of great importance to Ireland, and that immediately affected the interests of that kingdom, warrants, orders, and directions by the authority of the King and his predecessors, have been issued under the royal sign manual, without any previous reference or advice of His Majesty's officers of Ireland, which have always had their due force, and have been punctually complied with, and obeyed." It may be so, and I am heartily sorry for it, because it may prove an eternal source of discontent. However among all these precedents there is not one of a patent for coining money for Ireland.

There is nothing hath perplexed me more than this doctrine of precedents. If a job is to be done, and upon searching records you find it hath been done before, there will not want a lawyer to justify the legality of it, by producing his precedents, without ever considering the motives and circumstances that first introduced them, the necessity or turbulence or iniquity of times, the corruptions of ministers, or the arbitrary disposition of the prince then reigning. And I have been told by persons eminent in the law, that the worst actions which human nature is capable of, may be justified by the same doctrine. How the first precedents began of determining cases of the highest importance to Ireland, and immediately affecting its interest, without any previous reference or advice to the King's officers here, may soon be accounted for. Before this kingdom was entirely reduced by the submission of Tyrone in the last year of Queen Elizabeth's reign, there was a period of four hundred years, which was a various scene of war and peace between the English pale and the Irish natives, and the government of that part of this island which lay in the English hands, was, in many things under the immediate administration of the King. Silver and copper were often coined here among us, and once at least upon great necessity, a mixed or base metal was sent from England. The reign of King James Ist. was employed in settling the kingdom after Tyrone's rebellion, and this nation flourished extremely till the time of the massacre 1641. In that difficult juncture of affairs, the nobility and gentry coined their own plate here in Dublin.

By all that I can discover, the copper coin of Ireland for three hundred years past consisted of small pence and halfpence, which particular men had licence to coin, and were current only within certain towns and districts, according to the personal credit of the owner who uttered them, and was bound to receive them again, whereof I have seen many sorts; neither have I heard of any patent granted for coining copper for Ireland till the reign of King Charles II. which was in the year 1680. to George Legge Lord Dartmouth, and renewed by King James II. in the first year of his reign to John Knox. Both patents were passed in Ireland, and in both the patentees were obliged to receive their coin again to any that would offer then twenty shillings of it, for which they were obliged to pay gold or silver.

The patents both of Lord Dartmouth and Knox were referred to the Attorney-general here, and a report made accordingly, and both, as I have already said, were passed in this kingdom. Knox had only a patent for the remainder of the term granted to Lord Dartmouth, the patent expired in 1701, and upon a petition by Roger Moor to have it renewed, the matter was referred hither, and upon the report of the attorney and solicitor, that it was not for His Majesty's service or the interest of the nation to have it renewed, it was rejected by King William. It should therefore seem very extraordinary, that a patent for coining copper halfpence, intended and professed for the good of the kingdom, should be passed without once consulting that kingdom, for the good of which it is declared to be intended, and this upon the application of a "poor, private obscure mechanic;" and a patent of such a nature, that as soon as ever the kingdom is informed of its being passed, they cry out unanimously against it as ruinous and destructive. The representative of the nation in Parliament, and the Privy-council address the King to have it recalled; yet the patentee, such a one as I have described, shall prevail to have this patent approved, and his private interest shall weigh down the application of a whole kingdom. St. Paul says, "All things are lawful, but all things are not expedient." We are answered that this patent is lawful, but is it expedient? We read that the high-priest said "It was expedient that one Man should die for the people;" and this was a most wicked proposition. But that a whole nation should die for one man, was never heard of before.

But because much weight is laid on the precedents of other patents, for coining copper for Ireland, I will set this matter in as clear a light as I can. Whoever hath read the Report, will be apt to think, that a dozen precedents at least could be produced of copper coined for Ireland, by virtue of patents passed in England, and that the coinage was there too; whereas I am confident, there cannot be one precedent shewn of a patent passed in England for coining copper for Ireland, for above an hundred years past, and if there were any before, it must be in times of confusion. The only patents I could ever hear of, are those already mentioned to Lord Dartmouth and Knox; the former in 1680. and the latter in 1685. Now let us compare these patents with that granted to Wood. First, the patent to Knox, which was under the same conditions as that granted to Lord Dartmouth, was passed in Ireland, the government and the Attorney and Solicitor-general making report that it would be useful to this kingdom: [The patentee was obliged to make every halfpenny one hundred and ten grains Troy weight, whereby *2s. 2d.* only could be coined out of a pound of copper.][14] The patent was passed with the advice of the King's council here; The patentee was obliged to receive his coin from those who thought themselves surcharged, and to give gold and silver for it; Lastly, The patentee was to pay only *16l. 13s. 4d. per ann.* to the crown. Then, as to the execution of that patent. First, I find the halfpence were milled, which, as it is of great use to prevent counterfeits (and therefore industriously avoided by Wood) so it was an addition to the charge of coinage. And for the weight and goodness of the metal; I have several halfpence now by me, many of which weigh a ninth part more than those coined by Wood, and bear the fire and hammer a great deal better; and which is no trifle, the impression fairer and deeper. I grant indeed, that many of the latter coinage yield in weight to some of Wood's, by a fraud natural to such patentees; but not so immediately after the grant, and before the coin grew current: For in this circumstance Mr. Wood must serve for a precedent in future times.

[Footnote 14: The portion here in square brackets was printed in the fourth edition of this Letter and in the work entitled, "Fraud

Detected." It is not given in Faulkner's first collected edition issued in 1735, nor in "The Hibernian Patriot," issued in 1730. [T.S.]]

Let us now examine this new patent granted to William Wood. It passed upon very false suggestions of his own, and of a few confederates: It passed in England, without the least reference hither. It passed unknown to the very Lord Lieutenant, then in England. Wood is empowered to coin one hundred and eight thousand pounds, "and all the officers in the kingdom (civil and military) are commanded" in the Report to countenance and assist him. Knox had only power to utter what we would take, and was obliged "to receive his coin back again at our demand," and to "enter into security for so doing." Wood's halfpence are not milled, and therefore more easily counterfeited by himself as well as by others: Wood pays a thousand pounds *per ann.* for 14 years, Knox paid only *16l. 13s. 4d. per ann.* for 21 years.

It was the Report that set me the example of making a comparison between those two patents, wherein the committee was grossly misled by the false representation of William Wood, as it was by another assertion, that seven hundred ton of copper were coined during the 21 years of Lord Dartmouth's and Knox's patents. Such a quantity of copper at the rate of *2s. 8d. per* pound would amount to about an hundred and ninety thousand pounds, which was very near as much as the current cash of the kingdom in those days; yet, during that period, Ireland was never known to have too much copper coin, and for several years there was no coining at all: Besides I am assured, that upon enquiring into the custom-house books, all the copper imported into the kingdom, from 1683 to 1692, which includes 8 years of the 21 (besides one year allowed for the troubles) did not exceed 47 tons, and we cannot suppose even that small quantity to have been wholly applied to coinage: So that I believe there was never any comparison more unluckily made or so destructive of the design for which it was produced.

The Psalmist reckons it an effect of God's anger, when "He selleth His people for nought, and taketh no money for them." That we have greatly offended God by the wickedness of our lives is not to be disputed: But our King we have not offended in word or deed; and although he be God's vicegerent upon earth, he will not punish us for any offences, except those which we shall commit against his legal authority, his sacred person (which God preserve) or the laws of the land.

The Report is very profuse in arguments, that Ireland is in great want of copper money.[15] Who were the witnesses to prove it, hath been shewn already, but in the name of God, Who are to be judges? Does not the nation best know its own wants? Both Houses of Parliament, the Privy-council and the whole body of the people declare the contrary: Or let the wants be what they will, We desire they may not be supplied by Mr. Wood. We know our own wants but too well; they are many and grievous to be borne, but quite of another kind. Let England be satisfied: As things go, they will in a short time have all our gold and silver, and may keep their adulterate copper at home, for we are determined not to purchase it with our manufactures, which Wood hath graciously offered to accept. Our wants are not so bad by an hundredth part as the method he hath taken to supply them. He hath already tried his faculty in New-England,[16] and I hope he will meet at least with an equal reception here; what *that* was I leave to public intelligence. I am supposing a wild case, that if there should be any person already receiving a monstrous pension out of this kingdom, who was instrumental in procuring this patent, they have either not well consulted their own interests, or Wood must[17] put more dross into his copper and still diminish its weight.

[Footnote 15: On this subject of the want of small money in Ireland, Monck Mason traverses the Report in the following manner:

"There appears to be a manifest prevarication in their lordships' report upon this part of the subject; they state, that the witnesses testified, that there was a want of small money in Ireland; they attempt, therefore, to impose a copper currency, which certainly was not wanted. To satisfy the reader upon this point, I shall quote, from the unpublished correspondence of Archbishop King, the following extracts: the first, from his letter to General Gorge, dated the 17th October, 1724, is to the following purpose.

"'... As to our wanting halfpence for change, it is most false; we have more halfpence than we need, already; it is true, we want change; but it is sixpences, shillings, half-crowns, and crowns; our silver and our guineas being almost gone; and the general current coin of the kingdom is now moydores, which are thirty shillings a-piece; at least nine pence above the value in silver: now, they would have us change these for halfpence, and so the whole cash of the kingdom would be these halfpence.' ...

"But the true state of the case, as to coin, is more circumstantially developed in the following letter of the same prelate to Mr. Southwell, which was written a few months before, viz., on the 9th June, 1724.

"'... And yet, after all, we want change, and I will take leave to acquaint you with the state of this kingdom as to coin. We used to have hardly any money passing here, but foreign ducatoons, plate pieces, perns, dollars, etc. but, when the East India Company were forbid sending the coin of England abroad, they continued to buy up all our foreign coin, and give us English money in lieu of some part of it; by which we lost twopence in every ounce, the consequence of this was, that in two years there was not to be seen in Ireland a piece of foreign silver.

"'If any be brought, it is immediately sent away, the two, or as I am informed, the three pence in the ounce, given by the East India Company, being a temptation not to be resisted; but, the truth is, very little is brought in, for the merchants that carry our commodities to foreign markets, find it more to their advantage to carry directly to London whatever they receive in cash; and whereas formerly they used, when they had disposed of their cargo, to load their vessels with such commodities as there was a demand for in Ireland, and bring the rest in cash, they bring now only the commodities, and send the silver to London; and when they have got the twopence in every ounce from the East India Company, the rest serves to answer the returns we are obliged to make to England, for the rents we are obliged to pay to noblemen and gentlemen who have estates in Ireland and live in England, and for the pensions, and other occasions which are many; by this means they gain likewise the exchange, which is commonly four or five per cent, better to them than if they sent cash.

"'It Is farther to be observed, that 21 shillings, which is the value of a guinea in England, makes in Ireland 22 shillings and 9 pence, whereas a guinea passes for 23 shillings with us, therefore, he who sends silver into England, gains three pence more by it than if he sent guineas; this advantage, though it may seem little, yet in a manner has entirely drained us of our English money which was given in lieu of foreign silver.

"'But farther, if any carry foreign gold to England, they cannot easily pass it, and if they do, it is at a greater loss than there is in the guineas, this has taken away our guineas, so that there is hardly one to be seen; we have hardly any coin left but a few moydores and pistoles, which can, by no means, serve the inland trade of the kingdom.

"'To give, therefore, a short view of our case, it is thus; We can have English coin but by stealth, there being an act of parliament forbidding the exportation of English coin; if, therefore, we should send our gold or silver to England to be coined, we cannot have it back again, or if we could, we cannot keep it for the reason above; we cannot for the same reason have foreign silver; let us add to these, that by the act of navigation and other acts, we cannot make our markets of buying where we make our markets for selling; though we might have the commodities we want much cheaper there, than we can have them in England, viz. all East India and Turkey goods, with many others: nor is it to be expected that any nation will trade with us with their silver only, when we will not exchange commodities with them.

"'Except, therefore, England designs entirely to ruin Ireland, a kingdom by which it is demonstrable that she gains yearly thirteen or fourteen hundred thousand pounds, she ought to think of giving us some relief'" ("History of St. Patrick's," pp. xciii-xciv). [T.S.]]

[Footnote 16: See note on p. 14. [T.S.]]

[Footnote 17: Another hint at the Duchess of Kendal and her connection with the patent. [T.S.]]

Upon Wood's complaint that the officers of the King's revenue here had already given orders to all the inferior officers not to receive any of his coin, the Report says, That "this cannot but be looked upon as a very extraordinary proceeding," and being contrary to the powers given in the patent, the Committee say, They "cannot advise His Majesty to give directions to the officers of the revenue here, not to receive or utter any of the said coin as has been desired in the addresses of both Houses," but on the contrary, they "think it both just and reasonable that the King should immediately give orders to the commissioners of the revenue, &c. to revoke all orders, &c. that may have been given by them to hinder or obstruct the receiving the said coin." And accordingly, we are told, such orders are arrived.[18]. Now this was a cast of Wood's politics; for his information was wholly false and groundless, which he knew very well; and that the commissioners of the revenue here were all, except one, sent us from England, and love their employments too well to have taken such a step: But Wood was wise enough to consider, that such orders of revocation would be an open declaration of the crown in his favour, would put the government here under a difficulty, would make a noise, and possibly create some terror in the poor people of Ireland. And one great point he hath gained, that although any orders of revocation will be needless, yet a new order is to be sent, and perhaps already here, to the commissioners of the revenue, and all the King's officers in Ireland, that Wood's "halfpence be suffered and permitted, without any let, suit, trouble, molestation or denial of any of the King's officers or ministers whatsoever, to pass and be received as current money by such as shall be willing to receive them." In this order there is no exception, and therefore, as far as I can judge, it includes all officers both civil and military, from the Lord High Chancellor to a justice of peace, and from the general to an ensign: So that Wood's project is not likely to fail for want of managers enough. For my own part, as things stand, I have but little regret to find myself out of the number, and therefore I shall continue in all humility to exhort and warn my fellow-subjects never to receive or utter this coin, which will reduce the kingdom to beggary by much quicker and larger steps than have hitherto been taken.[19]

[Footnote 18: Archbishop King's letter, quoted by Monck Mason, explains why it was that the revenue officers refused to receive Wood's coins. It seems the officers had been advised by lawyers that, in the event of their taking the coins, it might be quite likely they would be compelled to make them good, should such a demand be made of them. Precedents could easily be cited by those taking action, since all previous patents issued to private individuals for coining money, required of the patentee to take them back and pay for them with gold or silver. [T. S.]]

[Footnote 19: The suggestion thus made by the Lords of the Committee, although coupled with the reduction in the amount of money Wood was to be permitted to introduce, did not do any good. Archbishop King argued rightly that this was treating the people of Ireland as if they were fools and children. If Wood could coin £40,000, what was to prevent him coining £200,000? The suggestion indeed irritated the people almost as much as did the patent itself. [T.S.]]

But it is needless to argue any longer. The matter is come to an issue. His Majesty pursuant to the law, hath left the field open between Wood and the kingdom of Ireland. Wood hath liberty to offer his coin, and we have law, reason, liberty and necessity to refuse it. A knavish jockey may ride an old foundered jade about the market, but none are obliged to buy it. I hope the words "voluntary" and "willing to receive it" will be understood, and applied in their true natural meaning, as commonly understood by Protestants. For if a fierce captain comes to my shop to buy six yards of scarlet cloth, followed by a porter laden with a sack of Wood's coin upon his shoulders, if we are agreed about the price, and my scarlet lies ready cut upon the counter, if he then gives me the word of command, to receive my money in Wood's coin, and calls me a "disaffected Jacobite dog" for refusing it (although I am as loyal a subject as himself, and without hire) and thereupon seizes my cloth, leaving me the price in his odious copper, and bids me take my remedy: In this case, I shall hardly be brought to think that I am left to my own will. I shall therefore on such occasions, first order the porter aforesaid to go off with his pack, and then see the money in silver and gold in my possession before I cut or measure my cloth. But if a common soldier drinks his pot first, and then offers payment in Wood's halfpence, the landlady may be under some difficulty; For if she complains to his captain or ensign, they are likewise officers, included in this general order for encouraging these halfpence to pass as current money. If she goes to a justice of peace, he is also an officer, to whom this general order is directed. I do therefore advise her to follow my practice, which I have already begun, and be paid for her goods before she parts with them. However I should have been content, for some reasons, that the military gentlemen had been excepted by name, because I have heard it said, that their discipline is best confined within their own district.

His Majesty in the conclusion of his answer to the address of the House of Lords against Wood's coin, is pleased to say that "he will do everything in his power for the satisfaction of his people." It should seem therefore, that the recalling the patent is not to be understood as a thing in his power. But however since the law does not oblige us to receive this coin, and consequently the patent leaves it to our voluntary choice, there is nothing remaining to preserve us from rain but that the whole kingdom should continue in a firm determinate resolution never to receive or utter this fatal coin:[20]

[Footnote 20: So ready was the response to this suggestion of Swift's, that it was found necessary for tradesmen to take precautions to have it publicly known that they were in no way connected with Wood and his money, The following is a copy of an advertisement which illustrates this:

"Whereas several persons in this kingdom suspect that John Molyneux of Meath Street, ironmonger, and his brother Daniel Molyneux, of Essex Street, ironmonger, are interested in the patent obtained by William Wood for coining of halfpence and farthings for this kingdom.

"Now we the said John Molyneux and Daniel Molyneux, in order to satisfy the public, do hereby declare, that we are in no way concerned with the said Wood in relation to his said patent; And that we never were possessed of any of the said halfpence or farthings, except one halfpence and one farthing, which I the said John Molyneux received in a post-letter, and which I immediately afterwards delivered to one of the Lords-Justices of Ireland.

"And we do further declare, that we will not directly or indirectly, be anyways concerned with the said Wood's halfpence or farthings; but on the contrary, act to the great advantage and satisfaction of this kingdom, as good, loving and faithful subjects ought to do. And we do further declare, that to the best of our knowledge, the said William Wood is not in this kingdom.

"Given under our hands in Dublin this 22d. day of August 1724.

"JOHN MOLYNEUX

"DAN. MOLYNEUX."

Another ran as follows:

"ADVERTISEMENT.

"Whereas, I, Thomas Handy, of Meath Street, Dublin, did receive by the last packet, from a person in London, to whom I am an entire stranger, bills of lading for eleven casks of Wood's halfpence, shipped at Bristol, and consigned to me by the said person on his own proper account, of which I had not the least notice until I received the said bills of lading.

"Now I, the said Thomas Handy, being highly sensible of the duty and regard which every honest man owes to his country and to his fellow-subjects, do hereby declare, that I will not be concerned, directly or indirectly, in entering, landing, importing, receiving, or uttering any of the said Wood's halfpence, for that I am fully convinced, as well from the addresses of both Houses of Parliament, as otherwise, that the importing and uttering the said halfpence will be destructive to this nation, and prejudicial to his Majesty's revenue.

"And of this my resolution I gave notice by letter to the person who sent me the bills of lading, the very day I received them, and have sent back the said bills to him.

"THO. HANDY.

"Dublin, 29th. August, 1724." [T.S.]]

After which, let the officers to whom these orders are directed, (I would willingly except the military) come with their exhortations, their arguments and their eloquence, to persuade us to find our interest in our undoing. Let Wood and his accomplices travel about the country with cart-loads of their ware, and see who will take it off their hands, there will be no fear of his being robbed, for a highwayman would scorn to touch it.

I am only in pain how the commissioners of the revenue will proceed in this juncture; because I am told they are obliged by act of Parliament to take nothing but gold and silver in payment for His Majesty's customs, and I think they cannot justly offer this coinage of Mr. Wood to others, unless they will be content to receive it themselves.

The sum of the whole is this. The "Committee advises the King to send immediate orders to all his officers here, that Wood's coin be suffered and permitted without any let, suit, trouble, &c. to pass and be received as current money by such as shall be willing to receive the same." It is probable, that the first willing receivers may be those who must receive it whether they will or no, at least under the penalty of losing an office. But the landed undepending men, the merchants, the shopkeepers and bulk of the people, I hope, and am almost confident, will never receive it. What must the consequence be? The owners will sell it for as much as they can get. Wood's halfpence will come to be offered for six a penny (yet then he will be a sufficient gainer) and the necessary receivers will be losers of two-thirds in their salaries or pay.

This puts me in mind of a passage I was told many years ago in England. At a quarter-sessions in Leicester, the justices had wisely decreed, to take off a halfpenny in a quart from the price of ale. One of them, who came in after the thing was determined, being informed of what had passed, said thus: "Gentlemen; you have made an order, that ale should be sold in our country for three halfpence a quart: I desire you will now make another to appoint who must drink it, for *by G— I will not*."[21]

[Footnote 21: The following broadside, ascribed to Swift, but written probably by Sheridan, further amusingly illustrates the point Swift makes. The broadside was printed by John Harding:

"Another Letter to Mr. Harding the printer, upon occasion of the Report of the Committee of the Lords of His Majesty's Most Honourable Privy-Council, in relation to Mr. Wood's halfpence and farthings, etc., lately published.

"Mr. Harding,—Although this letter also is directed to you, yet you know that it is intended for the benefit of the whole kingdom, and therefore I pray make it public, and take care to disperse it.

"The design of it is only to desire all people to take notice, That whatever apprehensions some persons seem to be under on account of the above-mentioned report concerning Mr. Wood's halfpence and farthings, yet the utmost advice which the right honourable Committee have thought fit to give His Majesty, is, That a certain sum of the said halfpence and farthings may be received as current money by such as shall be willing to receive the same. And if we are willing to ruin ourselves and our country, I think we are not to be pitied.

"Upon this occasion I would only tell my countrymen a short story.

"A certain King of Great Britain who spoke broad Scotch, and being himself a man of wit, loved both to hear and speak things that were humorous, had once a petition preferred to him, in which the petitioner, having set forth his own merits, most humbly prayed His Majesty to grant him letters-patent for receiving a shilling from every one of his subjects who should be willing to give so much to him. 'In gude troth,' said the King, 'a very reasonable petition. Let every man give thee twa shillings gin he be willing so to do, and thou shalt have full liberty to receive it.' 'But,' says the petitioner, 'I desire that this clause may be inserted in my patent, That every man who refuses to give me a shilling, should appear at Westminster Hall to shew cause why he so refuses.' 'This also,' says the King, 'shall be granted thee, but always with this proviso, that the man be willing to come.'

"I am your, etc.

"MISOXULOS."]

I must beg leave to caution your lordships and worships in one particular. Wood hath graciously promised to load us at present only with forty thousand pounds of his coin, till the exigences of the kingdom require the rest. I entreat you will never suffer Mr. Wood to be a judge of your exigences. While there is one piece of silver or gold remaining in the kingdom he will call it an exigency, he will double his present *quantum* by stealth as soon as he can, and will have the remainder still to the good. He will pour his own raps[22] and counterfeits upon us: France and Holland will do the same; nor will our own coiners at home be behind them: To confirm which I have now in my pocket a rap or counterfeit halfpenny in imitation of his, but so ill performed, that in my conscience I believe it is not of his coining.

[Footnote 22: The word Rap is probably a contraction of "raparee," and was the name given to the tokens that passed current in Ireland for copper coins of small value. Generally it referred to debased coins; hence it may be allied to "raparee," who might be considered as a debased citizen. The raparees were so called from the rapary or half-pike they carried. [T.S.]]

I must now desire your lordships and worships that you will give great allowance for this long undigested paper, I find myself to have gone into several repetitions, which were the effects of haste, while new thoughts fell in to add something to what I had said before. I think I may affirm that I have fully answered every paragraph in the Report, which although it be not unartfully drawn, and is perfectly in the spirit of a pleader who can find the most plausible topics in behalf of his client, yet there was no great skill required to detect the many mistakes contained in it, which however are by no means to be charged upon the right honourable Committee, but upon the most false impudent and fraudulent representations of Wood and his accomplices. I desire one particular may dwell upon your minds, although I have mentioned it more than once; That after all the weight laid upon precedents there is not one produced in the whole Report, of a patent for coining copper in England to pass in Ireland, and only two patents referred to (for indeed there were no more) which were both passed in Ireland, by references to the King's Council here, both less advantageous to the coiner than this of Wood, and in both securities given to receive the coin at every call, and give gold and silver in lieu of it. This demonstrates the most flagrant falsehood and impudence of Wood, by which he would endeavour to make the right honourable Committee his instruments, (for his own illegal and exorbitant gain,) to ruin a kingdom, which hath deserved quite different treatment.

I am very sensible that such a work as I have undertaken might have worthily employed a much better pen. But when a house is attempted to be robbed it often happens that the weakest in the family runs first to stop the door. All the assistance I had were some informations from an eminent person,[23] whereof I am afraid I have spoiled a few by endeavouring to make them of a piece with my own productions, and the rest I was not able to manage: I was in the case of David who could not move in the armour of Saul, and therefore I rather chose to attack this "uncircumcised Philistine (Wood I mean) with a sling and a stone." And I may say for Wood's honour as well as my own, that he resembles Goliath in many circumstances, very applicable to the present purpose; For Goliath had "a helmet of brass upon his head, and he was armed with a coat of mail, and the weight of the coat was five thousand shekels of brass, and he had greaves of brass upon his legs, and a target of brass between his shoulders." In short he was like Mr. Wood, all over brass; And "he defied the armies of the living God." Goliath's condition of combat were likewise the same with those of Wood. "If he prevail against us, then shall we be his servants:" But if it happens that I prevail over him, I renounce the other part of the condition, he shall never be a servant of mine, for I do not think him fit to be trusted in any honest man's shop.

[Footnote 23: Mr. Robert Lindsay, a Dublin lawyer, assisted Swift on the legal points raised in the Drapier's letters. This is the Mr. Lindsay, counsellor-at-law, to whom Swift submitted a case concerning a Mr. Gorman (see Scott's edit., vol. xix., p. 294). Mr. Lindsay is supposed to be the author of two letters addressed to Chief Justice Whitshed on the matter of his conduct towards the grand jury which discharged Harding the printer (see Scott's edit., vol. vi., p. 467). [T.S.]]

I will conclude with my humble desire and request which I made in my second letter; That your lordships and worships would please to order a declaration to be drawn up expressing, in the strongest terms, your firm resolutions never to receive or utter any of Wood's halfpence or farthings, and forbidding your tenants to receive them. That the said declaration may be signed by as many persons as possible who have estates in this kingdom, and be sent down to your several tenants aforesaid.[24]

[Footnote 24: A Declaration, pursuant to this request, was signed soon after by the most considerable persons of the kingdom, which was universally spread and of great use. [F.]

"The humble petition of the lord-mayor, sheriffs, commons, and citizens of the city of Dublin, in Common Council assembled," was issued as a broadside on 8th September, 1724. See also Appendix IX. [T.S.]]

And if the dread of Wood's halfpence should continue till next quarter-sessions (which I hope it will not) the gentlemen of every county will then have a fair opportunity of declaring against them with unanimity and zeal.

I am with the greatest respect,
 (May it please your lordships and worships)
  Your most dutiful
   and obedient servant,
    M.B.

Aug. 25, 1724.

LETTER IV.

A LETTER TO THE WHOLE PEOPLE OF IRELAND.

NOTE

The country was now in a very fever of excitement. Everywhere meetings were held for the purpose of expressing indignation against the imposition, and addresses from brewers, butchers, flying stationers, and townspeople generally, were sent in embodying the public protest against Wood and his coins. Swift fed the flame by publishing songs and ballads well fitted for the street singers, and appealing to the understandings of those who he well knew would effectively carry his message to the very hearths of the poorest labourers. Courtier and student, tradesman and freeman, thief and prostitute, beggar and loafer, all were alike carried by an indignation which launched them on a maelstrom of enthusiasm. So general became the outcry that, in Coxe's words, "the lords justices refused to issue the orders for the circulation of the coin.... People of all descriptions and parties flocked in crowds to the bankers to demand their money, and drew their notes with an express condition to be paid in gold and silver. The publishers of the most treasonable pamphlets escaped with impunity, provided Wood and his patent were introduced into the work. The grand juries could scarcely be induced to find any bill against such delinquents; no witnesses in the prosecution were safe in their persons; and no juries were inclined, or if inclined could venture, to find them guilty."

In such a state of public feeling Swift assumed an entirely new attitude. He promulgated his "Letter to the Whole People of Ireland"—a letter which openly struck at the very root of the whole evil, and laid bare to the public eye the most secret spring of its righteous indignation. It was not Wood nor his coins, it was the freedom of the people of Ireland and their just rights and privileges that were being fought for. He wrote them the letter "to refresh and continue that spirit so seasonably raised among" them, and in order that they should plainly understand "that by the laws of God, of NATURE, of NATIONS, and of your COUNTRY, you ARE, and OUGHT to be as FREE a people as your brethren in England." The King's prerogative had been held threateningly over them. What was the King's prerogative? he asked in effect. It was but the right he enjoyed within the bounds of the law as made by the people in parliament assembled. The law limits him with his subjects. Such prerogative he respected and would take up arms to protect against any who should rebel. But "all government without the consent of the governed, is the very definition of slavery." The condition of the Irish nation was such that it was to be expected eleven armed men should overcome a single man in his shirt; but even if those in power exercise then power to cramp liberty, a man on the rack may still have "the liberty of roaring as loud as he thought fit." And the men on the rack roared to a tune that Walpole had never before heard.

The letter appeared on the 13th October, 1724.[1] The Duke of Grafton had been recalled and Carteret had taken up the reins of government. For reasons, either personal or politic, he took Walpole's side. Coxe goes into considerations on this attitude of Carteret's, but they hardly concern us here. Suffice it that the Lord Lieutenant joined forces with the party in the Irish Privy Council, among whom were Midleton and St. John Brodrick, and on October 27th issued a proclamation offering a reward of £300[2] for the discovery of the author of this "wicked and malicious pamphlet" which highly reflected on his Majesty and his ministers, and which tended "to alienate the affections of his good subjects of England and Ireland from each other."

[Footnote 1: Not on October 23rd as the earlier editors print it, and as
Monck Mason, Scott and Mr. Churton Collins repeat.]

[Footnote 2: See Appendix, No. VI.]

The author's name was not made public, nor was it likely to be. There is no doubt that it was generally known who the author was. In that general knowledge lies the whole pith of the Biblical quotation circulated abroad on the heels of the proclamation: "And the people said unto Saul, shall *Jonathan* die, who had wrought this great salvation in Israel? God forbid: as the Lord liveth there shall not one hair of his head fall to the ground, for he hath wrought with God this day: So the people rescued *Jonathan* that he died not."

Swift remained very much alive. Harding, for printing the obnoxious letter, had been arrested and imprisoned, and the Crown proceeded with his prosecution. In such circumstances Swift was not likely to remain idle. On the 26th October he addressed a letter to Lord Chancellor Midleton in defence of the Drapier's writings, and practically acknowledged himself to be the author.[3] It was not actually printed until 1735, but there is no doubt that Midleton received it at the time it was written. What effect it had on the ultimate issue is not known; but Midleton's conduct justifies the confidence Swift placed in him. The Grand Jury of the Michaelmas term of 1724 sat to consider the bill against Harding. On the 11th of November Swift addressed to them his "Seasonable Advice." The bill was thrown out. Whitshed, the Chief Justice, consistently with his action on a previous occasion (see vol. vii.), angrily remonstrated with the jury, demanded of them their reasons for such a decision, and finally dissolved them. This unconstitutional, and even disgraceful conduct, however, served but to accentuate the resentment of the people against Wood and the patent, and the Crown fared no better by a second Grand Jury. The second jury accompanied its rejection of the bill by a presentment against the patent,[4] and the defeat of the "prerogative" became assured. Every where the Drapier was acclaimed the saviour of his country. Any person who could scribble a doggerel or indite a tract rushed into print, and now Whitshed was harnessed to Wood in a pillory of contemptuous ridicule. Indeed, so bitter was the outcry against the Lord Chief Justice, that it is said to have hastened his death. The cities of Dublin, Cork and Waterford passed resolutions declaring the uttering of Wood's halfpence to be highly prejudicial to his Majesty's revenue and to the trades of the kingdom. The Drapier was now the patriot, and the whole nation responded to his appeal to assist him in its own defence.

[Footnote 3: The highly wrought up story about Swift's butler, narrated by Sheridan, Deane Swift and Scott, is nothing but a sample of eighteenth century "sensationalism." Swift never bothered himself about what his servants would say with regard to the authorship of the Letters. Certainly this letter to Midleton proves that he was not at all afraid of the consequences of discovery.]

[Footnote 4: See Appendix V.]

The text of the present reprint is based on that given by Sir Walter Scott, collated with the original edition and with that reprinted in "Fraud Detected" (1725). Faulkner's text of 1735 has also been consulted.

[T.S.]

A

LETTER

TO THE
WHOLE People
OF

IRELAND.

By M.B. *Drapier*.

AUTHOR of the LETTER to the *SHOP-KEEPERS*, &c.

DUBLIN:

LETTER IV.

A LETTER TO THE WHOLE PEOPLE OF IRELAND.

MY DEAR COUNTRYMEN,

Having already written three letters upon so disagreeable a subject as Mr. Wood and his halfpence; I conceived my task was at an end: But I find, that cordials must be frequently applied to weak constitutions, political as well as natural. A people long used to hardships, lose by degrees the very notions of liberty, they look upon themselves as creatures at mercy, and that all impositions laid on them by a stronger hand, are, in the phrase of the Report, legal and obligatory. Hence proceeds that poverty and lowness of spirit, to which a kingdom may be subject as well as a particular person. And when Esau came fainting from the field at the point to die, it is no wonder that he sold his birthright for a mess of pottage.

I thought I had sufficiently shewn to all who could want instruction, by what methods they might safely proceed, whenever this coin should be offered to them; and I believe there hath not been for many ages an example of any kingdom so firmly united in a point of great importance, as this of ours is at present, against that detestable fraud. But however, it so happens that some weak people begin to be alarmed anew, by rumours industriously spread. Wood prescribes to the newsmongers in London what they are to write. In one of their papers published here by some obscure printer (and probably with no good design) we are told, that "the Papists in Ireland have entered into an association against his coin," although it be notoriously known, that they never once offered to stir in the matter; so that the two Houses of Parliament, the Privy-council, the great number of corporations, the lord mayor and aldermen of Dublin, the grand juries, and principal gentlemen of several counties are stigmatized in a lump under the name of "Papists."

This impostor and his crew do likewise give out, that, by refusing to receive his dross for sterling, we "dispute the King's prerogative, are grown ripe for rebellion, and ready to shake off the dependency of Ireland upon the crown of England." To countenance which reports he hath published a paragraph in another newspaper, to let us know that "the Lord Lieutenant is ordered to come over immediately to settle his halfpence."

I entreat you, my dear countrymen, not to be under the least concern upon these and the like rumours, which are no more than the last howls of a dog dissected alive, as I hope he hath sufficiently been. These calumnies are the only reserve that is left him. For surely our continued and (almost) unexampled loyalty will never be called in question for not suffering ourselves to be robbed of all that we have, by one obscure ironmonger.

As to disputing the King's prerogative, give me leave to explain to those who are ignorant, what the meaning of that word *prerogative* is.

The Kings of these realms enjoy several powers, wherein the laws have not interposed: So they can make war and peace without the consent of Parliament; and this is a very great prerogative. But if the Parliament doth not approve of the war, the King must bear the charge of it out of his own purse, and this is as great a check on the crown. So the King hath a prerogative to coin money without consent of Parliament. But he cannot compel the subject to take that money except it be sterling, gold or silver; because herein he is limited by law. Some princes have indeed extended their prerogative further than the law allowed them; wherein however, the lawyers of succeeding ages, as fond as they are of precedents, have never dared to justify them. But to say the truth, it is only of late times that prerogative hath been fixed and ascertained. For whoever reads the histories of England, will find that some former Kings, and these none of the worst, have upon several occasions ventured to control the laws with very little ceremony or scruple, even later than the days of Queen Elizabeth. In her reign that pernicious counsel of sending base money hither, very narrowly failed of losing the kingdom, being complained of by the lord-deputy, the council, and the whole body of the English here:[5] So that soon after her death it was recalled by her successor, and lawful money paid in exchange.

[Footnote 5: See Moryson's "Itinerary" (Pt. ii., pp. 90, 196 and 262), where an account is given which fully bears out Swift.[T.S.]]

Having thus given you some notion of what is meant by the King's "prerogative," as far as a tradesman can be thought capable of explaining it, I will only add the opinion of the great Lord Bacon: That "as God governs the world by the settled laws of nature, which he hath made, and never transcends those laws but upon high important occasions; so among earthly princes, those are the wisest and the best, who govern by the known laws of the country, and seldomest make use of their prerogative."[6]

[Footnote 6: The words in inverted commas appear to be a reminiscence rather than a quotation. I have not traced the sentence, as it stands, in Bacon; but the regular government of the world by the laws of nature, as contrasted with the exceptional disturbance of these laws, is enunciated in Bacon's "Confession of Faith," while the dangers of a strained prerogative are urged in the

"Essay on Empire." Bacon certainly gives no support to Swift's limits of the prerogative as regards coinage. [CRAIK.]]

Now, here you may see that the vile accusation of Wood and his accomplices, charging us with "disputing the King's prerogative" by refusing his brass, can have no place, because compelling the subject to take any coin which is not sterling is no part of the King's prerogative, and I am very confident if it were so, we should be the last of his people to dispute it, as well from that inviolable loyalty we have always paid to His Majesty, as from the treatment we might in such a case justly expect from some who seem to think, we have neither common sense nor common senses. But God be thanked, the best of them are only our fellow-subjects, and not our masters. One great merit I am sure we have, which those of English birth can have no pretence to, that our ancestors reduced this kingdom to the obedience of England, for which we have been rewarded with a worse climate, the privilege of being governed by laws to which we do not consent, a ruined trade, a House of Peers without jurisdiction, almost an incapacity for all employments; and the dread of Wood's halfpence.

But we are so far from disputing the King's prerogative in coining, that we own he has power to give a patent to any man for setting his royal image and superscription upon whatever materials he pleases, and liberty to the patentee to offer them in any country from England to Japan, only attended with one small limitation, That nobody alive is obliged to take them.

Upon these considerations I was ever against all recourse to England for a remedy against the present impending evil, especially when I observed that the addresses of both Houses, after long expectance, produced nothing but a REPORT altogether in favour of

Wood, upon which I made some observations in a former letter, and might at least have made as many more. For it is a paper of as singular a nature as I ever beheld.

But I mistake; for before this Report was made, His Majesty's most gracious answer to the House of Lords was sent over and printed, wherein there are these words, "granting the patent for coining halfpence and farthings AGREEABLE TO THE PRACTICE OF HIS ROYAL PREDECESSORS, &c." That King Charles 2d. and King James 2d. (AND THEY ONLY) did grant patents for this purpose is indisputable, and I have shewn it at large. Their patents were passed under the great seal of Ireland by references to Ireland, the copper to be coined in Ireland, the patentee was bound on demand to receive his coin back in Ireland, and pay silver and gold in return. Wood's patent was made under the great seal of England, the brass coined in England, not the least reference made to Ireland, the sum immense, and the patentee under no obligation to receive it again and give good money for it: This I only mention, because in my private thoughts I have sometimes made a query, whether the penner of those words in His Majesty's most gracious answer, "agreeable to the practice of his royal predecessors," had maturely considered the several circumstances, which, in my poor opinion seem to make a difference.

Let me now say something concerning the other great cause of some people's fear, as Wood has taught the London newswriter to express it. That "his Excellency the Lord Lieutenant is coming over to settle Wood's halfpence."

We know very well that the Lords Lieutenants for several years past have not thought this kingdom worthy the honour of their residence, longer than was absolutely necessary for the King's business, which consequently wanted no speed in the dispatch; and therefore it naturally fell into most men's thoughts, that a new governor coming at an unusual time must portend some unusual business to be done, especially if the common report be true, that the Parliament prorogued to I know not when, is by a new summons (revoking that prorogation) to assemble soon after his arrival: For which extraordinary proceeding the lawyers on t'other side the water have by great good fortune found two precedents.

All this being granted, it can never enter into my head that so little a creature as Wood could find credit enough with the King and his ministers to have the Lord Lieutenant of Ireland sent hither in a hurry upon his errand.

For let us take the whole matter nakedly as it lies before us, without the refinements of some people, with which we have nothing to do. Here is a patent granted under the great seal of England, upon false suggestions, to one William Wood for coining copper halfpence for Ireland: The Parliament here, upon apprehensions of the worst consequences from the said patent, address the King to have it recalled; this is refused, and a committee of the Privy-council report to His Majesty, that Wood has performed the conditions of his patent. He then is left to do the best he can with his halfpence; no man being obliged to receive them; the people here, being likewise left to themselves, unite as one man, resolving they will have nothing to do with his ware. By this plain account of the fact it is manifest, that the King and his ministry are wholly out of the case, and the matter is left to be disputed between him and us. Will any man therefore attempt to persuade me, that a Lord Lieutenant is to be dispatched over in great haste before the ordinary time, and a Parliament summoned by anticipating a prorogation, merely to put an hundred thousand pounds into the pocket of a sharper, by the ruin of a most loyal kingdom.

But supposing all this to be true. By what arguments could a Lord Lieutenant prevail on the same Parliament which addressed with so much zeal and earnestness against this evil, to pass it into a law? I am sure their opinion of Wood and his project is not mended since the last prorogation; and supposing those methods should be used which detractors tell us have been sometimes put in practice for gaining votes. It is well known that in this kingdom there are few employments to be given, and if there were more, it is as well known to whose share they must fall.

But because great numbers of you are altogether ignorant in the affairs of your country, I will tell you some reasons why there are so few employments to be disposed of in this kingdom. All considerable offices for life here are possessed by those to whom the reversions were granted, and these have been generally followers of the chief governors, or persons who had interest in the Court of England. So the Lord Berkeley of Stratton[7] holds that great office of master of the rolls, the Lord Palmerstown[8] is first remembrancer worth near 2000_l. per ann._ One Dodington[9] secretary to the Earl of Pembroke,[10] begged the reversion of clerk of the pells worth 2500_l._ a year, which he now enjoys by the death of the Lord Newtown. Mr. Southwell is secretary of state,[11] and the Earl of Burlington[12] lord high treasurer of Ireland by inheritance. These are only a few among many others which I have been told of, but cannot remember. Nay the reversion of several employments during pleasure are granted the same way. This among many others is a circumstance whereby the kingdom of Ireland is distinguished from all other nations upon earth, and makes it so difficult an affair to get into a civil employ, that Mr.

Addison was forced to purchase an old obscure place, called keeper of the records of Bermingham's Tower of ten pounds a year, and to get a salary of 400_l._ annexed to it,[13] though all the records there are not worth half-a-crown, either for curiosity or use. And we lately saw a favourite secretary descend to be master of the revels, which by his credit and extortion he hath made pretty considerable.[14] I say nothing of the under-treasurership worth about 8000_l_. a year, nor the commissioners of the revenue, four of whom generally live in England; For I think none of these are granted in reversion. But the test is, that I have known upon occasion some of these absent officers as keen against the interest of Ireland as if they had never been indebted to her for a single groat.

[Footnote 7: Berkeley was one of the Junta in Harley's administration of 1710-1714. He had married Sir John Temple's daughter. His connection with a person so disliked by Swift may account for his inclusion here. [T.S.]]

[Footnote 8: This was Henry Temple, first Viscount Palmerston, with whom Swift later had an unpleasant correspondence. Palmerston could not have been more than seven years old when he was appointed (September 21st, 1680), with Luke King, chief remembrancer of the Court of Exchequer in Ireland, for their joint lives. King died in 1716, but the grant was renewed to Palmerston and his son Henry for life. He was raised to the peerage as Baron Temple of Mount Temple, and Viscount Palmerston of Palmerston, in March, 1722-1723. Sir Charles Hanbury Williams called him "Little Broadbottom Palmerston." He died in 1757. [T.S.]]

[Footnote 9: George Bubb (1691-1762) was Chief Secretary during Wharton's Lord lieutenancy in 1709. He took the name of Doddington on the death of his uncle in 1720. [T.S.]]

[Footnote 10: Thomas Herbert, eighth Earl of Pembroke (1656-1733), had preceded the Earl of Wharton as Lord lieutenant of Ireland. He bears a high character in history and on four successive coronations, namely, those of William and Mary, Anne, George I. and George II., he acted as sword carrier. Although a Tory, even Macaulay acknowledges Pembroke's high breeding and liberality. [T.S.]]

[Footnote 11: This is the Edward Southwell to whom Archbishop King wrote the letters quoted from Monck Mason in previous notes. He was the son of Sir Robert Southwell, the diplomatist and friend of Sir William Temple, to whom Swift bore a letter of introduction from the latter, soliciting the office of amanuensis. In June, 1720, Edward Southwell had his salary as secretary increased by £300; and in July of the same year the office was granted to him and his son for life. The Southwell family first came to Ireland in the reign of James I., at the time of the plantation of Munster. [T.S.]]

[Footnote 12: Richard Boyle, third Earl of Burlington (or Bridlington of Yorks), and fourth Earl of Cork (1695-1753), was appointed Lord High-Treasurer of Ireland in August, 1715. His great-grandfather, the first Earl of Cork, had held the same office in 1631. The Lord-lieutenancy of the West Riding of Yorkshire, and the office of Custos Rotulorum of the North and West Ridings, seem also to have been inheritances of this family. The third Earl had a taste for architecture, and spent enormous sums of money in the reconstruction of Burlington House, a building that was freely satirized by Hogarth and Lord Hervey. His taste, however, seems to have run to the ornamental rather than the useful, and its gratification involved him in such serious financial difficulties, that he was compelled to sell some of his Irish estates. Swift notes that "My Lord Burlington is now selling in one article £9,000 a year in Ireland for £200,000 which must pay his debts" (Scott's edit. 1814, vol. xix., p. 129). [T.S.]]

[Footnote 13: This post was found for Addison on his appointment in 1709 as secretary to the Earl of Wharton, Lord-lieutenant of Ireland. Tickell, in his preface to his edition of Addison's works, says the post was granted to Addison as a mark of Queen Anne's special favour. Bermingham's Tower was that part of Dublin Castle in which the records were kept. [T.S.]]

[Footnote 14: Mr. Hopkins, secretary to the Duke of Grafton. The exactions made by this gentleman upon the players, in his capacity of Master of the Revels, are the subject of two satirical poems. [S.]

This may have been John Hopkins, the second son of the Bishop of Londonderry, who was the author of "Amasia," dedicated to the Duchess of Grafton. [T.S.]]

I confess, I have been sometimes tempted to wish that this project of Wood might succeed, because I reflected with some pleasure what a jolly crew it would bring over among us of lords and squires, and pensioners of both sexes, and officers civil and military, where we should live together as merry and sociable as beggars, only with this one abatement, that we should neither have meat to feed, nor manufactures to clothe us, unless we could be content to prance about in coats of mail, or eat brass as ostriches do iron.

I return from this digression to that which gave me the occasion of making it: And I believe you are now convinced, that if the Parliament of Ireland were as temptable as any other assembly within a mile of Christendom (which God forbid) yet the managers must of necessity fail for want of tools to work with. But I will yet go one step further, by supposing that a hundred new employments were erected on purpose to gratify compilers; yet still an insuperable difficulty would remain; for it happens, I know not how, that money is neither Whig nor Tory, neither of town nor country party, and it is not improbable, that a gentleman would rather choose to live upon his own estate which brings him gold and silver, than with the addition of an employment, when his rents and salary must both be paid in Wood's brass, at above eighty *per cent.* discount.

For these and many other reasons, I am confident you need not be under the least apprehensions from the sudden expectation of the Lord Lieutenant,[15] while we continue in our present hearty disposition; to alter which there is no suitable temptation can possibly be offered: And if, as I have often asserted from the best authority, the law hath not left a power in the crown to force any money except sterling upon the subject, much less can the crown devolve such a power upon another.

[Footnote 15: Lord Carteret, afterwards Earl Granville. See note to "A
Vindication of Lord Carteret," in vol. vii. of present edition of Swift's works. [T.S.]]

This I speak with the utmost respect to the person and dignity of his Excellency the Lord Carteret, whose character hath been given me by a gentleman that hath known him from his first appearance in the world: That gentleman describes him as a young nobleman of great accomplishments, excellent learning, regular in his life, and of much spirit and vivacity. He hath since, as I have heard, been employed abroad, was principal secretary of state, and is now about the 37th year of his age appointed Lord Lieutenant of Ireland. From such a governor this kingdom may reasonably hope for as much prosperity as, under so many discouragements, it can be capable of receiving.[16]

[Footnote 16: Carteret was an old friend of Swift. On the Earl's appointment to the Lord-lieutenancy, in April, 1724, Swift wrote him a letter on the matter of Wood's halfpence, in which he took the liberty of "an old humble servant, and one who always loved and esteemed" him, to make known to him the apprehensions the people were under concerning Mr. Wood's patent. "Neither is it doubted," he wrote, "that when your excellency shall be thoroughly informed, your justice and compassion for an injured people, will force you to employ your credit for their relief." Swift waited for more than a month, and on receiving no reply, sent a second letter, which Sir Henry Craik justly calls, "a masterpiece of its kind." It was as follows:

"June 9, 1724.

"**MY LORD,**

"It is above a month since I took the boldness of writing to your excellency, upon a subject wherein the welfare of this kingdom is highly concerned.

"I writ at the desire of several considerable persons here, who could not be ignorant that I had the honour of being well known to you.

"I could have wished your excellency had condescended so far, as to let one of your under clerks have signified to me that a letter was received.

"I have been long out of the world; but have not forgotten what used to pass among those I lived with while I was in it: and I can say, that during the experience of many years, and many changes in affairs, your excellency, and one more, who is not worthy to be compared to you, are the only great persons that ever refused to answer a letter from me, without regard to business, party, or greatness; and if I had not a peculiar esteem for your personal qualities, I should think myself to be acting a very inferior part in making this complaint.

"I never was so humble, as to be vain upon my acquaintance with men in power, and always rather chose to avoid it when I was not called. Neither were their power or titles sufficient, without merit, to make me cultivate them; of which I have witnesses enough left, after all the havoc made among them, by accidents of time, or by changes of persons, measures, and opinions.

"I know not how your conception of yourself may alter, by every new high station; but mine must continue the same, or alter for the worse.

"I often told a great minister, whom you well know, that I valued him for being the same man through all the progress of power and place. I expected the like in your lordship; and still hope that I shall be the only person who will ever find it otherwise.

"I pray God to direct your excellency in all your good undertakings, and especially in your government of this kingdom.

"I shall trouble you no more; but remain, with great respect, my Lord,

"Your excellency's most obedient,

"and most humble servant,

"JON. SWIFT."

This letter brought an immediate reply from Carteret, who confessed himself in the wrong for his silence, and trusted he had not forfeited Swift's friendship by it. With regard to Mr. Wood's patent, he said that the matter was under examination, "and till that is over I am not informed sufficiently to make any other judgment of the matter, than that which I am naturally led to make, by the general aversion which appears to it in the whole nation." Swift replied in a charming vein, and elegantly put his scolding down to the testiness of old age. His excellency had humbled him. "Therefore, I fortel that you, who could so easily conquer so captious a person, and of so little consequence, will quickly subdue this whole kingdom to love and reverence you" (Scott's ed. 1824, vol. xvi., pp. 430-435). [T.S.]]

It is true indeed, that within the memory of man, there have been governors of so much dexterity, as to carry points of terrible consequence to this kingdom, by their power with *those who were in office*, and by their arts in managing or deluding others with oaths, affability, and even with dinners. If Wood's brass had in those times been upon the anvil, it is obvious enough to conceive what methods would have been taken. Depending persons would have been told in plain terms, that it was a "service expected from them, under pain of the public business being put into more complying hands." Others would be allured by promises. To the country gentleman, besides good words, burgundy and closeting. It would perhaps have been hinted how "kindly it would be taken to comply with a royal patent, though it were not compulsory," that if any inconveniences ensued, it might be made up with other "graces or favours hereafter." That "gentlemen ought to consider whether it were prudent or safe to disgust England:" They would be desired to "think of some good bills for encouraging of trade, and setting the poor to work, some further acts against Popery and for uniting Protestants." There would be solemn engagements that we should "never be troubled with above forty thousand pounds in his coin, and all of the best and weightiest sort, for which we should only give our manufactures in exchange, and keep our gold and silver at home." Perhaps a "seasonable report of some invasion would have been spread in the most proper juncture," which is a great smoother of rubs in public proceedings; and we should have been told that "this was no time to create differences when the kingdom was in danger."

These, I say, and the like methods would in corrupt times have been taken to let in this deluge of brass among us; and I am confident would even then have not succeeded, much less under the administration of so excellent a person as the Lord Carteret, and in a country where the people of all ranks, parties and denominations are convinced to a man, that the utter undoing of themselves and their posterity for ever will be dated from the admission of that execrable coin; that if it once enters, it can be no more confined to a small or moderate quantity, than the plague can be confined to a few families, and that no equivalent can be given by any earthly power, any more than a dead carcass can be recovered to life by a cordial.

There is one comfortable circumstance in this universal opposition to Mr. Wood, that the people sent over hither from England to fill up our vacancies ecclesiastical, civil and military, are all on our side: Money, the great divider of the world, hath by a strange revolution, been the great uniter of a most divided people. Who would leave a hundred pounds a year in England (a country of freedom) to be paid a thousand in Ireland out of Wood's exchequer. The gentleman they have lately made primate[17] would never quit his seat in an English House of Lords, and his preferments at Oxford and Bristol, worth twelve hundred pounds a year, for four times the denomination here, but not half the value; therefore I expect to hear he will be as good an Irishman, upon this article, as any of his brethren, or even of us who have had the misfortune to be born in this island. For those, who, in the common phrase, do not "come hither to learn the language," would never change a better country for a worse, to receive brass instead of gold.

[Footnote 17: Hugh Boulter (1672-1742) was appointed Archbishop of Armagh, August 31st, 1724. He had been a fellow of Magdalen College, Oxford, and had served the King as chaplain in Hanover, in 1719. In this latter year he was promoted to the Bishopric of Bristol, and the Deanery of Christ Church, Oxford. His appointment as Primate of Ireland, was in accordance with Walpole's plan for governing Ireland from England. Walpole had no love for Carteret, and no faith in his power or willingness to aid him in his policy. Indeed, Carteret was sent to Ireland to be got out of the way. He was governor nominally; the real governor being Walpole in the person of the new Primate. What were Boulter's instructions may be gathered from the manner in which he carried out his purpose. Of a strong character and of untiring energy, Boulter set about his work in a fashion which showed that Walpole had chosen well. Nothing of any importance that transpired in Ireland, no fact of any interest about the individuals in office, no movement of any suspected or suspicious person escaped his vigilance. His letters testify to an unabating zeal for the English government of Irish affairs by Englishmen in the English interest. His perseverance knew no obstacles; he continued against all difficulties in his dogged and yet able manner to establish some order out of the chaos of Ireland's condition. But his government was the outcome of a profound conviction that only in the interest of England should Ireland be governed. If Ireland could be made prosperous and contented, so much more good would accrue to England. But that prosperity and that contentment had nothing whatever to do with safeguarding Irish institutions, or recognizing the rights of the Irish people. If he gave way to popular opinion at all, it was because it was either expedient or beneficial to the English interest. If he urged, as he did, the founding of Protestant Charter schools, it was because this would strengthen the English power. To preserve that he obtained the enactment of a statute which excluded Roman Catholics from the legal profession and the offices of legal administration; and another act of his making actually disfranchised them altogether. Boulter was also a member of the Irish Privy Council, and Lord Justice of Ireland. The latter office he held under the vice-regencies of Carteret, Dorset and Devonshire. His secretary, Ambrose Philips, had been connected with him, in earlier years, in contributing to a periodical entitled, "The Free Thinker," which appeared in 1718. Philips, in 1769, supervised the publication of Boulter's "Letters," which were published at Oxford. [T.S.]]

Another slander spread by Wood and his emissaries is, that by opposing him we discover an inclination to "shake off our dependence upon the crown of England." Pray observe how important a person is this same William Wood, and how the public weal of two kingdoms is involved in his private interest. First, all those who refuse to take his coin are Papists; for he tells us that "none but Papists are associated against him;" Secondly, they "dispute the King's prerogative;" Thirdly, "they are ripe for rebellion," and Fourthly, they are going to "shake off their dependence upon the crown of England;" That is to say, "they are going to choose another king;" For there can be no other meaning in this expression, however some may pretend to strain it.

And this gives me an opportunity of explaining, to those who are ignorant, another point, which hath often swelled in my breast. Those who come over hither to us from England, and some weak people among ourselves, whenever in discourse we make mention of liberty and property, shake their heads, and tell us, that Ireland is a "depending kingdom," as if they would seem, by this phrase, to intend that the people of Ireland is in some state of slavery or dependence different from those of England; Whereas a "depending kingdom" is a modern term of art, unknown, as I have heard, to all ancient civilians, and writers upon government; and Ireland is on the contrary called in some statutes an "imperial crown," as held only from God; which is as high a style as any kingdom is capable of receiving. Therefore by this expression, a "depending kingdom," there is no more understood than that by a statute made here in the 33d year of Henry 8th. "The King and his successors are to be kings imperial of this realm as united and knit to the imperial crown of England." I have looked over all the English and Irish statutes without finding any law that makes Ireland depend upon England, any more than England does upon Ireland. We have indeed obliged ourselves to have the same king with them, and consequently they are obliged to have the same king with us. For the law was made by our own Parliament, and our ancestors then were not such fools (whatever they were in the preceding reign) to bring themselves under I know not what dependence, which is now talked of without any ground of law, reason or common sense.[18]

[Footnote 18: This was the passage selected by the government upon which to found its prosecution. As Sir Walter Scott points out, it "contains the pith and essence of the whole controversy." [T.S.]]

Let whoever think otherwise, I M.B. Drapier, desire to be excepted,[19] for I declare, next under God, I *depend* only on the King my sovereign, and on the laws of my own country; and I am so far from *depending* upon the people of England, that if they should ever rebel against my sovereign (which God forbid) I would be ready at the first command from His Majesty to take arms against them, as some of *my* countrymen did against *theirs* at Preston. And if such a rebellion should prove so successful as to fix the Pretender on the throne of England, I would venture to transgress that statute so far as to lose every drop of my blood to hinder him from being King of Ireland.[20]

[Footnote 19: For a humorous story which accounts for Swift's use of the words "desire to be excepted," see the Drapier's sixth letter. [T.S.]]

[Footnote 20: Great offence was taken at this paragraph. Swift refers to it again in his sixth letter. Sir Henry Craik, in his "Life of Jonathan Swift" (vol. ii., p. 74), has an acute note on this paragraph, and the one already alluded to in the sixth letter. I take the liberty of transcribing it: "The manoeuvre by which Swift managed to associate a suspicion of Jacobitism with his opponents, is one peculiarly characteristic; and so is the skill with which, in the next letter, he meets the objections to this paragraph, by half offering an extent of submission that might equally be embarrassing—a submission even to Jacobitism, if Jacobitism were to become strong enough. He does not commit himself, however: he fears a 'spiteful interpretation.' In short, he places the English Cabinet on the horns of a dilemma. 'Am I to resist Jacobitism? Then what becomes of your doctrine of Ireland's dependency?' or, 'Am I to become a Jacobite, if England bids me? Then what becomes of your Protestant succession? Must even that give way to your desire to tyrannize?'" [T.S.]]

'Tis true indeed, that within the memory of man, the Parliaments of England have sometimes assumed the power of binding this kingdom by laws enacted there,[21] wherein they were at first openly opposed (as far as truth, reason and justice are capable of opposing) by the famous Mr. Molineux,[22] an English gentleman born here, as well as by several of the greatest patriots, and best Whigs in England; but the love and torrent of power prevailed. Indeed the arguments on both sides were invincible. For in reason, all government without the consent of the governed is the very definition of slavery: But in fact, eleven men well armed will certainly subdue one single man in his shirt. But I have done. For those who have used power to cramp liberty have gone so far as to resent even the liberty of complaining, although a man upon the rack was never known to be refused the liberty of roaring as loud as he thought fit.

[Footnote 21: Particularly in the reign of William III., when this doctrine of English supremacy was assumed, in order to discredit the authority of the Irish Parliament summoned by James II. [S.]

See note on Poyning's Law, p. 77. [T.S.]]

[Footnote 22: See note on p. 167. [T.S.]]

And as we are apt to sink too much under unreasonable fears, so we are too soon inclined to be raised by groundless hopes (according to the nature of all consumptive bodies like ours) thus, it hath been given about for several days past, that somebody in England empowered a second somebody to write to a third somebody here to assure us, that we "should no more be troubled with those halfpence." And this is reported to have been done by the same person, who was said to have sworn some months ago, that he would "ram them down our throats" (though I doubt they would stick in our stomachs) but whichever of these reports is true or false, it is no concern of ours. For in this point we have nothing to do with English ministers, and I should be sorry it lay in their power to redress this grievance or to enforce it: For the "Report of the Committee" hath given me a surfeit. The remedy is wholly in your own hands, and therefore I have digressed a little in order to refresh and continue that spirit so seasonably raised amongst you, and to let you see that by the laws of GOD, of NATURE, of NATIONS, and of your own COUNTRY, you ARE and OUGHT to be as FREE a people as your brethren in England.

If the pamphlets published at London by Wood and his journeymen in defence of his cause, were reprinted here, and that our countrymen could be persuaded to read them, they would convince you of his wicked design more than all I shall ever be able to say. In short I make him a perfect saint in comparison of what he appears to be from the writings of those whom he hires to justify his project. But he is so far master of the field (let others guess the reason) that no London printer dare publish any paper written in favour of Ireland, and here nobody hath yet been so bold as to publish anything in favour of him.

There was a few days ago a pamphlet sent me of near 50 pages written in favour of Mr. Wood and his coinage, printed in London; it is not worth answering, because probably it will never be published here: But it gave me an occasion to reflect upon an unhappiness we lie under, that the people of England are utterly ignorant of our case, which however is no wonder, since it is a point they do not in the least concern themselves about, farther than perhaps as a subject of discourse in a coffee-house when they have nothing else to talk of. For I have reason to believe that no minister ever gave himself the trouble of reading any papers written in our defence, because I suppose their opinions are already determined, and are formed wholly upon the reports of Wood and his accomplices; else it would be impossible that any man could have the impudence to write such a pamphlet as I have mentioned.

Our neighbours whose understandings are just upon a level with ours (which perhaps are none of the brightest) have a strong contempt for most nations, but especially for Ireland: They look upon us as a sort of savage Irish, whom our ancestors conquered several hundred years ago, and if I should describe the Britons to you as they were in Caesar's time, when they painted their bodies, or clothed themselves with the skins of beasts, I would act full as reasonably as they do: However they are so far to be excused in relation to the present subject, that, hearing only one side of the cause, and having neither opportunity nor curiosity to examine the other, they believe a lie merely for their ease, and conclude, because Mr. Wood pretends to have power, he hath also reason on his side.

Therefore to let you see how this case is represented in England by Wood and his adherents, I have thought it proper to extract out of that pamphlet a few of those notorious falsehoods in point of fact and reasoning contained therein; the knowledge whereof will confirm my countrymen in their own right sentiments, when they will see by comparing both, how much their enemies are in the wrong.

First, The writer, positively asserts, "That Wood's halfpence were current among us for several months with the universal approbation of all people, without one single gainsayer, and we all to a man thought ourselves happy in having them."

Secondly, He affirms, "That we were drawn into a dislike of them only by some cunning evil-designing men among us, who opposed this patent of Wood to get another for themselves."

Thirdly, That "those who most declared at first against Wood's patent were the very men who intended to get another for their own advantage."

Fourthly, That "our Parliament and Privy-council, the Lord Mayor and aldermen of Dublin, the grand juries and merchants, and in short the whole kingdom, nay the very dogs" (as he expresseth it) "were fond of those halfpence, till they were inflamed by those few designing persons aforesaid."

Fifthly, He says directly, That "all those who opposed the halfpence were Papists and enemies to King George."

Thus far I am confident the most ignorant among you can safely swear from your own knowledge that the author is a most notorious liar in every article; the direct contrary being so manifest to the whole kingdom, that if occasion required, we might get it confirmed under five hundred thousand hands.

Sixthly, He would persuade us, that "if we sell five shillings worth of our goods or manufactures for two shillings and fourpence worth of copper, although the copper were melted down, and that we could get five shillings in gold or silver for the said goods, yet to take the said two shillings and fourpence in copper would be greatly for our advantage."

And Lastly, He makes us a very fair offer, as empowered by Wood, that "if we will take off two hundred thousand pounds in his halfpence for our goods, and likewise pay him three *per cent.* interest for thirty years, for an hundred and twenty thousand pounds (at which he computes the coinage above the intrinsic value of the copper) for the loan of his coin, he, will after that time give us good money for what halfpence will be then left."

Let me place this offer in as clear a light as I can to shew the unsupportable villainy and impudence of that incorrigible wretch. First (says he) "I will send two hundred thousand pounds of my coin into your country, the copper I compute to be in real value eighty thousand pounds, and I charge you with an hundred and twenty thousand pounds for the coinage; so that you see I lend you an hundred and twenty thousand pounds for thirty years, for which you shall pay me three *per cent.* That is to say three thousand six hundred pounds *per ann.* which in thirty years will amount to an hundred and eight thousand pounds. And when these thirty years are expired, return me my copper and I will give you good money for it."

This is the proposal made to us by Wood in that pamphlet written by one of his commissioners; and the author is supposed to be the same infamous Coleby one of his under-swearers at the committee of council, who was tried for robbing the treasury here, where he was an under-clerk.[23]

[Footnote 23: See note on p. 61. [T.S.]]

By this proposal he will first receive two hundred thousand pounds, in goods or sterling for as much copper as he values at eighty thousand pounds, but in reality not worth thirty thousand pounds. Secondly, He will receive for interest an hundred and eight thousand pounds. And when our children came thirty years hence to return his halfpence upon his executors (for before that time he will be probably gone to his own place) those executors will very reasonably reject them as raps and counterfeits, which probably they will be, and millions of them of his own coinage.

Methinks I am fond of such a dealer as this who mends every day upon our hands, like a Dutch reckoning, where if you dispute the unreasonableness and exorbitance of the bill, the landlord shall bring it up every time with new additions.

Although these and the like pamphlets published by Wood in London be altogether unknown here, where nobody could read them without as much indignation as contempt would allow, yet I thought it proper to give you a specimen how the man employs his time, where he rides alone without one creature to contradict him, while our FEW FRIENDS there wonder at our silence, and the English in general, if they think of this matter at all, impute our refusal to wilfulness or disaffection, just as Wood and his hirelings are pleased to represent.

But although our arguments are not suffered to be printed in England, yet the consequence will be of little moment. Let Wood endeavour to persuade the people there that we ought to receive his coin, and let me convince our people here that they ought to reject it under pain of our utter undoing. And then let him do his best and his worst.

Before I conclude, I must beg leave in all humility to tell Mr. Wood, that he is guilty of great indiscretion, by causing so honourable a name as that of Mr. Walpole to be mentioned so often, and in such a manner, upon his occasion: A short paper printed at Bristol and reprinted here reports Mr. Wood to say, that he "wonders at the impudence and insolence of the Irish in refusing his coin, and what he will do when Mr. Walpole comes to town." Where, by the way, he is mistaken, for it is the true English people of Ireland who refuse it, although we take it for granted that the Irish will do so too whenever they are asked. He orders it to be printed in another paper, that "Mr. Walpole will cram this brass down our throats:" Sometimes it is given out that we must "either take these halfpence or eat our brogues," And, in another newsletter but of yesterday, we read that the same great man "hath sworn to make us swallow his coin in fire-balls."

This brings to my mind the known story of a Scotchman, who receiving sentence of death, with all the circumstances of hanging, beheading, quartering, embowelling and the like, cried out, "What need all this COOKERY?" And I think we have reason to ask the same question; for if we believe Wood, here is a dinner getting ready for us, and you see the bill of fare, and I am sorry the drink was forgot, which might easily be supplied with melted lead and flaming pitch.

What vile words are these to put into the mouth of a great councillor, in high trust with His Majesty, and looked upon as a prime-minister. If Mr. Wood hath no better a manner of representing his patrons, when I come to be a great man, he shall never be suffered to attend at my levee. This is not the style of a great minister, it savours too much of the kettle and the furnace, and came entirely out of Mr. Wood's forge.

As for the threat of making us eat our brogues, we need not be in pain; for if his coin should pass, that unpolite covering for the feet, would no longer be a national reproach; because then we should have neither shoe nor brogue left in the kingdom. But here the falsehood of Mr. Wood is fairly detected; for I am confident Mr. Walpole never heard of a brogue in his whole life.[24]

[Footnote 24: A biting sneer at Walpole's ignorance of Irish affairs. [T.S.]]

As to "swallowing these halfpence in fire-balls," it is a story equally improbable. For to execute this operation the whole stock of Mr. Wood's coin and metal must be melted down and moulded into hollow balls with wild-fire, no bigger than a reasonable throat can be able to swallow. Now the metal he hath prepared, and already coined will amount at least fifty millions of halfpence to be swallowed by a million and a half of people; so that allowing two halfpence to each ball, there will be about seventeen balls of wild-fire a-piece to be swallowed by every person in this kingdom, and to administer this dose, there cannot be conveniently fewer than fifty thousand operators, allowing one operator to every thirty, which, considering the squeamishness of some stomachs and the peevishness of young children, is but reasonable. Now, under correction of better judgments, I think the trouble and charge of such an experiment would exceed the profit, and therefore I take this report to be spurious, or at least only a new scheme of Mr.

Wood himself, which to make it pass the better in Ireland he would father upon a minister of state.

But I will now demonstrate beyond all contradiction that Mr. Walpole is against this project of Mr. Wood, and is an entire friend to Ireland, only by this one invincible argument, that he has the universal opinion of being a wise man, an able minister, and in all his proceedings pursuing the true interest of the King his master: And that as his integrity is above all corruption, so is his fortune above all temptation. I reckon therefore we are perfectly safe from that corner, and shall never be under the necessity of contending with so formidable a power, but be left to possess our brogues and potatoes in peace as remote from thunder as we are from Jupiter.

I am,
  My dear countrymen,
    Your loving fellow-subject,
      fellow-sufferer and humble servant.
              M.B.

Oct. 13. 1724.

SEASONABLE ADVICE TO THE GRAND JURY.

SEASONABLE ADVICE TO THE GRAND JURY,

CONCERNING THE BILL PREPARING AGAINST THE PRINTER OF THE DRAPIER'S FOURTH LETTER.

Since a bill is preparing for the grand jury, to find against the printer of the Drapier's last letter, there are several things maturely to be considered by those gentlemen, before whom this bill is to come, before they determine upon it.

FIRST, they are to consider, that the author of the said pamphlet, did write three other discourses on the same subject; which instead of being censured were universally approved by the whole nation, and were allowed to have raised, and continued that spirit among us, which hitherto hath kept out Wood's coin: For all men will allow, that if those pamphlets had not been writ, his coin must have overrun the nation some months ago.

SECONDLY, it is to be considered that this pamphlet, against which a proclamation hath been issued, is writ by the same author; that nobody ever doubted the innocence, and goodness of his design, that he appears through the whole tenor of it, to be a loyal subject to His Majesty, and devoted to the House of Hanover, and declares himself in a manner peculiarly zealous against the Pretender; And if such a writer in four several treatises on so nice a subject, where a royal patent is concerned, and where it was necessary to speak of England and of liberty, should in one or two places happen to let fall an inadvertent expression, it would be hard to condemn him after all the good he hath done; Especially when we consider, that he could have no possible design in view, either of honour or profit, but purely the GOOD of his country.

THIRDLY, it ought to be well considered, whether any one expression in the said pamphlet, be really liable to just exception, much less to be found "wicked, malicious, seditious, reflecting upon His Majesty and his ministry," &c.

The two points in that pamphlet, which it is said the prosecutors intend chiefly to fix on, are, First, where the author mentions the "penner of the King's answer." First, it is well known, His Majesty is not master of the English tongue, and therefore it is necessary that some other person should be employed to pen what he hath to say, or write in that language. Secondly, His Majesty's answer is not in the first person, but the third. It is not said "WE are concerned," or, "OUR royal predecessors," but "HIS MAJESTY is concerned;" and "HIS royal predecessors." By which it is plain these are properly not the words of His Majesty; but supposed to be taken from him, and transmitted hither by one of his ministers. Thirdly it will be easily seen, that the author of the pamphlet delivers his sentiments upon this particular, with the utmost caution and respect, as any impartial reader will observe.

The second paragraph, which it is said will be taken notice of as a motive to find the bill, is, what the author says of Ireland being a depending kingdom. He explains all the dependency he knows of it, which is a law made in Ireland, whereby it is enacted that "whoever is King of England, shall be King of Ireland." Before this explanation be condemned, and the bill found upon it, it would be proper, that some lawyers should fully inform the jury what other law there is, either statute or common for this dependency, and if there be no law, there is no transgression.

The Fourth thing very maturely to be considered by the jury, is, what influence their finding the bill may have upon the kingdom.

The people in general find no fault in the Drapier's last book, any more than in the three former, and therefore when they hear it is condemned by a grand jury of Dublin, they will conclude it is done in favour of Wood's coin, they will think we of this town have changed our minds, and intend to take those halfpence, and therefore that it will be in vain for them to stand out. So that the question comes to this, Which will be of the worst consequence, to let pass one or two expressions, at the worst only unwary, in a book written for the public service; or to leave a free open passage for Wood's brass to overrun us, by which we shall be undone for ever.

The fifth thing to be considered, is, that the members of the grand jury being merchants, and principal shopkeepers, can have no suitable temptation offered them, as a recompense for the mischief they will suffer by letting in this coin, nor can be at any loss or danger by rejecting the bill: They do not expect any employments in the state, to make up in their own private advantage, the destruction of their country. Whereas those who go about to advise, entice, or threaten them to find that bill, have great employments, which they have a mind to keep, or to get greater, which was likewise the case of all those who signed to have the author prosecuted. And therefore it is known, that his grace the Lord Archbishop of Dublin,[1] so renowned for his piety, and wisdom, and love of his country, absolutely refused to condemn the book, or the author.

[Footnote 1: The proclamation against the Drapier's fourth letter as given in Appendix IV. at the end of this volume, does not bear Archbishop King's signature. In a letter from that prelate, written on November 24th, 1724, to Samuel Molineux, secretary to the Prince of Wales, it appears that other persons of influence also refrained from sanctioning it. The following is an extract from this letter as given by Monck Mason for the first time:

"A great many pamphlets have been writ about it [Wood's patent], but I am told none of them are permitted to be printed in England. Two have come out since my Lord Lieutenant came here, written with sobriety, modesty, and great force, in my opinion, which put the matter in a fair and clear light, though not with all the advantage of which it is capable; four were printed before, by somebody that calleth himself a Drapier which were in a ludicrous and satyrical style; against the last of these the Lord Lieutenant procured a proclamation, signed by 17 of the Council; offering £300 for discovering the author. I thought the premium excessive, so I and three more refused to sign it, but declared, that if his excellency would secure us from the brass money, I would sign it, or any other, tending only to the disadvantage of private persons; but, till we had that security, I would look on this proclamation no otherwise than as a step towards passing that base and mischievous coin, and designed to intimidate those who opposed the passing it; and I declared, that I would not approve of anything that might countenance, or encourage such a ruinous project; that issuing such a proclamation would make all believe, that the government was engaged to support Wood's pretensions, and that would neither be for their honour nor ease. I was not able to stop the proclamation, but my refusing to sign it has not been without effect." ("History of St. Patrick's," p. 344, note n.). [T.S.]]

Lastly, it ought to be considered what consequence the finding the bill, may have upon a poor man perfectly innocent, I mean the printer. A lawyer may pick out expressions and make them liable to exception, where no other man is able to find any. But how can it be supposed, that an ignorant printer can be such a critic? He knew the author's design was honest, and approved by the whole kingdom, he advised with friends, who told him there was no harm in the book, and he could see none himself. It was sent him in an unknown hand, but the same in which he received the three former. He and his wife have offered to take their oaths that they knew not the author; and therefore to find a bill, that may bring a punishment upon the innocent, will appear very hard, to say no worse. For it will be impossible to find the author, unless he will please to discover himself, although I wonder he ever concealed his name. But I suppose what he did at first out of modesty, he now continues to do out of prudence. God protect us and him!

I will conclude all with a fable, ascribed to Demosthenes. He had served the people of Athens with great fidelity in the station of an orator, when upon a certain occasion, apprehending to be delivered over to his enemies, he told the Athenians, his countrymen, the following story. Once upon a time the wolves desired a league with the shepherds, upon this condition; that the cause of strife might be taken away, which was the shepherds and the mastiffs; this being granted, the wolves without all fear made havoc of the sheep.[2]

Novem. 11th, 1724.

[Footnote 2: The advice had the desired effect. The jury returned a verdict of "Ignoramus" on the bill, which so aroused Whitshed, the Chief Justice, that he discharged them. As a comment on Whitshed's illegal procedure, the following extract was circulated:

EXTRACT FROM A BOOK ENTITLED, "AN EXACT COLLECTION OF THE DEBATES OF THE HOUSE OF COMMONS HELD AT WESTMINSTER, OCTOBER 21, 1680," page 150.

Resolutions of the House of Commons, in England, November 13, 1680.

"Several persons being examined about the dismissing a grand jury in
Middlesex, the House came to the following resolutions:—

"*Resolved*, That the discharging of a grand-jury by any judge, before the end of the term, assizes, or sessions, while matters are under their consideration, and not presented, is arbitrary, illegal, destructive to public justice, a manifest violation of his oath, and is a means to subvert the fundamental laws of this kingdom.

"*Resolved*, That a committee be appointed to examine the proceedings of the judges in Westminster-hall, and report the same with their opinion therein to this House." [T.S.]]

LETTER V.

A LETTER TO THE LORD CHANCELLOR MIDDLETON.

NOTE.

I have departed from the order given by Faulkner and the earlier editors,[1] and followed by Sir W. Scott in arranging the series of the Drapier's Letters, by adhering to a more correct chronological sequence. This letter has always been printed as the sixth Drapier's letter, but I have printed it here as the fifth, since it was written prior to the letter addressed to Viscount Molesworth, which has hitherto been called the fifth. The Molesworth letter I print here as "Letter VI." As already noted the letter to Midleton was written on the 26th October, 1724, but its first publication in print did not occur until Faulkner included it in the fourth volume of his collected edition of Swift's works, issued in 1735. There it is signed "J.S." and is given as from the "Deanery House." All the other letters are printed as "By M.B. Drapier." The Advertisement to the Reader prefixed to the present fifth letter is from Faulkner's edition. Probably it was printed by Faulkner under Swift's direction.

[Footnote 1: Sheridan, Deane Swift, Hawkesworth and Nichols]

Swift's acquaintance with Midleton had been of long standing. The Chancellor had been an avowed opponent of the patent and yet, by his signature to the proclamation, he seemed to be giving the weight of his official position against the popular sentiment. In addressing him, Swift was endeavouring, apparently, to keep him to his original line of action and to destroy any influence the government party may have had on him, since he was well aware of Carteret's insinuating charm. Midleton, however, had always stood firm against the patent. His signature to the proclamation against the Drapier was justified by him when he said that the Drapier's letters tended to disturbance. Carteret had really tried to win him over, but he did not succeed "While he [Midleton] expressed the highest obligation to the Lord Lieutenant," writes Coxe, "he declared that his duty to his country was paramount to every other consideration, and refused to give any assistance to government, until the patent was absolutely surrendered."

The text here given of this letter is based on Faulkner's issue in vol. iv. of the 1735 edition of Swift's works. It has been collated with that given in the fifth volume of the "Miscellanies," printed in London in the same year.

[T.S.]

ADVERTISEMENT TO THE READER[2]

The former of the two following papers is dated Oct. 6th 1724[3], by which it appears to be written a little after the proclamation against the author of the Drapier's Fourth Letter. It is delivered with much caution, because the author confesseth himself to be Dean of St. Patrick's; and I could discover his name subscribed at the end of the original, although blotted out by some other hand, I can tell no other reason why it was not printed, than what I have heard; that the writer finding how effectually the Drapier had succeeded, and at the same time how highly the people in power seemed to be displeased, thought it more prudent to keep the paper in his cabinet. However, having received some encouragement to collect into one volume all papers relating to Ireland, supposed to be written by the Drapier; and knowing how favourably that author's writings in this kind have been received by the public; to make the volume more complete, [I procured a copy of the following letter from one of the author's friends, with whom it was left, while the author was in England; and][4] I have printed it as near as I could in the order of time.

[Footnote 2: Nichols, in the second volume of his Supplement to Swift's Works (1779, 8vo), prints a note on this "Advertisement," furnished him by Bowyer. It is as follows:

"1. The first of the papers is said to be dated Oct. 6, 1724; and that it appears from thence to be dated a little after the proclamation against the Drapier's fourth letter. Now the fourth letter itself is dated Oct. 23, 1724. This is a pardonable mistake anywhere, but, much more in a country where *going before just coming after* is the characteristic dialect. But I little thought that the Dean, in his zeal for Ireland, would vouchsafe to adopt the shibboleth of it.

"2. The Preface-writer, in the choice MS which he found, could discover the Dean's name subscribed at the end of the original; but *blotted out* by *some other hand*. As the former passage is a proof that the Advertisement was drawn up in Ireland, so this affords a strong presumption that it was under the direction of the Dean himself: for who else could divine that his name was struck out by another hand? Other ink it might be: but in these recent MSS. of our age, it is the first time I ever heard of a blot carrying the evidence of a handwriting. Whether the Dean or the printer hit this *blot*, I shall not inquire; but lay before you the pleasant procedure of the latter upon this discovery. He had got, we see, the original in the Dean's hand; but the name was obliterated. What does he, but send away to England for a copy which might authenticate *his original*; and from such a copy the public is favoured with it! I remember, in a cause before Sir Joseph Jekyll, a man began reading in court the title-deeds of an estate which was contested. 'The original is a little blind,' says he; 'I have got a very fair copy of it, which I beg leave to go on with'—'Hold,' says Sir Joseph, 'if the original is not good, the copy can never make it so.' I am far, however, from accusing the printer of intending any fraud on the world. He who tells his story so openly gives security enough for his honesty. I can easily conceive the Advertisement might be in a good measure the Dean's, who never was over-courteous to his readers, and might for once be content to be merry with them." [T.S.]]

[Footnote 3: Misprinted by Faulkner for Oct. 26th. [T.S.]]

[Footnote 4: This portion in square brackets is not given by Faulkner in his Advertisement. [T.S.]]

The next treatise is called "An Address, &c." It is without a date; but seems to be written during the first session of Parliament in Lord Carteret's government. The title of this Address is in the usual form, by M.B. Drapier. There is but a small part of it that relates to William Wood and his coin: The rest contains several proposals for the improvement of Ireland, the many discouragements it lies under, and what are the best remedies against them.

By many passages in some of the Drapier's former letters, but particularly in the following Address, concerning the great drain of money from Ireland by absentees, importation of foreign goods, balance of trade, and the like, it appears that the author had taken much pains, and been well informed in the business of computing; all his reasonings upon that subject, although he does not here descend to particular sums, agreeing generally with the accounts given by others who have since made that enquiry their particular study. And it is observable, that in this Address, as well as in one of his printed letters, he hath specified several important articles, that have not been taken notice of by others who came after him.

LETTER V.

A LETTER TO THE LORD CHANCELLOR MIDDLETON.[5]

My Lord, I desire you will consider me as a member who comes in at the latter end of a debate; or as a lawyer who speaks to a cause, when the matter hath been almost exhausted by those who spoke before.

[Footnote 5: Alan Brodrick, Lord Midleton (1660?-1728), came of a Surrey family that had greatly benefited by the forfeitures in Ireland. Adopting the profession of the law, Brodrick was, in 1695, appointed Solicitor-General for Ireland. He sat in the Irish House of Commons as the member for Cork, and in 1703 was chosen its Speaker. His strong opposition to the Sacramental Test Act lost him the favour of the government, and he was removed from his office of Solicitor-General. In 1707, however, he was appointed Attorney-General for Ireland, and in 1714 made Lord Chancellor. In the year following he was created Baron Brodrick of Midleton. His trimming with Walpole and Carteret did not, however, prevent him from opposing the Wood's patent, though he signed the proclamation against the Drapier. He thought the letters served to "create jealousies between the King and the people of Ireland." [T.S.]]

I remember some months ago I was at your house upon a commission, where I am one of the governors: But I went thither not so much on account of the commission, as to ask you some questions concerning Mr. Wood's patent to coin halfpence for Ireland; where you very freely told me, in a mixed company, how much you had been always against that wicked project, which raised in me an esteem for you so far, that I went in a few days to make you a visit, after many years' intermission. I am likewise told, that your son wrote two letters from London, (one of which I have seen) empowering those to whom they were directed, to assure his friends, that whereas there was a malicious report spread of his engaging himself to Mr. Walpole for forty thousand pounds of Wood's coin, to be received in Ireland, the said report was false and groundless; and he had never discoursed with that minister on the subject; nor would ever give his consent to have one farthing of the said coin current here. And although it be long since I have given myself the trouble of conversing with people of titles or stations; yet I have been told by those who can take up with such amusements, that there is not a considerable person of the kingdom, scrupulous in any sort to declare his opinion. But all this is needless to allege, when we consider, that the ruinous consequences of Wood's patent, have been so strongly represented by both Houses of Parliament; by the Privy-council; the Lord Mayor and Aldermen of Dublin; by so many corporations; and the concurrence of the principal gentlemen in most counties, at their quarter-sessions, without any regard to party, religion, or nation.

I conclude from hence, that the currency of these halfpence would, in the universal opinion of our people, be utterly destructive to this kingdom; and consequently, that it is every man's duty, not only to refuse this coin himself, but as far as in him lies, to persuade others to do the like: And whether this be done in private or in print, is all a case: As no layman is forbid to write, or to discourse upon religious or moral subjects; although he may not do it in a pulpit (at least in our church). Neither is this an affair of state, until authority shall think fit to declare it so: Or if you should understand it in that sense; yet you will please to consider that I am not now a preaching.

Therefore, I do think it my duty, since the Drapier will probably be no more heard of, so far to supply his place, as not to incur his fortune: For I have learnt from old experience, that there are times wherein a man ought to be cautious as well as innocent. I therefore hope, that preserving both those characters, I may be allowed, by offering new arguments or enforcing old ones, to refresh the memory of my fellow-subjects, and keep up that good spirit raised among them; to preserve themselves from utter ruin by lawful means, and such as are permitted by his Majesty.

I believe you will please to allow me two propositions: First, that we are a most loyal people; and, Secondly, that we are a free people, in the common acceptation of that word applied to a subject under a limited monarch. I know very well, that you and I did many years ago in discourse differ much, in the presence of Lord Wharton, about the meaning of that word *liberty*, with relation to Ireland. But if you will not allow us to be a free people, there is only another appellation left; which, I doubt, my Lord Chief Justice Whitshed would call me to an account for, if I venture to bestow: For, I observed, and I shall never forget upon what occasion, the device upon his coach to be *Libertas et natale solum;* at the very point of time when he was sitting in his court, and perjuring himself to betray both.[6]

[Footnote 6: On this motto of Whitshed's Swift wrote the following poetical paraphrase:

"*Libertas et natale solum:*
Fine words! I wonder where you stole 'em.
Could nothing but thy chief reproach
Serve for a motto on thy coach?
But let me now thy words translate:
Natale solum, my estate;
My dear estate, how well I love it,
My tenants, if you doubt, will prove it,

> They swear I am so kind and good,
> I hug them till I squeeze their blood.
> *Libertas* bears a large import:
> First, how to swagger in a court;
> And, secondly, to shew my fury
> Against an uncomplying jury;
> And, thirdly, 'tis a new invention,
> To favour Wood, and keep my pension;
> And, fourthly, 'tis to play an odd trick,
> Get the great seal and turn out Broderick;
> And, fifthly, (you know whom I mean,)
> To humble that vexatious Dean:
> And, sixthly, for my soul to barter it
> For fifty times its worth to Carteret.
> Now since your motto thus you construe,
> I must confess you've spoken once true.
> *Libertas et natale solum.*
> You had good reason when you stole 'em."

[T.S.]]

Now, as for our loyalty, to His present Majesty; if it hath ever been equalled in any other part of his dominions; I am sure it hath never been exceeded: And I am confident he hath not a minister in England who could ever call it once in question: But that some hard rumours at least have been transmitted from t'other side the water, I suppose you will not doubt: and rumours of the severest kind; which many good people have imputed to the indirect proceeding of Mr. Wood and his emissaries; as if he endeavoured it should be thought that our loyalty depended upon the test of refusing or taking his copper. Now, as I am sure you will admit us to be a loyal people; so you will think it pardonable in us to hope for all proper marks of favour and protection from so gracious a King, that a loyal and free people can expect: Among which, we all agree in reckoning this to be one; that Wood's halfpence may never have entrance into this kingdom. And this we shall continue to wish, when we dare no longer express our wishes; although there were no such mortal as a Drapier in the world.

I am heartily sorry, that any writer should, in a cause so generally approved, give occasion to the government and council to charge him with paragraphs "highly reflecting upon His Majesty and his ministers; tending to alienate the affections of his good subjects in England and Ireland from each other; and to promote sedition among the people."[7] I must confess, that with many others, I thought he meant well; although he might have the failing of better writers, to be not always fortunate in the manner of expressing himself.

[Footnote 7: Swift here quotes the words of the proclamation issued against the fourth Drapier's Letter. See Appendix IV. [T.S.]]

However, since the Drapier is but one man, I shall think I do a public service, by asserting that the rest of my countrymen are wholly free from learning out of *his* pamphlets to reflect on the King or his ministers, to breed sedition.

I solemnly declare, that I never once heard the least reflection cast upon the King, on the subject of Mr. Wood's coin: For in many discourses on this matter, I do not remember His Majesty's name to be so much as mentioned. As to the ministry in England, the only two persons hinted at were the Duke of Grafton, and Mr. Walpole:[8] The former, as I have heard you and a hundred others affirm, declared, that he never saw the patent in favour of Mr. Wood, before it was passed, although he were then lord lieutenant:

And therefore I suppose everybody believes, that his grace hath been wholly unconcerned in it since.

[Footnote 8: Walpole was created a Knight of the Bath in 1724, when that order was revived. In 1726 he was installed Knight of the Order of the Garter, being the only commoner who had been so distinguished since the reign of James I., except Admiral Montague, afterwards Earl of Sandwich. He had been offered a peerage in 1723, but declined it for himself, accepting it for his son, who was created Baron Walpole of Walpole, in Norfolk. [T.S.]]

Mr. Walpole was indeed supposed to be understood by the letter W. in several newspapers; where it is said, that some expressions fell from him not very favourable to the people of Ireland; for the truth of which, the kingdom is not to answer, any more than for the discretion of the publishers. You observe, the Drapier wholly clears Mr. Walpole of this charge, by very strong arguments and speaks of him with civility. I cannot deny myself to have been often present, where the company gave then opinion, that Mr. Walpole favoured Mr. Wood's project, which I always contradicted; and for my own part, never once opened my lips against that minister, either in mixed or particular meetings: And my reason for this reservedness was, because it pleased him, in the Queen's time (I mean Queen Anne of ever blessed memory) to make a speech directly against me, by name, in the House of Commons, as I was told a very few minutes after, in the Court of Requests, by more than fifty members.

But you, who are in a great station here, (if anything here may be called great) cannot be ignorant, that whoever is understood by public voice to be chief minister, will, among the general talkers, share the blame, whether justly or no, of every thing that is disliked;

which I could easily make appear in many instances, from my own knowledge, while I was in the world; and particularly in the case of the greatest, the wisest, and the most uncorrupt minister, I ever conversed with.[9]

[Footnote 9: Robert Harley, Earl of Oxford. [T.S.]]

But, whatever unpleasing opinion some people might conceive of Mr. Walpole, on account of those halfpence; I dare boldly affirm, it was entirely owing to Mr. Wood. Many persons of credit, come from England, have affirmed to me, and others, that they have seen letters under his hand, full of arrogance and insolence towards Ireland; and boasting of his favour with Mr. Walpole; which is highly probable: Because he reasonably thought it for his interest to spread such a report; and because it is the known talent of low and little spirits, to have a great man's name perpetually in their mouths.[10]

[Footnote 10: See Coxe's "Memoirs of Walpole" (vol. i., cap. 26, p. 389, ed. 1800), where Wood is blamed for his indiscretion on this matter. See also note prefixed to the Drapier's First Letter in the present edition. [T.S.]]

Thus I have sufficiently justified the people of Ireland, from learning any bad lessons out of the Drapier's pamphlets, with regard to His Majesty and his ministers: And, therefore, if those papers were intended to sow sedition among us, God be thanked, the seeds have fallen upon a very improper soil.

As to alienating the affections of the people of England and Ireland from each other; I believe, the Drapier, whatever his intentions were, hath left that matter just as he found it.

I have lived long in both kingdoms, as well in country as in town; and therefore, take myself to be as well informed as most men, in the dispositions of each people toward the other. By the people, I understand here, only the bulk of the common people; and I desire no lawyer may distort or extend my meaning.

There is a vein of industry and parsimony, that runs through the whole people of England; which, added to the easiness of their rents, makes them rich and sturdy. As to Ireland, they know little more than they do of Mexico; further than that it is a country subject to the King of England, full of bogs, inhabited by wild Irish Papists; who are kept in awe by mercenary troops sent from thence: And their general opinion is, that it were better for England if this whole island were sunk into the sea; for, they have a tradition, that every forty years there must be a rebellion in Ireland. I have seen the grossest suppositions pass upon them; "that the wild Irish were taken in toils; but that, in some time, they would grow so tame, as to eat out of your hands:" I have been asked by hundreds, and particularly by my neighbours, your tenants, at Pepper-harrow; "whether I had come from Ireland by sea:" And, upon the arrival of an Irishman to a country town, I have known crowds coming about him, and wondering to see him look so much better than themselves.

A gentleman now in Dublin, affirms, "that passing some months ago through Northampton, and finding the whole town in a flurry, with bells, bonfires, and illuminations, upon asking the cause, was told, it was for joy, that the Irish had submitted to receive Wood's halfpence." This, I think, plainly shews what sentiments that large town hath of us; and how little they made it their own case; although they be directly in our way to London, and therefore, cannot but be frequently convinced that we have human shapes.

As to the people of this kingdom, they consist either of Irish Papists; who are as inconsiderable, in point of power, as the women and children; or of English Protestants, who love their brethren of that kingdom; although they may possibly sometimes complain, when they think they are hardly used: However, I confess, I do not see any great consequence, how their personal affections stand to each other, while the sea divides them, and while they continue in their loyalty to the same prince. And yet, I will appeal to you; whether those from England have reason to complain, when they come hither in pursuit of their fortunes? Or, whether the people of Ireland have reason to boast, when they go to England on the same design?

My second proposition was, that we of Ireland are a free people: This, I suppose, you will allow; at least, with certain limitations remaining in your own breast. However, I am sure it is not criminal to affirm; because the words "liberty" and "property," as applied to the subject, are often mentioned in both houses of Parliament, as well as in yours, and other courts below; from whence it must follow, that the people of Ireland do, or ought to enjoy all the benefits of the common and statute law; such as to be tried by juries, to pay no money without their own consent, as represented in Parliament; and the like. If this be so, and if it be universally agreed, that a free people cannot, by law, be compelled to take any money in payment, except gold and silver; I do not see why any man should be hindered from cautioning his countrymen against this coin of William Wood; who is endeavouring by fraud to rob us of that property, which the laws have secured. If I am mistaken, and that this copper can be obtruded on us; I would put the Drapier's case in another light, by supposing, that a person going into his shop, should agree for thirty shillings' worth of goods, and force the seller to take his payment in a parcel of copper pieces, intrinsically not worth above a crown: I desire to know, whether the Drapier would not be actually robbed of five and twenty shillings, and how far he could be said to be master of his property? The same question may be applied to rents and debts, on bond or mortgage, and to all kind of commerce whatsoever.

Give me leave to do what the Drapier hath done more than once before me; which is, to relate the naked fact, as it stands in the view of the world.

One William Wood, Esq; and hardware-man, obtains, by fraud, a patent in England, to coin 108,000_l._ in copper, to pass in Ireland, leaving us liberty to take, or to refuse. The people here, in all sorts of bodies and representatives, do openly and heartily declare, that they will not accept this coin: To justify these declarations, they generally offer two reasons; first, because by the words of the patent, they are left to their own choice: And secondly, because they are not obliged by law: So that here you see there is, *bellum atgue virum*, a kingdom on one side, and William Wood on the other. And if Mr. Wood gets the victory, at the expense of Ireland's ruin, and the profit of one or two hundred thousand pounds (I mean by continuing, and counterfeiting as long as he lives) for himself; I doubt, both present and future ages will, at least, think it a very singular scheme.

If this fact be truly stated; I must confess, I look upon it as my duty, so far as God hath enabled me, and as long as I keep within the bounds of truth, of duty, and of decency, to warn my fellow-subjects, as they value their King, their country, and all that ought or can be dear to them, never to admit this pernicious coin; no not so much as one single halfpenny. For, if one single thief forces the door, it is in vain to talk of keeping out the whole crew behind.

And, while I shall be thus employed, I will never give myself leave to suppose, that what I say can either offend my Lord Lieutenant; whose person and great qualities I have always highly respected; (as I am sure his excellency will be my witness) or the ministers in England, with whom I have nothing to do, or they with me; much less the Privy-council here, who, as I am informed, did send an address to His Majesty against Mr. Wood's coin; which, if it be a mistake, I desire I may not be accused for a spreader of false news: But, I confess, I am so great a stranger to affairs, that for anything I know, the whole body of the council may since have been changed: And, although I observed some of the very same names in a late declaration against that coin, which I saw subscribed to the proclamation against the Drapier; yet possibly they may be different persons; for they are utterly unknown to me, and are like to continue so.

In this controversy, where the reasoners on each side are divided by St. George's Channel, His Majesty's prerogative, perhaps, would not have been mentioned; if Mr. Wood, and his advocates, had not made it necessary, by giving out, that the currency of his coin should be enforced by a proclamation. The traders and common people of the kingdom, were heartily willing to refuse this coin; but the fear of a proclamation brought along with it most dreadful apprehensions. It was therefore, absolutely necessary for the Drapier, to remove this difficulty; and accordingly, in one of his former pamphlets, he hath produced invincible arguments, (wherever he picked them up) that the King's prerogative was not at all concerned in the matter; since the law had sufficiently provided against any coin to be imposed upon the subject, except gold and silver; and that copper is not money, but as it hath been properly called *nummorum famulus*.

The three former letters from the Drapier, having not received any public censure, I look upon them to be without exception; and that the good people of the kingdom ought to read them often, in order to keep up that spirit raised against this destructive coin of Mr. Wood: As for this last letter, against which a proclamation is issued; I shall only say, that I could wish it were stripped of all that can be any way exceptionable; which I would not think it below me to undertake, if my abilities were equal; but being naturally somewhat slow of comprehension; no lawyer, and apt to believe the best of those who profess good designs, without any visible motive either of profit or honour; I might pore for ever, without distinguishing the cockle from the corn.

That which, I am told, gives greatest offence in this last letter, is where the Drapier affirms; "that if a rebellion should prove so successful, as to fix the Pretender on the throne of England, he would venture so far to transgress the Irish statute, (which unites Ireland to England under one King) as to lose every drop of his blood, to hinder him from being King of Ireland."

I shall not presume to vindicate any man, who openly declares he would transgress a statute; and a statute of such importance: But, with the most humble submission, and desire of pardon for a very innocent mistake, I should be apt to think that the loyal intention of the writer, might be at least some small extenuation of his crime. For, in this I confess myself to think with the Drapier.

I have not hitherto been told of any other objections against that pamphlet; but, I suppose, they will all appear at the prosecution of the Drapier. And, I think, whoever in his own conscience believes the said pamphlet to be "wicked and malicious, seditious and scandalous, highly reflecting upon His Majesty and his ministers,

&c." would do well to discover the author, (as little a friend as I am to the trade of informers) although the reward of 300_l_. had not been tacked to the discovery. I own, it would be a great satisfaction to me, to hear the arguments not only of judges, but of lawyers, upon this case. Because, you cannot but know, there often happens occasions, wherein it would be very convenient, that the bulk of the people should be informed how they ought to conduct themselves; and therefore, it hath been the wisdom of the English Parliaments, to be very reserved in limiting the press. When a bill is debating in either House of Parliament there, nothing is more usual, than to have the controversy handled by pamphlets on both sides; without the least animadversion upon the authors.

So here, in the case of Mr. Wood and his coin; since the two Houses gave their opinion by addresses, how dangerous the currency of that copper would be to Ireland; it was, without all question, both lawful and convenient, that the bulk of the people should be let more particularly into the nature of the danger they were in; and of the remedies that were in their own power, if they would have the sense to apply them; and this cannot be more conveniently done, than by particular persons, to whom God hath given zeal and understanding sufficient for such an undertaking. Thus it happened in the case of that destructive project for a bank in Ireland, which was brought into Parliament a few years ago; and it was allowed, that the arguments and writings of some without doors, contributed very much to reject it.[11]

[Footnote 11: Swift himself assisted in writing against this "destructive project" in a series of pamphlets (see vol. vii.). The arguments for and against the bank were thoroughly discussed by Hercules Rowley and Henry Maxwell in a series of controversial letters against each other. [T.S.]]

Now, I should be heartily glad if some able lawyers would prescribe the limits, how far a private man may venture in delivering his thoughts upon public matters: Because a true lover of his country, may think it hard to be a quiet stander-by, and an indolent looker-on, while a public error prevails; by which a whole nation may be ruined. Every man who enjoys property, hath some share in the public; and therefore, the care of the public is, in some degree, every such man's concern.

To come to particulars, I could wish to know, Whether it be utterly unlawful in any writer so much as to mention the prerogative; at least so far as to bring it into doubt, upon any point whatsoever? I know it is often debated in Westminster-hall; and Sir Edward Coke, as well as other eminent lawyers, do frequently handle that subject in their books.

Secondly, How far the prerogative extends to force coin upon the subject, which is not sterling; such as lead, brass, copper, mixt metal, shells, leather, or any other material; and fix upon it whatever denomination the crown shall think fit?

Thirdly, What is really and truly meant by that phrase of "a depending kingdom," as applied to Ireland; and wherein that dependency consisteth?

Lastly, In what points relating to liberty and property, the people of Ireland differ, or at least ought to differ, from those of England?

If these particulars were made so clear, that none could mistake them, it would be of infinite ease and use to the kingdom; and either prevent or silence all discontents.

My Lord Somers, the greatest man I ever knew of your robe; and whose thoughts of Ireland differed as far as heaven and earth, from those of some others among his brethren here; lamented to me, that the prerogative of the Crown, or the privileges of Parliament, should ever be liable to dispute, in any single branch of either; by which means, he said, the public often suffered great inconveniences; whereof he gave me several instances. I produce the authority of so eminent a person, to justify my desires, that some high points might be cleared.

For want of such known ascertainment, how far a writer may proceed in expressing his good wishes for his country; a person of the most innocent intentions, may possibly, by the oratory and comments of lawyers, be charged with many crimes, which from his very soul he abhors; and consequently may be ruined in his fortunes, and left to rot among thieves in some stinking jail; merely for mistaking the purlieus of the law. I have known, in my lifetime, a printer prosecuted and convicted, for publishing a pamphlet; where the author's intentions, I am confident, were as good and innocent, as those of a martyr at his last prayers.[12] I did very lately, as I thought it my duty, preach to the people under my inspection, upon the subject of Mr. Wood's coin; and although I never heard that my sermon gave the least offence, as I am sure none was intended; yet, if it were now printed and published, I cannot say, I would ensure it from the hands of the common hangman; or my own person from those of a messenger.[13]

[Footnote 12: Supposed to be "A proposal for the universal use of Irish manufactures," written by the author. [F.]]

[Footnote 13: The reference here is to Swift's sermon on "Doing Good."
See Swift's Works, vol. iv., p. 181, present edition. [T.S.]]

I have heard the late Chief Justice Holt[14]affirm, that in all criminal cases, the most favourable interpretation should be put upon words, that they can possibly bear. You meet the same position asserted in many trials, for the greatest crimes; though often very ill practised, by the perpetual corruption of judges. And I remember, at a trial in Kent, where Sir George Rook[15] was indicted for calling a gentleman knave and villain; the lawyer for the defendant brought off his client, by alleging, that the words were not injurious; for, *knave* in the old and true signification, imported only a servant; and *villain* in Latin, is *villicus*; which is no more than a man employed in country labour; or rather a bailiff.

[Footnote 14: Sir John Holt (1642-1710) held the recordership of London, in 1685, and was appointed Lord Chief Justice of the King's Bench in 1688. In the celebrated case, Ashby v.. White, Holt strongly upheld the rights of the voter as against the House of Commons. He was distinguished, in his time, for the fair and impartial hearing he always accorded a prisoner, and he even personally assisted the accused in cases where the law did not allow him to be represented by counsel. Many of Holt's opinions did become "standard maxims." [T.S.]]

[Footnote 15: Admiral Sir George Rooke (1650-1709), who, with Rear-Admiral Byng, captured Gibraltar in 1704. [T.S.]]

If Sir John Holt's opinion were a standard maxim for all times and circumstances, any writer, with a very small measure of discretion, might easily be safe; but, I doubt, in practice it hath been frequently controlled, at least before his time; for I take it to be an old rule in law.

I have read, or heard, a passage of Signor Leti, an Italian; who being in London, busying himself with writing the History of England, told King Charles the Second, that he endeavoured as much as he could to avoid giving offence, but found it a thing impossible; although he should have been as wise as Solomon: The King answered, that if this were the case, he had better employ his time in writing proverbs as Solomon did: But Leti lay under no public necessity of writing; neither would England have been one halfpenny the better, or the worse, whether he writ or no.

This I mention, because I know it will readily be objected, "What have private men to do with the public? What call had a Drapier to turn politician, to meddle in matters of state? Would not his time have been better employed in looking to his shop; or his pen in writing proverbs, elegies, ballads, garlands, and wonders? He would then have been out of all danger of proclamations, and prosecutions. Have we not able magistrates and counsellors hourly watching over the public weal?" All this may be true: And yet, when the addresses from both Houses of Parliament, against Mr. Wood's halfpence, failed of success; if some pen had not been employed, to inform the people how far they might legally proceed, in refusing that coin, to detect the fraud, the artifice, and insolence of the coiner; and to lay open the most ruinous consequences to the whole kingdom; which would inevitably follow from the currency of the said coin; I might appeal to many hundred thousand people, whether any one of them would ever have had the courage or sagacity to refuse it.

If this copper should begin to make its way among the common, ignorant people, we are inevitably undone; it is they who give us the greatest apprehension, being easily frighted, and greedy to swallow misinformations: For, if every man were wise enough to understand his own interest, which is every man's principal study, there would be no need of pamphlets upon this occasion. But, as things stand, I have thought it absolutely necessary, from my duty to God, my King, and my country, to inform the people, that the proclamation lately issued against the Drapier, doth not in the least affect the case of Mr. Wood and his coin; but only refers to certain paragraphs in the Drapier's last pamphlet, (not immediately relating to his subject, nor at all to the merits of the cause,) which the government was pleased to dislike; so that any man has the same liberty to reject, to write, and to declare against this coin, which he had before: Neither is any man obliged to believe, that those honourable persons (whereof you are the first) who signed that memorable proclamation against the Drapier, have at all changed their opinions, with regard to Mr. Wood or his coin.

Therefore concluding myself to be thus far upon a safe and sure foot; I shall continue, upon any proper occasion, as God enables me, to revive and preserve that spirit raised in the nation, (whether the real author were a real Drapier or no is little to the purpose) against this horrid design of Mr. Wood; at the same time carefully watching every stroke of my pen, and venturing only to incur the public censure of the world as a writer; not of my Lord Chief Justice Whitshed, as a criminal. Whenever an order shall come out by authority, forbidding all men upon the highest penalties, to offer anything in writing or discourse against Mr. Wood's halfpence; I shall certainly submit. However, if that should happen, I am determined to be somewhat more than the last man in the kingdom to receive them; because I will never receive them at all:

For, although I know how to be silent; I have not yet learned to pay active obedience against my conscience, and the public safety.

I desire to put a case, which I think the Drapier, in some of his books, hath put before me; although not so fully as it requires.

You know the copper halfpence in England are coined by the public; and every piece worth pretty tolerably near the value of the copper. Now suppose, that, instead of the public coinage, a patent had been granted to some private, obscure person, for coining a proportionable quantity of copper in that kingdom, to what Mr. Wood is preparing in this; and all of it at least five times below the intrinsic value: The current money of England is reckoned to be twenty millions; and ours under five hundred thousand pounds: By this computation, as Mr. Wood hath power to give us 108,000 pound; so the patentee in England, by the same proportion, might circulate four millions three hundred and twenty thousand pounds; besides as much more by stealth and counterfeits: I desire to know from you, whether the Parliament might not have addressed upon such an occasion; what success they probably would have had; and how many Drapiers would have risen to pester the world with pamphlets: Yet that kingdom would not be so great a sufferer as ours in the like case; because their cash would not be conveyed into foreign countries, but lie hid in the chests of cautious, thrifty men, until better times. Then I desire, for the satisfaction of the public, that you will please to inform me why this country is treated in so very different a manner, in a point of such high importance; whether it be on account of Poining's act; of subordination; dependence; or any other term of art; which I shall not contest, but am too dull to understand.

I am very sensible, that the good or ill success of Mr. Wood, will affect you less than any person of consequence in the kingdom; because I hear you are so prudent as to make all your purchases in England; and truly so would I, if I had money, although I were to pay a hundred years' purchase; because I should be glad to possess a freehold that could not be taken from me by any law to which I did not give my own consent; and where I should never be in danger of receiving my rents in mixed copper, at the loss of sixteen shillings in the pound. You can live in ease and plenty at Pepper-harrow, in Surrey; and therefore I thought it extremely generous and public-spirited in you to be of the kingdom's side in this dispute, by shewing, without reserve, your disapprobation of Mr. Wood's design; at least if you have been so frank to others as you were to me; which indeed I could not but wonder at, considering how much we differ in other points; and therefore I could get but few believers, when I attempted to justify you in this article from your own words.

I would humbly offer another thought, which I do not remember to have fallen under the Drapier's observation. If these halfpence should once gain admittance; it is agreed, that in no long space of time, what by the clandestine practices of the coiner, what by his own counterfeits, and those of others, either from abroad or at home; his limited quantity would be trebled upon us, until there would not be a grain of gold or silver visible in the nation. This, in my opinion would lay a heavy charge upon the crown, by creating a necessity of transmitting money from England to pay the salaries at least of the principal civil officers: For I do not conceive how a judge (for instance) could support his dignity with a thousand pounds a year in Wood's coin; which would not intrinsically be worth near two hundred. To argue that these halfpence, if no other coin were current, would answer the general ends of commerce among ourselves, is a great mistake; and the Drapier hath made that matter too clear to admit an answer; by shewing us what every owner of land must be forced to do with the products of it in such a distress. You may read his remarks at large in his second and third letter; to which I refer you.

Before I conclude, I cannot but observe, that for several months past, there have more papers been written in this town, such as they are, all upon the best public principle, the love of our country, than, perhaps, hath been known in any other nation, and in so short a time: I speak in general, from the Drapier down to the maker of ballads; and all without any regard to the common motives of writers: which are profit, favour, and reputation. As to profit, I am assured by persons of credit, that the best ballad upon Mr. Wood will not yield above a groat to the author; and the unfortunate adventurer Harding, declares he never made the Drapier any present, except one pair of scissors. As to favour, whoever thinks to make his court by opposing Mr. Wood is not very deep in politics. And as to reputation, certainly no man of worth and learning, would employ his pen upon so transitory a subject, and in so obscure a corner of the world, to distinguish himself as an author. So that I look upon myself, the Drapier, and my numerous brethren, to be all true patriots in our several degrees.

All that the public can expect for the future, is only to be sometimes warned to beware of Mr. Wood's halfpence; and refer them for conviction to the Drapier's reasons. For, a man of the most superior understanding, will find it impossible to make the best use of it, while he writes in constraint; perpetually softening, correcting, or blotting out expressions, for fear of bringing his printer, or himself, under a prosecution from my Lord Chief-Justice Whitshed. It calls to my remembrance the madman in Don Quixote, who being soundly beaten by a weaver for letting a stone (which he always carried on his shoulder) fall upon a spaniel, apprehended that every cur he met was of the same species.

For these reasons, I am convinced, that what I have now written will appear low and insipid; but if it contributes, in the least, to preserve that union among us for opposing this fatal project of Mr. Wood, my pains will not be altogether lost.

I sent these papers to an eminent lawyer (and yet a man of virtue and learning into the bargain) who, after many alterations returned them back, with assuring me, that they are perfectly innocent; without the least mixture of treason, rebellion, sedition, malice, disaffection, reflection, or wicked insinuation whatsoever.

If the bellman of each parish, as he goes his circuit, would cry out, every night, "Past twelve o'clock; Beware of Wood's halfpence;" it would probably cut off the occasion for publishing any more pamphlets; provided that in country towns it were done upon market days. For my own part, as soon as it shall be determined, that it is not against law, I will begin the experiment in the liberty of St. Patrick's; and hope my example may be followed in the whole city But if authority shall think fit to forbid all writings, or discourses upon this subject, except such as are in favour of Mr. Wood, I will obey as it becomes me; only when I am in danger of bursting, I will go and whisper among the reeds, not any reflection upon the wisdom of my countrymen; but only these few words, BEWARE OF WOOD'S HALFPENCE.

I am,
  With due Respect,
    Your Most Obedient,

Humble Servant,
J.S.

Deanery House,
Oct. 26, 1724.

LETTER VI

A LETTER TO THE RIGHT HONOURABLE THE LORD VISCOUNT MOLESWORTH.

NOTE.

This letter, hitherto styled the Drapier's fifth letter, is here printed as the sixth, for the reasons already stated. It was published on the 14th December, 1724, at a time when the Drapier agitation had reached its last stage. The Drapier had taught his countrymen that "to be brave is to be wise," and he now struck the final blow that laid prostrate an already tottering opposition.

Walpole realized that to govern Ireland from England he must have a trustier aid, a heavier hand, and a more vigilant eye, than were afforded in Carteret. Carteret, however, was better away in Ireland, and, moreover, as Lord-Lieutenant, he was an ameliorating influence on the Irish patriotic party in Dublin. But that party was now backed by a very important popular opinion. For the present, therefore, he gave way; but his real feelings might have been discovered by an interpretation of his appointment of Hugh Boulter as Archbishop of Armagh and Primate of Ireland.[1] Boulter's letter to the Duke of Newcastle, written after his arrival in Dublin towards the end of November, 1724, gave a very unambiguous account of the state of the country towards the patent. On the 3rd of December, he wrote, "We are at present in a very bad state, and the people so poisoned with apprehensions of Wood's halfpence, that I do not see there can be any hopes of justice against any person for seditious writings, if he does but mix somewhat about Wood in them.... But all sorts here are determinedly set against Wood's halfpence, and look upon their estates as half sunk in their value, whenever they shall pass upon the nation."[2] On January

19th 1724-1725, the Primate wrote again to the same effect. On the 3rd of July, he hopes that, as parliament is about to meet, the Lord-Lieutenant "will be impowered in his speech to speak clearly as to the business of the halfpence, and thoroughly rid this nation of their fear on that head."[3] Boulter's advice was taken. On the 14th August, 1725, a vacation of the patent was issued, and when parliament met shortly after, the Lord-Lieutenant was able, in his speech, to announce that his Majesty had put an entire end to the patent granted Wood for coining copper halfpence and farthings. He alluded to the surrender as a remarkable instance of royal favour and condescension which should fill the hearts of a loyal and obedient people with the highest sense of duty and gratitude. He doubted not the Houses would make suitable acknowledgment of their sense of happiness enjoyed under his Majesty's most mild and gracious government.[4]

[Footnote 1: See note on pp. 111-112.]

[Footnote 2: Boulter's letter, vol. i., p. 3. Dublin edition, 1770.]

[Footnote 3: *Ibid.*, p. 29.]

[Footnote 4: Comm. Journals, vol. iii., p. 398.]

The Commons unanimously voted an address suitable to the occasion and in harmony with the Lord-Lieutenant's suggestion. But the Lords procrastinated in debates. It was a question whether their address should or should not include the words "great wisdom" in addition to the word "condescension" to express their sense of his Majesty's action. Finally, however, the address was forthcoming, though not before some strenuous expressions of opinion had been made by Midleton and Archbishop King against Walpole's administration. As passed, their Address included the debated words; as presented the Address omitted them.

Thus ended this famous agitation in which the people of Ireland won their first victory over England by constitutional means. Wood was no loser by the surrender; indeed, he was largely the gainer, since he was given a pension of £3,000 per annum for twelve years.[5]

[Footnote 5: Coxe says for eight years.]

Now that the fight was over the people, to use Scott's words, "turned their eyes with one consent on the man, by whose unbending fortitude, and pre-eminent talents, this triumph was accomplished." He was hailed joyously and blessed fervently wherever he went; the people almost idolized him; he was their defender and their liberator. No monarch visiting his domains could have been received with greater honour than was Swift when he came into a town. Medals and medallions were struck in his honour. A club was formed to the memory of the Drapier; shops and taverns bore the sign of the Drapier's Head; children and women carried handkerchiefs with the Drapier's portrait woven in them. All grades of society respected him for an influence that, founded in sincerity and guided by integrity and consummate ability, had been used patriotically. The DEAN became Ireland's chiefest citizen; and Irishmen will ever revere the memory of the man who was the first among them to precipitate their national instincts into the abiding form of national power—the reasoned opinion of a free people.

The text of this letter is based on that given by Sir Walter Scott, collated with the original edition and with the text given in "Fraud Detected" (1725).

[T.S.]

A

LETTER

To the Right Honourable the *Lord Viscount Molesworth.*

* * * * *

By *M.B. Drapier*, Author of the Letter to the *Shop-keepers*, &c.

* * * * *

They compassed me about also with Words of Deceit, and fought against me without a Cause.

For my Love they are my Adversaries, but I give my self unto Prayer.

And they have rewarded me Evil for Good, and Hatred for my Love. *Psalm* 109. *v.* 3, 4, 5.

Seek not to be Judge, being not able to take away Iniquity, lest at any Time thou fear the Person of the Mighty, and lay a stumbling Block in the Way of thy Uprightness.

Offend not against the Multitude of a City, and then thou shalt not cast thy self down among the People.

Bind not one Sin upon another, for in One thou shalt not be Unpunished. *Ecclus.* Ch. 7. V. 6, 7, 8.

* * * * *

Non jam prima peto Mnesttheus, neque vincere certo: Quanquam O! Sed superent, quibus Hoc, Neptune, dedisti.

* * * * *

DIRECTIONS TO THE PRINTER.

MR. HARDING, When I sent you my former papers, I cannot say I intended you either good or hurt, and yet you have happened through my means to receive both. I pray God deliver you from any more of the latter, and increase the former. Your trade, particularly in this kingdom, is of all others the most unfortunately circumstantiated; For as you deal in the most worthless kind of trash, the penny productions of pennyless scribblers, so you often venture your liberty and sometimes your lives, for the purchase of half-a-crown, and by your own ignorance are punished for other men's actions.

I am afraid, you in particular think you have reason to complain of me for your own and your wife's confinement in prison, to your great expense, as well as hardship, and for a prosecution still impending. But I will tell you, Mr. Harding, how that matter stands. Since the press hath lain under so strict an inspection, those who have a mind to inform the world are become so cautious, as to keep themselves if possible out of the way of danger. My custom is to dictate to a 'prentice who can write in a feigned hand, and what is written we send to your house by a blackguard boy. But at the same time I do assure you upon my reputation, that I never did send you anything, for which I thought you could possibly be called to an account. And you will be my witness that I always desired you by a letter to take some good advice before you ventured to print, because I knew the dexterity of dealers in the law at finding out something to fasten on where no evil is meant; I am told indeed, that you did accordingly consult several very able persons, and even some who afterwards appeared against you: To which I can only answer, that you must either change your advisers, or determine to print nothing that comes from a Drapier.

I desire you will send the enclosed letter, directed "To my Lord Viscount Molesworth at his house at Brackdenstown near Swords;" but I would have it sent printed for the convenience of his Lordship's reading, because this counterfeit hand of my 'prentice is not very legible. And if you think fit to publish it, I would have you first get it read over carefully by some notable lawyer: I am assured you will find enough of them who are friends to the Drapier, and will do it without a fee, which I am afraid you can ill afford after all your expenses. For although I have taken so much care, that I think it impossible to find a topic out of the following papers for sending you again to prison; Yet I will not venture to be your guarantee.

This ensuing letter contains only a short account of myself, and an humble apology for my former pamphlets, especially the last, with little mention of Mr. Wood or his halfpence, because I have already said enough upon that subject, until occasion shall be given for new fears; and in that case you may perhaps hear from me again.

I am,
 Your Friend
  and Servant,
   M.B.

From my shop in
St. Francis-street
Dec. 14. 1724.

P.S. For want of intercourse between you and me, which I never will suffer, your people are apt to make very gross errors in the press, which I desire you will provide against.

LETTER VI

A LETTER TO THE RIGHT HONOURABLE THE LORD VISCOUNT MOLESWORTH, AT HIS HOUSE AT BRACKDENSTOWN NEAR SWORDS.[6]

My Lord, I reflect too late on the maxim of common observers, that "those who meddle in matters out of their calling, will have reason to repent;" which is now verified in me: For by engaging in the trade of a writer, I have drawn upon myself the displeasure of the government, signified by a proclamation promising a reward of three hundred pounds to the first faithful subject who shall be able and inclined to inform against me. To which I may add the laudable zeal and industry of my Lord Chief Justice [Whitshed] in his endeavours to discover so dangerous a person. Therefore whether I repent or no, I have certainly cause to do so, and the common observation still stands good.

[Footnote 6: Robert, Viscount Molesworth (1656-1725), born in Dublin and educated at the University there, was a prominent adherent of the Prince of Orange during the Revolution of 1688. In 1692 William sent him to Denmark as envoy-extraordinary to the Court at Copenhagen; but he left abruptly because of the offence he gave there. Retiring to Flanders, Molesworth revenged himself by writing, "An Account of Denmark as it was in 1692," in which he described that country as no fit place for those who held their liberties dearly. Molesworth had been strongly imbued with the republican teachings of Algernon Sidney, and his book affords ample proof of the influence. Its publication aroused much indignation, and a controversy ensued in which Swift's friend, Dr. William King, took part. In 1695 Molesworth returned to Ireland, became a Privy Councillor in 1697, sat in the Irish parliament in

1703-1705, and in the English House of Commons from 1705 to 1708. In 1713 he was removed from the Irish Privy Council on a charge of a treasonable utterance, which Steele vindicated in "The Englishman" and "The Crisis." The accession of George I., however, brought Molesworth into his honours again, and he was created Baron Molesworth of Philipstown, and Viscount Molesworth of Swords, in 1719. His work entitled "Considerations for Promoting Agriculture," issued in 1723, was considered by Swift as "an excellent discourse, full of most useful hints." At the time Swift addressed him this sixth letter, Molesworth was living in retirement at Brackdenstown. [T.S.]]

It will sometimes happen, I know not how in the course of human affairs, that a man shall be made liable to legal animadversions, where he has nothing to answer for, either to God or his country; and condemned at Westminster-hall for what he will never be charged with at the Day of Judgment.

After strictly examining my own heart, and consulting some divines of great reputation, I cannot accuse myself of any "malice or wickedness against the public;" of any "designs to sow sedition," of "reflecting on the King and his ministers," or of endeavouring "to alienate the affections of the people of this kingdom from those of England."[7] All I can charge myself with, is a weak attempt to serve a nation in danger of destruction by a most wicked and malicious projector, without waiting until I were called to its assistance; which attempt, however it may perhaps give me the title of *pragmatical* and *overweening* will never lie a burthen upon my conscience. God knows whether I may not with all my caution have already run myself into danger, by offering thus much in my own vindication. For I have heard of a judge, who, upon the criminal's appeal to the dreadful Day of Judgment, told him he had incurred a *premunire* for appealing to a foreign jurisdiction: And of another in Wales, who severely checked the prisoner for offering the same plea, taxing him with reflecting on the Court by such a comparison, because "comparisons were odious."

[Footnote 7: The quotations are from the charges stated in the indictment and proclamation against the writer and printer of the previous letters. [T.S.]]

But in order to make some excuse for being more speculative than others of my condition, I desire your lordship's pardon, while I am doing a very foolish thing, which is, to give you some little account of myself.

I was bred at a free school where I acquired some little knowledge in the Latin tongue, I served my apprenticeship in London, and there set up for myself with good success, till by the death of some friends, and the misfortunes of others, I returned into this kingdom, and began to employ my thoughts in cultivating the woollen manufacture through all its branches Wherein I met with great discouragement and powerful opposers, whose objections appeared to me very strange and singular They argued that the people of England would be offended if our manufactures were brought to equal theirs; and even some of the weaving trade were my enemies, which I could not but look upon as absurd and unnatural I remember your lordship at that time did me the honour to come into my shop, where I shewed you a piece of black and white stuff just sent from the dyer, which you were pleased to approve of, and be my customer for it.[8]

[Footnote 8: The "piece of black and white stuff just sent from the dyer," refers to his pamphlet, issued in 1720, "The Proposal for the Universal Use of Irish Manufactures." See vol. vii. [T.S.]]

However I was so mortified, that I resolved for the future to sit quietly in my shop, and deal in common goods like the rest of my brethren; till it happened some months ago considering with myself that the lower and poorer sort of people wanted a *plain strong coarse stuff to defend them against cold easterly winds, which then blew very fierce and blasting for a long time together,* I contrived one on purpose, which sold very well all over the kingdom, and preserved many thousands from agues I then made a second and a third kind of stuffs for the gentry with the same success, insomuch that an ague hath hardly been heard of for some time.[9]

[Footnote 9: The "cold easterly winds" refer to the demands made on the Irish people to accept Wood's halfpence. The three different kinds of "stuffs" are the three letters written under the *nom de guerre,* "M.B. Drapier." [T.S.]]

This incited me so far, that I ventured upon a fourth piece made of the best Irish wool I could get, and I thought it grave and rich enough to be worn by the best lord or judge of the land. But of late some great folks complain as I hear, "that when they had it on, they felt a shuddering in their limbs," and have thrown it off in a rage, cursing to hell the poor Drapier who invented it, so that I am determined never to work for persons of quality again, except for your lordship and a very few more.[10]

[Footnote 10: This refers to the fourth letter of the Drapier, which brought forth the proclamation, and for the author of which the reward of £300 was offered. [T.S.]]

I assure your lordship upon the word of an honest citizen, that I am not richer by the value of one of Mr. Wood's halfpence with the sale of all the several stuffs I have contrived; for I give the whole profit to the dyers and pressers.[11] And therefore I hope you will please to believe, that no other motive beside the love of my country could engage me to busy my head and hands to the loss of my time and the gain of nothing but vexation and ill-will.

[Footnote 11: The printers [F.]]

I have now in hand one piece of stuff to be woven on purpose for your lordship, although I might be ashamed to offer it you, after I have confessed that it will be made only from the shreds and remnants of the wool employed in the former. However I shall work it up as well as I can, and at worst, you need only give it among your tenants.

I am very sensible how ill your lordship is like to be entertained with the pedantry of a drapier in the terms of his own trade. How will the matter be mended, when you find me entering again, though very sparingly, into an affair of state; for such is now grown the controversy with Mr. Wood, if some great lawyers are to be credited. And as it often happens at play, that men begin with farthings, and go on to gold, till some of them lose their estates, and die in jail; so it may possibly fall out in my case, that by playing too long with Mr. Wood's halfpence, I may be drawn in to pay a fine, double to the reward for betraying me, be sent to prison, and "not be delivered thence till I shall have paid the uttermost farthing."

There are my lord, three sorts of persons with whom I am resolved never to dispute: A highwayman with a pistol at my breast, a troop of dragoons who come to plunder my house, and a man of the law who can make a merit of accusing me. In each of these cases, which are almost the same, the best method is to keep out of the way, and the next best is to deliver your money, surrender your house, and confess nothing.

I am told that the two points in my last letter, from which an occasion of offence hath been taken, are where I mention His Majesty's answer to the address of the House of Lords upon Mr. Wood's patent, and where I discourse upon Ireland's being a dependent kingdom. As to the former, I can only say, that I have treated it with the utmost respect and caution, and I thought it necessary to shew where Wood's patent differed in many essential parts from all others that ever had been granted, because the contrary had for want of due information been so strongly and so largely asserted. As to the other, of Ireland's dependency, I confess to have often heard it mentioned, but was never able to understand what it meant. This gave me the curiosity to enquire among several eminent lawyers, who professed they knew nothing of the matter. I then turned over all the statutes of both kingdoms without the least information, further than an Irish act, that I quoted, of the 33d of Henry 8th, uniting Ireland to England under one king. I cannot say I was sorry to be disappointed in my search, because it is certain, I could be contented to depend only upon God and my prince and the laws of my own country, after the manner of other nations. But since my betters are of a different opinion, and desire further dependencies, I shall readily submit, not insisting on the exception I made of M.B. Drapier. For indeed that hint was borrowed from an idle story I had heard in England, which perhaps may be common and beaten, but because it insinuates neither treason nor sedition, I will just barely relate it.

Some hundred years ago when the peers were so great that the commons were looked upon as little better than their dependents, a bill was brought in for making some new additions to the power and privileges of the peerage. After it was read, one Mr. Drewe a member of the house, stood up, and said, he very much approved the bill, and would give his vote to have it pass; but however, for some reasons best known to himself, he desired that a clause might be inserted for excepting the family of the Drewes. The oddness of the proposition taught others to reflect a little, and the bill was thrown out.

Whether I were mistaken, or went too far in examining the dependency must be left to the impartial judgment of the world, as well as to the courts of judicature, although indeed not in so effectual and decisive a manner. But to affirm, as I hear some do, in order to countenance a fearful and servile spirit, that this point did not belong to my subject, is a false and foolish objection. There were several scandalous reports industriously spread by Wood and his accomplices to discourage all opposition against his infamous project. They gave it out that we were prepared for a rebellion, that we disputed the King's prerogative, and were shaking off our dependency. The first went so far, and obtained so much belief against the most visible demonstrations to the contrary, that a great person of this kingdom, now in England, sent over such an account of it to his friends, as would make any good subject both grieve and tremble. I thought it therefore necessary to treat that calumny as it deserved. Then I proved by an invincible argument that we could have no intention to dispute His Majesty's prerogative, because the prerogative was not concerned in the question, the civilians and lawyers of all nations agreeing that copper is not money. And lastly to clear us from the imputation of shaking off our dependency, I shewed wherein as I thought this dependency consisted, and cited the statute above mentioned made in Ireland, by which it is enacted, that "whoever is King of

England shall be King of Ireland," and that the two kingdoms shall be "for ever knit together under one King." This, as I conceived, did wholly acquit us of intending to break our dependency, because it was altogether out of our power, for surely no King of England will ever consent to the repeal of that statute.

But upon this article I am charged with a heavier accusation. It is said I went too far, when I declared, that "if ever the Pretender should come to be fixed upon the throne of England (which God forbid) I would so far venture to transgress this statute, that I would lose the last drop of my blood before I would submit to him as King of Ireland."

This I hear on all sides, is the strongest and weightiest objection against me, and which hath given the most offence; that I should be so bold to declare against a direct statute, and that any motive how strong soever, could make me reject a King whom England should receive. Now if in defending myself from this accusation I should freely confess, that I "went too far," that "the expression was very indiscreet, although occasioned by my zeal for His present Majesty and his Protestant line in the House of Hanover," that "I shall be careful never to offend again in the like kind." And that "I hope this free acknowledgment and sorrow for my error, will be some atonement and a little soften the hearts of my powerful adversaries." I say if I should offer such a defence as this, I do not doubt but some people would wrest it to an ill meaning by some spiteful interpretation, and therefore since I cannot think of any other answer, which that paragraph can admit, I will leave it to the mercy of every candid reader.

I will now venture to tell your lordship a secret, wherein I fear you are too deeply concerned You will therefore please to know that this habit of writing and discoursing, wherein I unfortunately differ from almost the whole kingdom, and am apt to grate the ears of more than I could wish, was acquired during my apprenticeship in London, and a long residence there after I had set up for myself. Upon my return and settlement here, I thought I had only changed one country of freedom for another. I had been long conversing with the writings of your lordship,[12] Mr. Locke, Mr. Molineaux,[13] Colonel Sidney[14] and other dangerous authors, who talk of "liberty as a blessing, to which the whole race of mankind hath an original title, whereof nothing but unlawful force can divest them." I knew a good deal of the several Gothic institutions in Europe, and by what incidents and events they came to be destroyed; and I ever thought it the most uncontrolled and universally agreed maxim, that *freedom* consists in a people being governed by laws made with their own consent; and *slavery* in the contrary. I have been likewise told, and believe it to be true, that *liberty* and *property* are words of known use and signification in this kingdom, and that the very lawyers pretend to understand, and have them often in their mouths. These were the errors which have misled me, and to which alone I must impute the severe treatment I have received. But I shall in time grow wiser, and learn to consider my driver, the road I am in, and with whom I am yoked. This I will venture to say, that the boldest and most obnoxious words I ever delivered, would in England have only exposed me as a stupid fool, who went to prove that the sun shone in a clear summer's day; and I have witnesses ready to depose that your lordship hath said and writ fifty times worse, and what is still an aggravation, with infinitely more wit and learning, and stronger arguments, so that as politics run, I do not know a person of more exceptionable principles than yourself; and if ever I shall be discovered, I think you will be bound in honour to pay my fine and support me in prison; or else I may chance to inform against you by way of reprisal.[15]

[Footnote 12: See note *ante*, p. 161. [T.S.]]

[Footnote 13: William Molyneux (1656-1698), the correspondent of John Flamsteed and Locke. His "Dioptrica Nova" contains a warm appreciation of Locke's "Essay on the Human Understanding." He died in October, 1698, but in the early part of this year, he published his famous inquiry into the effect of English legislation on Irish manufactures. The work was entitled, "The Case of Ireland's being bound by Acts of Parliament in England stated," and its publication made a great stir both in England and in Ireland. Molyneux attempted to show that the Irish Parliament was independent of the English Parliament. His book was reported by a Committee of the House of Commons, on June 22nd, 1698, to be "of dangerous consequence to the Crown and Parliament of England," but the matter went no further than embodying this resolution of the committee in an address to the King. [T.S.]]

[Footnote 14: Algernon Sidney (1622-1682), the author of the well known "Discourses concerning Government," and the famous republican of the Cromwellian and Restoration years, was the second surviving son of the second Earl of Leicester His career as soldier, statesman, agitator, ambassador and author, forms an interesting and even fascinating chapter of the story of this interesting period of English history. He was tried for treason before Jeffreys, and in spite of a most excellent defence, sentenced to death. His execution took place on December 7th, 1682. [T. S.]]

[Footnote 15: A writer, signing himself M.M., replying to this letter of Swift's in a broadside entitled, "Seasonable Advice to M.B. Drapier, Occasioned by his Letter to the R—t. Hon. the Lord Visct.

Molesworth," actually takes this paragraph to mean that Swift intended seriously to turn informer: "Now sir, some people are of opinion that you carried this too far, inasmuch as you become a precedent to informers: others think that you intimate to his lordship, the miserable circumstance you are in by the menaces of the prentice to whom you dictate; they conceive your declaring to inform, if not fee'd, to the contrary, signifies your said prentice on the last occasion to swear, if you don't forthwith deliver him his indentures, and half of your stock to set up trade with, he will inform against you, bring you to justice, be dismissed by law, and get the promised £300 to begin trade with; how near these conceptions be to truth I can't tell; but I know people think that word *inform* unseasonable. . . ." [T.S.]]

In the meantime, I beg your lordship to receive my confession, that if there be any such thing as a dependency of Ireland upon England, otherwise than as I have explained it, either by the law of God, of nature, of reason, of nations, or of the land (which I shall never hereafter contest,) then was the proclamation against me, the most merciful that ever was put out, and instead of accusing me as malicious, wicked and seditious, it might have been directly as guilty of high treason.

All I desire is, that the cause of my country against Mr. Wood may not suffer by any inadvertency of mine; Whether Ireland depends upon England, or only upon God, the King and the law, I hope no man will assert that it depends upon Mr. Wood. I should be heartily sorry that this commendable resentment against me should accidentally (and I hope, what was never intended) strike a damp upon that spirit in all ranks and corporations of men against the desperate and ruinous design of Mr. Wood. Let my countrymen blot out those parts in my last letter which they dislike, and let no rust remain on my sword to cure the wounds I have given to our most mortal enemy. When Sir Charles Sidley[16] was taking the oaths, where several things were to be renounced, he said "he loved renouncing," asked "if any more were to be renounced, for he was ready to renounce as much as they pleased." Although I am not so thorough a renouncer; yet let me have but good city security against this pestilent coinage, and I shall be ready not only to renounce every syllable in all my four letters, but to deliver them cheerfully with my own hands into those of the common hangman, to be burnt with no better company than the coiner's *effigies,* if any part of it hath escaped out of the secular hands of the rabble.

[Footnote 16: This must be Sir Charles Sedley (properly Sidley), the famous wit and dramatist of Charles II.'s reign. In his reprint of 1735, Faulkner prints the name "Sidley," though the original twopenny tract and the "Hibernian Patriot" print it as "Sidney." Sir W. Scott corrects it to "Sedley." [T.S.]]

But whatever the sentiments of some people may be, I think it is agreed that many of those who subscribed against me, are on the side of a vast majority in the kingdom who opposed Mr. Wood; and it was with great satisfaction that I observed some right honourable names very amicably joined with my own at the bottom of a strong declaration against him and his coin. But if the admission of it among us be already determined the worthy person who is to betray me ought in prudence to do it with all convenient speed, or else it may be difficult to find three hundred pounds in sterling for the discharge of his hire; when the public shall have lost five hundred thousand, if there be so much in the nation; besides four-fifths of its annual income for ever.

I am told by lawyers, that in all quarrels between man and man, it is of much weight, which of them gave the first provocation or struck the first blow. It is manifest that Mr. Wood hath done both, and therefore I should humbly propose to have him first hanged and his dross thrown into the sea; after which the Drapier will be ready to stand his trial. "It must needs be that offences come, but woe unto him by whom the offence cometh." If Mr. Wood had held his hand every body else would have held their tongues, and then there would have been little need of pamphlets, juries, or proclamations upon this occasion. The provocation must needs have been great, which could stir up an obscure indolent Drapier to become an author. One would almost think the very stones in the street would rise up in such a cause: And I am not sure they will not do so against Mr. Wood if ever he comes within their reach. It is a known story of the dumb boy, whose tongue forced a passage for speech by the horror of seeing a dagger at his father's throat. This may lessen the wonder that a tradesman hid in privacy and silence should cry out when the life and being of his political mother are attempted before his face, and by so infamous a hand.

But in the meantime, Mr. Wood the destroyer of a kingdom walks about in triumph (unless it be true that he is in jail for debt) while he who endeavoured to assert the liberty of his country is forced to hide his head for occasionally dealing in a matter of controversy. However I am not the first who hath been condemned to death for gaining a great victory over a powerful enemy, by disobeying for once the strict orders of military discipline.

I am now resolved to follow (after the usual proceeding of mankind, because it is too late) the advice given me by a certain Dean. He shewed the mistake I was in of trusting to the general good-will of the people, "that I had succeeded hitherto better than could be expected, but that some unfortunate circumstantial lapse would probably bring me within the reach of power. That my good intentions would be no security against those who watched every motion of my pen, in the bitterness of my soul." He produced an instance of "a writer as innocent, as disinterested, and as well meaning as myself, where the printer, who had the author in his power, was prosecuted with the utmost zeal, the jury sent back nine times, and the man given up to the mercy of the court."[17] The Dean further observed "that I was in a manner left alone to stand the battle, while others who had ten thousand times better talents than a Drapier, were so prudent to lie still, and perhaps thought it no unpleasant amusement to look on with safety, while another was giving them diversion at the hazard of his liberty and fortune, and thought they made a sufficient recompense by a little applause." Whereupon he concluded with a short story of a Jew at Madrid, who being condemned to the fire on account of his religion, a crowd of school-boys following him to the stake, and apprehending they might lose their sport, if he should happen to recant, would often clap him on the back, and cry, "*Sta firme Moyse* (Moses, continue steadfast)."

[Footnote 17: This was for the publication of "A Proposal for the Universal Use of Irish Manufactures." [T.S.]]

I allow this gentleman's advice to have been good, and his observations just, and in one respect my condition is worse than that of the Jew, for no recantation will save me. However it should seem by some late proceedings, that my state is not altogether deplorable. This I can impute to nothing but the steadiness of two impartial grand juries, which hath confirmed in me an opinion I have long entertained, that, as philosophers say, "virtue is seated in the middle," so in another sense, the little virtue left in the world is chiefly to be found among the middle rank of mankind, who are neither allured out of her paths by ambition, nor driven by poverty.

Since the proclamation occasioned by my last letter, and a due preparation for proceeding against me in a court of justice, there have been two printed papers clandestinely spread about, whereof no man is able to trace the original further than by conjecture, which with its usual charity lays them to my account. The former is entitled, "Seasonable Advice,"[18] and appears to have been intended for information of the grand jury, upon the supposition of a bill to be prepared against that letter. The other[19] is an extract from a printed book of Parliamentary Proceedings in the year 1680 containing an angry resolution of the House of Commons in England against dissolving grand juries. As to the former, your lordship will find it to be the work of a more artful hand than that of a common Drapier. It hath been censured for endeavouring to influence the minds of a jury, which ought to be wholly free and unbiassed, and for that reason it is manifest that no judge was ever known either upon or off the bench, either by himself or his dependents, to use the least insinuation that might possibly affect the passions or interests of any one single juryman, much less of a whole jury; whereof every man must be convinced who will just give himself the trouble to dip into the common printed trials; so as, it is amazing to think, what a number of upright judges there have been in both kingdoms for above sixty years past, which, considering how long they held their offices during pleasure, as they still do among us, I account next to a miracle.

[Footnote 18: See p. 123. [T.S.]]

[Footnote 19: See note on p. 127. [T.S.]]

As to the other paper I must confess it is a sharp censure of an English House of Commons against dissolving grand juries by any judge before the end of the term, assizes, or sessions, while matters are under their consideration, and not presented; is arbitrary, illegal, destructive to public justice, a manifest violation of his oath, and is a means to subvert the fundamental laws of the kingdom.

However, the publisher seems to have been mistaken in what he aimed at. For, whatever dependence there may be of Ireland upon England, I hope he would not insinuate, that the proceedings of a lord chief justice in Ireland must depend upon a resolution of an English House of Commons. Besides, that resolution although it were levelled against a particular lord chief justice, Sir William Scroggs,[20] yet the occasion was directly contrary: For Scroggs dissolved the grand jury of London for fear they should present, but ours in Dublin was dissolved because they would not present, which wonderfully alters the case. And therefore a second grand jury supplied that defect by making a presentment[21] that hath pleased the whole kingdom. However I think it is agreed by all parties, that both the one and the other jury behaved themselves in such a manner, as ought to be remembered to their honour, while there shall be any regard left among us for virtue or public spirit.

[Footnote 20: Sir William Scroggs (1623?-1683) was appointed Lord Chief Justice of England on the removal of Sir Thomas Ramsford in 1678. One of the eight articles of impeachment against Scroggs, in 1680, was for illegally discharging the grand jury of Middlesex before the end of the term. Although the articles of impeachment were carried to the House of Lords in 1681, the proceedings went no farther than ordering him to find bail and file his answer by a certain time. Scroggs was removed, on account of his unpopularity, on April 11th, 1681. As a lawyer, Scroggs has no great reputation; as a judge he must be classed with the notorious Jeffreys. [T.S.]]

[Footnote 21: See Appendix No. V. [T.S.]]

I am confident your lordship will be of my sentiments in one thing, that some short plain authentic tract might be published for the information both of petty and grand juries, how far their power reacheth, and where it is limited, and that a printed copy of such a treatise might be deposited in every court, to be consulted by the jurymen before they consider of their verdict; by which abundance of inconveniences would be avoided, whereof innumerable instances might be produced from former times, because I will say nothing of the present.

I have read somewhere of an eastern king who put a judge to death for an iniquitous sentence, and ordered his hide to be stuffed into a cushion, and placed upon the tribunal for the son to sit on, who was preferred to his father's office. I fancy such a memorial might not have been unuseful to a son of Sir William Scroggs, and that both he and his successors would often wriggle in their seats as long as the cushion lasted. I wish the relater had told us what number of such cushions there might be in that country.

I cannot but observe to your lordship how nice and dangerous a point it is grown for a private person to inform the people even in an affair where the public interest and safety are so highly concerned as that of Mr. Wood, and this in a country where loyalty is woven into the very hearts of the people, seems a little extraordinary. Sir William Scroggs was the first who introduced that commendable acuteness into the courts of judicature; but how far this practice hath been imitated by his successors or strained upon occasion, is out of my knowledge. When pamphlets unpleasing to the ministry were presented as libels, he would order the offensive paragraphs to be read before him, and said it was strange that the judges and lawyers of the King's Bench should be duller than all the people of England; and he was often so very happy in applying the initial letters of names, and expounding dubious hints (the two common expedients among writers of that class for escaping the law) that he discovered much more than ever the authors intended, as many of them or their printers found to their cost. If such methods are to be followed in examining what I have already written or may write hereafter upon the subject of Mr. Wood, I defy any man of fifty times my understanding and caution to avoid being entrapped, unless he will be content to write what none will read, by repeating over the old arguments and computations, whereof the world is already grown weary. So that my good friend Harding lies under this dilemma, either to let my learned works hang for ever a drying upon his lines, or venture to publish them at the hazard of being laid by the heels.

I need not tell your lordship where the difficulty lies. It is true, the King and the laws permit us to refuse this coin of Mr. Wood, but at the same time it is equally true, that the King and the laws permit us to receive it. Now it is most certain the ministers in England do not suppose the consequences of uttering that brass among us to be so ruinous as we apprehend; because doubtless if they understood it in that light, they are persons of too much honour and justice not to use their credit with His Majesty for saving a most loyal kingdom from destruction. But as long as it shall please those great persons to think that coin will not be so very pernicious to us, we lie under the disadvantage of being censured as obstinate in not complying with a royal patent. Therefore nothing remains, but to make use of that liberty which the King and the laws have left us, by continuing to refuse this coin, and by frequent remembrances to keep up that spirit raised against it, which otherwise may be apt to flag, and perhaps in time to sink altogether. For, any public order against receiving or uttering Mr. Wood's halfpence is not reasonably to be expected in this kingdom, without directions from England, which I think nobody presumes, or is so sanguine to hope.

But to confess the truth, my lord, I begin to grow weary of my office as a writer, and could heartily wish it were devolved upon my brethren, the makers of songs and ballads, who perhaps are the best qualified at present to gather up the gleanings of this controversy. As to myself, it hath been my misfortune to begin and pursue it upon a wrong foundation. For having detected the frauds and falsehoods of this vile impostor Wood in every part, I foolishly disdained to have recourse to whining, lamenting, and crying for mercy, but rather chose to appeal to law and liberty and the common rights of mankind, without considering the climate I was in.

Since your last residence in Ireland, I frequently have taken my nag to ride about your grounds, where I fancied myself to feel an air of freedom breathing round me, and I am glad the low condition of a tradesman did not qualify me to wait on you at your house, for then I am afraid my writings would not have escaped severer censures. But I have lately sold my nag, and honestly told his greatest fault, which was that of snuffing up the air about Brackdenstown, whereby he became such a lover of liberty, that I could scarce hold him in. I have likewise buried at the bottom of a strong chest your lordship's writings under a heap of others that treat of liberty, and spread over a layer or two of Hobbes, Filmer, Bodin[22] and many more authors of that stamp, to be readiest at hand whenever I shall be disposed to take up a new set of principles in government. In the mean time I design quietly to look to my shop, and keep as far out of your lordship's influence as possible; and if you ever see any more of my writings upon this subject, I promise you shall find them as innocent, as insipid and without a sting as what I have now offered you. But if your lordship will please to give me an easy lease of some part of your estate in Yorkshire,[23] thither will I carry my chest and turning it upside down, resume my political reading where I left it off; feed on plain homely fare, and live and die a free honest English farmer: But not without regret for leaving my countrymen under the dread of the brazen talons of Mr. Wood: My most loyal and innocent countrymen, to whom I owe so much for their good opinion of me, and of my poor endeavours to serve them,

I am
 with the greatest respect,
  My Lord
 Your Lordship's most obedient
  and most humble servant,
   M.B.

From my shop in St. Francis-Street, Dec. 14. 1724.

[Footnote 22: Sir Robert Filmer, the political writer who suffered for his adhesion to the cause of Charles I. His chief work was published after his death in 1680. It is entitled, "Patriarcha," and defends the patriarchal theory of government against the social-compact theory of Hobbes. Locke vigorously attacked it in his "Two Treatises on Government" published in 1690.

Jean Bodin, who died in 1596, wrote the "Livres de la Republique," a remarkable collection of information and speculation on the theoretical basis of political government. [T.S.]]

[Footnote 23: Molesworth's estate in Yorkshire was at Edlington, near Tickhill. [T.S.]]

LETTER VII.

AN HUMBLE ADDRESS TO BOTH HOUSES OF PARLIAMENT.

BY M.B. DRAPIER.

"Multa gemens ignominiam Plagasque superbi Victoris.—"

[VIRGIL, *Georg. III.*, 226-7.]

NOTE.

This letter was published in the fourth volume of the collected edition of Swift's Works, issued by Faulkner, in Dublin, in 1735. It is there stated that it was written "before the Lord Carteret came over, and soon after the fourth Drapier's letter." If Faulkner be correct, and he probably is, the subject matter of the letter shows that it was not to be printed until after the agitation had subsided. The letter is in an entirely different spirit from the other letters, and deals with suggestions and methods of action for a general righting of the wrongs under which Ireland was suffering. In matter as well as in manner it is not a continuation of the contest against Wood, but an effort to send the people along paths which would lead to their general welfare and prosperity. As such it properly concludes the Drapier series.

The text of the letter here printed is that of Faulkner collated with that given in the fifth volume of "Miscellanies," issued in London in. 1735.

[T.S.]

LETTER VII.

AN HUMBLE ADDRESS TO BOTH HOUSES OF PARLIAMENT.

I have been told, that petitions and addresses, either to King or Parliament, are the right of every subject; providing they consist with that respect, which is due to princes and great assemblies. Neither do I remember, that the modest proposals, or opinions of private men, have been ill-received, when they have not been delivered in the style of advice; which is a presumption far from my thoughts. However, if proposals should be looked upon as too assuming; yet I hope, every man may be suffered to declare his own and the nation's wishes. For instance; I may be allowed to wish, that some further laws were enacted for the advancement of trade, for the improvement of agriculture, now strangely neglected, against the maxim of all wise nations: For supplying the manifest defects in the acts concerning plantation of trees: For setting the poor to work, and many others.

Upon this principle, I may venture to affirm; it is the hearty wish of the whole nation, very few excepted; that the Parliament in this session would begin by strictly examining into the detestable fraud of one William Wood, now or late of London, hardwareman; who illegally and clandestinely, as appears by your own votes and addresses, procured a patent in England, for coining halfpence in that kingdom, to be current here. This, I say, is the wish of the whole nation, very few excepted; and upon account of those few, is more strongly and justly the wish of the rest: Those few consisting either of Wood's confederates, some obscure tradesmen, or certain bold UNDERTAKERS[1] of weak judgment, and strong ambition; who think to find their accounts in the ruin of the nation, by securing or advancing themselves. And, because such men proceed upon a system of politics, to which I would fain hope you will be always utter strangers, I shall humbly lay it before you.

[Footnote 1: This was a phrase used in the time of Charles II. to express those dashing ministers who obtained power by undertaking to carry through particular favourite measures of the crown. But the Dean applies it with his usual studied ambiguity, so that it may be explained as meaning schemers or projectors in general. [S.]]

Be pleased to suppose me in a station of fifteen hundred pounds a year, salary and perquisites; and likewise possessed of 800_l_. a year, real estate. Then, suppose a destructive project to be set on foot; such, for instance, as this of Wood; which if it succeed, in all the consequences naturally to be expected from it, must sink the rents and wealth of the kingdom one half, (although I am confident, it would have done so five-sixths.) Suppose, I conceive that the countenancing, or privately supporting this project, will please those by whom I expect to be preserved, or higher exalted. Nothing then remains, but to compute and balance my gain and my loss, and sum up the whole. I suppose that I shall keep my employment ten years, (not to mention the fair chance of a better.) This at 1500_l_. a year, amounts, in ten years, to 15,000_l_. My estate, by the success of the said project, sinks 400_l_. a year; which at twenty years' purchase, is but 8000_l_. so that I am a clean gainer of 7000_l_. upon the balance. And during all that period, I am possessed of power and credit, can gratify my favourites, and take vengeance of mine enemies. And if the project miscarry, my private merit is still entire. This arithmetic, as horrible as it appears, I knowingly affirm to have been practised, and applied in conjunctures, whereon depended the ruin or safety of a nation: Although, probably the charity and virtue of a senate, will hardly be induced to believe, that there can be such monsters among mankind. And yet, the wise Lord Bacon mentions a sort of people, (I doubt the race is not yet extinct) who would "set a house on fire, for the convenience of roasting their own eggs at the flame."

But whoever is old enough to remember, and hath turned his thoughts to observe the course of public affairs in this kingdom, from the time of the Revolution; must acknowledge, that the highest points of interest and liberty, have been often sacrificed to the avarice and ambition of particular persons, upon the very principles and arithmetic that I have supposed: The only wonder is, how these artists were able to prevail upon numbers; and influence even public assemblies to become instruments for effecting their execrable designs.

It is, I think, in all conscience, latitude enough for vice, if a man in station be allowed to act injustice, upon the usual principles of getting a bribe, wreaking his malice, serving his party, or consulting his preferment; while his wickedness terminates in the ruin only of particular persons: But, to deliver up our whole country, and every living soul who inhabits it, to certain destruction; hath not, as I remember, been permitted by the most favourable casuists on the side of corruption. It were far better, that all who have had the misfortune to be born in this kingdom, should be rendered incapable of holding any employment whatsoever, above the degree of a constable, (according to the scheme and intention of a great minister[2] *gone to his own place*)than to live under the daily apprehension of a few false brethren among ourselves. Because, in the former case we should be wholly free from the danger of being betrayed; since none could then have impudence enough to pretend any public good.

[Footnote 2: The Earl of Sunderland. See note on p. 377 of vol. *v.* of present edition. [T.S.]]

It is true, that in this desperate affair of the new halfpence, I have not heard of any man above my own degree of a shopkeeper, to have been hitherto so bold, as, in direct terms, to vindicate the fatal project; although I have been told of some very mollifying expressions which were used, and very gentle expedients proposed and handed about, when it first came under debate: But, since the eyes of the people have been so far opened, that the most ignorant can plainly see their own ruin, in the success of Wood's attempt; these grand compounders have been more cautious.[3]

[Footnote 3: Alluding to Walpole's overture for reducing the amount to be coined to £40,000. [T.S.]]

But that the same spirit still subsists, hath manifestly appeared (among other instances of great compliance) from certain circumstances, that have attended some late proceedings in a court of judicature. There is not any commonplace more frequently insisted on, by those who treat of our constitution, than the great happiness and excellency of trials by juries; yet if this blessed part of our law be eludible at pleasure, by the force of power, frowns, and artifice; we shall have little reason to boast of our advantage, in this particular, over other states or kingdoms in Europe. And surely, these high proceedings, exercised in a point that so nearly concerned the life-blood of the people, their necessary subsistence, their very food and raiment, and even the public peace; will not allow any favourable appearance; because it was obvious, that so much superabundant zeal could have no other design, or produce any other effect, than to damp that spirit raised in the nation against this accursed scheme of William Wood, and his abettors; to which spirit alone, we owe, and for ever must owe, our being hitherto preserved, and our hopes of being preserved for the future; if it can be kept up, and strongly countenanced by your wise assemblies. I wish I could account for such a demeanour upon a more charitable foundation, than that of putting our interest in over balance with the ruin of our country.

I remember some months ago, when this affair was fresh in discourse; a person near allied to SOMEBODY, or (as the hawkers called him) NOBODY, who was thought deeply concerned, went about very diligently among his acquaintance, to shew the bad consequences that might follow from any public resentment to the disadvantage of his ally Mr. Wood; principally alleging the danger of all employments being disposed of from England. One of these emissaries came to me, and urged the same topic: I answered, naturally, that I knew there was no office of any kind, which a man from England might not have, if he thought it worth his asking; and that I looked upon all who had the disadvantage of being born here, as only in the condition of leasers and gleaners. Neither could I forbear mentioning the known fable of the countryman, who entreated his ass to fly for fear of being taken by the enemy; but the ass refused to give himself that trouble; and upon a very wise reason, because he could not possibly change his present master for a worse: The enemy could not make him fare harder; beat him more cruelly; nor load him with heavier burthens.

Upon these, and many other considerations, I may affirm it to be the wish of the whole nation, that the power and privileges of juries were declared, ascertained, and confirmed by the legislature; and that whoever hath been manifestly known to violate them, might be stigmatized by public censure; not from any hope that such a censure will amend their practices, or hurt their interest, (for it may probably operate quite contrary in both:) but that the nation may know their enemies from their friends.

I say not this with any regard or view to myself; for I write in great security; and am resolved that none shall merit at my expense further than by shewing their zeal to discover, prosecute, and condemn me, for endeavouring to do my duty in serving my country: And yet I am conscious to myself that I never had the least intention to reflect on His Majesty's ministers, nor on any other person, except William Wood, whom I neither did, nor do yet conceive to be of that number. However, some would have it, that I went too far; but I suppose they will now allow themselves mistaken. I am sure I might easily have gone further; and I think I could not easily have fared worse. And therefore I was no further affected with their proclamation, and subsequent proceedings, than a good clergyman is with the sins of the people. And as to the poor printer, he is now gone to appear before a higher, and before a righteous tribunal.

As my intention is only to lay before your great assemblies, the general wishes of the nation; and as I have already declared it our principal wish that your first proceeding would be to examine into the pernicious fraud of William Wood; so I must add, as the universal opinion, that all schemes of commutation, composition, and the like expedients, either avowed or implied, will be of the most pernicious consequences to the public; against the dignity of a free kingdom; and prove an encouragement to future adventurers in the same destructive projects. For, it is a maxim, which no man at present disputes, that even a connivance to admit one thousand pounds in these halfpence, will produce, in time, the same ruinous effects, as if we openly consented to admit a million. It were, therefore, infinitely more safe and eligible, to leave things in the doubtful, melancholy state they are at present, (which, however, God forbid) and trust entirely to the general aversion of our people against this coin; using all honest endeavours to preserve, continue, and increase that aversion, than submit to apply those palliatives which weak, perfidious, or abject politicians, are, upon all occasions, and in all diseases, so ready to administer.

In the small compass of my reading, (which, however, hath been more extensive than is usual to men of my inferior calling) I have observed that grievances have always preceded supplies; and if ever grievances had a title to such a pre-eminence, it must be this of Wood; because it is not only the greatest grievance that any country could suffer, but a grievance of such a kind that, if it should take effect, would make it impossible for us to give any supplies at all; except in adulterate copper; unless a tax were laid for paying the civil and military lists, and the large pensions, with real commodities instead of money; which, however, might be liable to some few objections as well as difficulties: For although the common soldiers might be content with beef and mutton, and wool, and malt, and leather; yet I am in some doubt as to the generals, the colonels, the numerous pensioners, the civil officers, and others, who all live in England upon Irish pay; as well as those few who reside among us only because they cannot help it.

There is one particular, which although I have mentioned more than once in some of my former papers, yet I cannot forbear to repeat, and a little enlarge upon it; because I do not remember to have read or heard of the like in the history of any age or country; neither do I ever reflect upon it without the utmost astonishment.

After the unanimous addresses to his Sacred Majesty, against this patent of Wood, from both Houses of Parliament, which are the three estates of the kingdom; and likewise an address from the Privy-council, to whom, under the chief governors, the whole administration is entrusted; the matter is referred to a committee of council in London. Wood, and his adherents, are heard on one side; and a few volunteers, without any trust or direction from hence, on the other. The question (as I remember) chiefly turned upon the want of halfpence in Ireland: Witnesses are called on the behalf of Wood (of what credit I have formerly shewn :) Upon the issue the patent is found good and legal; all His Majesty's officers here, (not excepting the military) commanded to be aiding and assisting to make it effectual. The addresses of both Houses of Parliament, of the Privy-council; and of the city of Dublin: The declarations of most counties and corporations through the kingdom, are altogether laid aside, as of no weight, consequence, or consideration whatsoever: And the whole kingdom of Ireland nonsuited, in default of appearance; as if it were a private cause between John Doe, plaintiff, and William Roe, defendant.

With great respect to those-honourable persons, the committee of council in London, I have not understood them to be our governors, councillors, or judges. Neither did our case turn at all upon the question, whether Ireland wanted halfpence or no. For there is no doubt, but we do want both halfpence, gold, and silver; and we have numberless other wants, and some that we are not so much as allowed to name; although they are peculiar to this nation; to which no other is subject, whom God hath blessed with religion and laws, or any degree of soil and sunshine: But, for what demerits on our side, I am altogether in the dark.

But, I do not remember, that our want of halfpence was either affirmed, or denied in any of our addresses or declarations, against those of Wood: We alleged, the fraudulent obtaining and executing his patent, the baseness of his metal, the prodigious sum to be coined, which might be increased by stealth, from foreign importation and his own counterfeits, as well as those at home; whereby we must infallibly lose all our little gold and silver, and all our poor remainder of a very limited and discouraged trade: We urged, that the patent was passed without the least reference hither; and without mention of any security given by Wood, to receive his own halfpence upon demand; both which are contrary to all former proceedings in the like cases. These, and many other arguments we offered; but still the patent went on, and at this day our ruin would have been half completed; if God, in His mercy, had not raised an universal detestation of these halfpence, in the whole kingdom; with a firm resolution never to receive them; since we are not under obligations to do so by any law, either human or divine.

But, in the Name of God, and of all justice and piety; when the King's Majesty was pleased that this patent should pass; is it not to be understood, that he conceived, believed, and intended it as a gracious act, for the good and benefit of his subjects, for the advantage of a great and fruitful kingdom; of the most loyal kingdom upon earth, where no hand or voice was ever lifted up against him; a kingdom where the passage is not of three hours from Britain; and a kingdom where Papists have less power, and less land, than in England? Can it be denied, or doubted, that His Majesty's ministers understood and proposed the same end, the good of this nation, when they advised the passing this patent? Can the person of Wood be otherwise regarded, than as the instrument, the mechanic, the head-workman, to prepare his furnace, his fuel, his metal, and his stamps? If I employ a shoe-boy, is it in view to his advantage, or to my own convenience? I mention the person of William Wood alone, because no other appears, and we are not to reason upon surmises; neither would it avail, if they had a real foundation.

Allowing therefore, (for we cannot do less) that this patent, for the coining of halfpence, was wholly intended, by a gracious king, and a wise public-spirited ministry, for the advantage of Ireland; yet when the whole kingdom to a man, for whose good the patent was designed, do, upon maturest consideration, universally join, in openly declaring, protesting, addressing, petitioning, against these halfpence, as the most ruinous project that ever was set on foot, to complete the slavery and destruction of a poor innocent country: Is it, was it, can it, or will it ever be a question, not whether such a kingdom, or William Wood, should be a gainer; but whether such a kingdom should be wholly undone, destroyed, sunk, depopulated, made a scene of misery and desolation, for the sake of William Wood? God, of His infinite mercy, avert this dreadful judgment; and it is our universal wish, that God would put it into your hearts to be His instruments for so good a work.

For my own part, who am but one man, of obscure condition, I do solemnly declare, in the presence of Almighty God, that I will suffer the most ignominious and torturing death, rather than submit to receive this accursed coin, or any other that shall be liable to the same objections, until they shall be forced upon me, by a law of my own country; and if that shall ever happen, I will transport myself into some foreign land, and eat the bread of poverty among a free people.

Am I legally punishable for these expressions? Shall another proclamation issue against me, because I presume to take my country's part against William Wood; where her final destruction is intended? But, whenever you shall please to impose silence upon me, I will submit; because, I look upon your unanimous voice to be the voice of the nation; and this I have been taught, and do believe to be, in some manner, the voice of God.

The great ignominy of a whole kingdom, lying so long at mercy, under so vile an adversary, is such a deplorable aggravation, that the utmost expressions of shame and rage, are too low to set it forth; and therefore, I shall leave it to receive such a resentment, as is worthy of a parliament.

It is likewise our universal wish, that His Majesty would grant liberty to coin halfpence in this kingdom, for our own use; under such restrictions as a parliament here shall advise: Since the power of coining even gold and silver, is possessed by every petty prince abroad; and was always practised by Scotland, to the very time of the Union; yet surely Scotland, as to soil, climate, and extent, is not, in itself, a fourth part the value of Ireland; (for Bishop Burnet says, it is not above a fortieth part in value, to the rest of Britain) and with respect to the profit that England gains from hence, not the forty thousandth part. Although I must confess, that a mote in the eye, or a thorn in the side, is more dangerous and painful than a beam, or a spike at a distance.

The histories of England, and of most other countries, abound in relating the miserable, and sometimes the most tragical effects, from the abuses of coin; by debasing the metal, by lessening, or enhancing the value upon occasions, to the public loss; of which we have an example, within our own memory in England, and another very lately in France. It is the tenderest point of government, affecting every individual, in the highest degree. When the value of money is arbitrary, or unsettled; no man can well be said to have any property at all; nor is any wound so suddenly felt, so hardly cured, or that leaves such deep and lasting scars behind it.

I conceive this poor unhappy island, to have a title to some indulgence from England; not only upon the score of Christianity, natural equity, and the general rights of mankind; but chiefly on account of that immense profit they receive from us; without which, that kingdom would make a very different figure in Europe, from what it doth at present.

The rents of land in Ireland, since they have been of late so enormously raised, and screwed up, may be computed to about two millions; whereof one-third part, at least, is directly transmitted to those, who are perpetual absentees in England; as I find by a computation made with the assistance of several skilful gentlemen.

The other articles by which we are altogether losers, and England a gainer; we found to amount to almost as much more. I will only set down as many heads of them as I can remember; and leave them to the consideration of those, who understand accounts better than I pretend to do.

The occasional absentees, for business, health, or diversion.

Three-fourths of the revenue of the chief governor, during his absence; which is usually four-fifths of his government.

The whole revenue of the post-office.

The numerous pensions paid to persons in England.

The pay of the chief officers of the army absent in England, which is a great sum.

Four commissioners of the revenue, always absent.

Civil employments very numerous, and of great income.

The vast charge of appeals to the House of Lords, and to the Court of
Delegates.

Students at the Inns of Court, and the two Universities.

Eighty thousand pounds sent yearly to England, for coals; whereof the prime cost is nothing; and therefore, the profit wholly theirs.

One hundred thousand pounds paid several years past, for corn sent over hither from England; the effect of our own great wisdom in discouraging agriculture.

The kind liberty granted us of wearing Indian stuffs, and calicoes, to gratify the vanity and folly of our women; which, beside the profit to England, is an unconceivable loss to us; forcing the weavers to beg in our streets, or transport themselves to foreign countries.

The prodigious loss to us, and gain to England, by selling them all our wool at their own rates; whereof the manufacture exceeds above ten times the prime cost: A proceeding without example in the Christian or heathen world.

Our own wool returned upon us, in English manufactures, to our infinite shame and damage; and the great advantage of England.

The full profit of all our mines accruing to England; an effect of great negligence and stupidity.

An affectation among us, of liking all kinds of goods made in England.

NOTE, Many of the above articles have been since particularly computed by another writer, to whose treatise the reader is referred.[4]

[Footnote 4: The work referred to is "A List of the Absentees of Ireland, and the yearly value of their estates and Incomes spent abroad," by Thomas Prior, Esq. Prior was a native of Ireland and the schoolfellow and life-long friend of Berkeley, the philosopher. In concert with Samuel Madden and other friends, he founded, in 1731, the Dublin Society for the Promotion of Agriculture, Manufactures, Arts and Sciences. This society was the parent of the present Royal Dublin Society. His "List of the Absentees of Ireland" was published in 1729. He also issued "Observations on Coin" (1730), and "An Authentic Narrative of the Success of Tar Water in Curing a great number and variety of Distempers" (1746), to which Berkeley contributed. [T.S.]]

These and many other articles, which I cannot recollect at present, are agreed by judicious men to amount to near seven hundred thousand pounds *per ann.* clear profit to England. And, upon the whole, let any man look into those authors who write upon the subject of commerce, he shall find, that there is not one single article in the essentials, or circumstances of trade, whereby a country can be a loser, which we do not possess in the highest perfection; somewhat, in every particular, that bears a kind of analogy to William Wood; and now the branches are all cut off, he stands ready with his axe at the root.

Upon this subject of perpetual absentees, I have spent some time in very insignificant reflections; and considering the usual motives of human actions, which are pleasure, profit, and ambition, I cannot yet comprehend how those persons find their account in any of the three. I speak not of those English peers or gentlemen, who, beside their estates at home, have possessions here; for, in that case, the matter is desperate; but I mean those lords, and wealthy knights, or squires, whose birth, and partly their education, and all their fortune (except some trifle, and that in very few instances) are in this kingdom. I knew many of them well enough, during several years, when I resided in England; and truly I could not discover that the figure they made was, by any means, a subject for envy; at least it gave me two very different passions: For, excepting the advantage of going now and then to an opera, or sometimes appearing behind a crowd at Court; or adding to the ring of coaches in Hyde Park, or losing their money at the Chocolate House; or getting news, votes, and minutes, about five days before us in Dublin, I say, besides these, and a few other privileges of less importance, their temptations to live in London, were beyond my knowledge or conception. And I used to wonder, how a man of birth and spirit, could endure to be wholly insignificant and obscure in a foreign country, when he might live with lustre in his own; and even at less than half that expense, which he strains himself to make, without obtaining any one end; except that which happened to the frog when he would needs contend for size with the ox. I have been told by scholars, that Caesar said, he would rather be the first man, in I know not what village, than the second in Rome. This, perhaps, was a thought only fit for Caesar: But to be preceded by thousands, and neglected by millions; to be wholly without power, figure, influence, honour, credit, or distinction, is not, in my poor opinion, a very amiable situation of life, to a person of title, or wealth, who can so cheaply and easily shine in his native country.

But, besides the depopulating of the kingdom, the leaving so many parts of it wild and uncultivated, the ruin of so many country-seats and plantations, the cutting down all the woods to supply expenses in England; the absence of so many noble and wealthy persons, hath been the cause of another fatal consequence, which few perhaps have been aware of. For if that very considerable number of lords, who possess the amplest fortunes here, had been content to live at home, and attend the affairs of their own country in Parliament; the weight, reputation, and dignity thereby added to that noble House, would, in all human probability, have prevented certain proceedings, which are now ever to be lamented; because they never can be remedied: And we might have then decided our own properties among ourselves, without being forced to travel five hundred miles by sea and land, to another kingdom, for justice; to our infinite expense, vexation, and trouble: Which is a mark of servitude without example, from the practice of any age or nation in the world.

I have sometimes wondered, upon what motive the peerage of England were so desirous to determine our controversies; because I have been assured, and partly know, that the frequent appeals from hence, have been very irksome to that illustrious body; and whoever hath frequented the Painted Chamber, and Court of Requests, must have observed, that they are never so nobly filled, as when an Irish appeal is under debate.

The peers of Scotland, who are very numerous, were content to reside in their castles and houses, in that bleak and barren climate; and although some of them made frequent journeys to London, yet I do not remember any of their greatest families, till very lately, to have made England their constant habitation, before the Union: Or, if they did, I am sure it was generally to their own advantage; and whatever they got, was employed to cultivate and increase their own estates; and by that means enrich themselves and their country.

As to the great number of rich absentees, under the degree of peers; what particular ill effects their absence may have upon this kingdom, besides those already mentioned, may perhaps be too tender a point for me to touch. But whether those who live in another kingdom, upon great estates here; and have lost all regards to their own country, further than upon account of the revenues they receive from it: I say, whether such persons may not be prevailed on to recommend others to vacant seats, who have no interest here, except a precarious employment; and consequently can have no views, but to preserve what they have got, or to be higher advanced: This, I am sure, is a very melancholy question, if it be a question at all.

But, besides the prodigious profit which England receives by the transmittal thither of two-thirds of the revenues of this whole kingdom; it hath another mighty advantage by making our country a receptacle, wherein to disburthen themselves of their supernumerary pretenders to offices; persons of second-rate merit in their own country; who, like birds of passage, most of them thrive and fatten here, and fly off when their credit and employments are at an end. So that Ireland may justly say what Luther said of himself; POOR Ireland maketh many rich.

If amidst all our difficulties, I should venture to assert, that we have one great advantage, provided we could improve it as we ought; I believe most of my readers would be long in conjecturing what possible advantage could ever fall to our share. However, it is certain, that all the regular seeds of party and faction among us are entirely rooted out, and if any new ones shall spring up, they must be of equivocal generation, without any seed at all; and will justly be imputed to a degree of stupidity beyond even what we have been ever charged with upon the score of our birth-place and climate.

The parties in this kingdom (including those of modern date) are, First, of those who have been charged or suspected to favour the Pretender; and those who were zealous opposers of him. Secondly, of those who were for and against a toleration of Dissenters by law. Thirdly, of High and Low Church; or, (to speak in the cant of the times) of Whig and Tory: And, Fourthly, of court and country. If there be any more, they are beyond my observation or politics: For as to subaltern or occasional parties, they have all been derivations from the same originals.

Now, it is manifest, that all these incitements to faction, party, and division are wholly removed from among us. For, as to the Pretender, his cause is both desperate and obsolete: There are very few now alive who were *men* in his father's time, and in that prince's interest; and in all others, the obligation of conscience hath no place;[5] even the Papists in general, of any substance, or estates, and their priests almost universally, are what we call Whigs in the sense which by that word is generally understood. They feel the smart, and see the scars of their former wounds; and very well know, that they must be made a sacrifice to the least attempts towards a change; although it cannot be doubted, that they would be glad to have their superstition restored, under any prince whatsoever.

[Footnote 5: That is to say, they had not sworn any allegiance to him.
[T.S.]]

Secondly, The Dissenters are now tolerated by law; neither do we observe any murmurs at present from that quarter, except those reasonable complaints they make of persecution, because they are excluded from civil employments; but their number being very small in either House of Parliament, they are not yet in a situation to erect a party: Because, however indifferent men may be with regard to religion, they are now grown wise enough to know, that if such a latitude were allowed to Dissenters; the few small employments left us in cities and corporations, would find other hands to lay hold on them.

Thirdly, The dispute between High and Low Church is now at an end; two-thirds of the bishops having been promoted in this reign, and most of them from England, who have bestowed all preferments in their gift to those they could well confide in: The deaneries all except three, and many principal church-livings, are in the donation of the crown: So that we already possess such a body of clergy as will never engage in controversy upon that antiquated and exploded subject.

Lastly, As to court and country parties, so famous and avowed under most reigns in English Parliaments: This kingdom hath not, for several years past been a proper scene whereon to exercise such contentions; and is now less proper than ever; many great employments for life being in distant hands, and the reversions diligently watched and secured; the temporary ones of any inviting value are all bestowed elsewhere as fast as they drop; and the few remaining, are of too low consideration to create contests about them, except among younger brothers, or tradesmen like myself. And, therefore, to institute a court and country party without materials, would be a very new system in politics, and what I believe was never thought on before; nor, unless in a nation of idiots, can ever succeed. For the most ignorant Irish cottager will not sell his cow for a groat.

Therefore, I conclude, that all party and faction, with regard to public proceedings, are now extinguished in this kingdom; neither doth it appear in view how they can possibly revive; unless some new causes be administered; which cannot be done without crossing the interests of those who are greatest gainers by continuing the same measures. And, general calamities without hope of redress, are allowed to be the great uniters of mankind.

However we may dislike the causes; yet this effect of begetting an universal concord among us in all national debates, as well as in cities, corporations, and country neighbourhoods, may keep us at least alive, and in a condition to eat the little bread allowed us in peace and amity. I have heard of a quarrel in a tavern, where all were at daggers-drawing, till one of the company cried out, desiring to know the subject of the quarrel; which, when none of them could tell, they put up their swords, sat down, and passed the rest of the evening in quiet. The former part hath been our case; I hope the latter will be so too; that we shall sit down amicably together, at least until we have something that may give us a title to fall out; since nature hath instructed even a brood of goslings to stick together while the kite is hovering over their heads.

It is certain, that a firm union in any country, where every man wishes the same thing with relation to the public, may, in several points of the greatest importance, in some measure, supply the defect of power; and even of those rights which are the natural and undoubted inheritance of mankind. If the universal wish of the nation upon any point, were declared by the unanimous vote of the House of Commons, and a reasonable number of Lords; I should think myself obliged in conscience to act in my sphere according to that vote; because, in all free nations, I take the proper definition of law to be the will of the majority of those who have the property in land; which, if there be a monarchy, is to be confirmed by the royal assent. And, although such votes or declarations have not received such a confirmation, for certain accidental reasons; yet I think they ought to be of much weight with the subject; provided they neither oppose the King's prerogative, endanger the peace of the nation, nor infringe any law already in force; none of which, however, can reasonably be supposed. Thus, for instance, if nine in ten of the House of Commons, and a reasonable number of native temporal peers, should declare, that whoever received or uttered brass coin, except under certain limitations and securities, should be deemed as enemies to the King and the nation; I should think it a heinous sin in myself to act contrary to such a vote: And, if the same power should declare the same censure against those who wore Indian stuffs and calicoes, or woollen manufactures imported from abroad, whereby this nation is reduced to the lowest ebb of misery; I should readily, heartily, and cheerfully pay obedience; and to my utmost power persuade others to do the like: Because, there is no law of this land obliging us either to receive such coin, or to wear such foreign manufactures.

Upon this last article, I could humbly wish that the reverend the clergy would set us an example, by contenting themselves with wearing gowns, and other habiliments of Irish drapery; which, as it would be some incitement to the laity, and set many hands to work; so they would find their advantage in the cheapness; which is a circumstance not to be neglected by too many among that venerable body.[6] And, in order to this, I could heartily desire, that the most ingenious artists of the weaving trade, would contrive some decent stuffs and silks for clergymen, at reasonable rates.[7]

[Footnote 6: This hath since been put in practice, by the persuasions, and influence of the supposed author; but much defeated by the most infamous fraud of shop-keepers. [F.]]

[Footnote 7: This scheme was likewise often urged to the weavers by the supposed author; but he could never prevail upon them to put it in practice. [F.]]

I have pressed several of our most substantial brethren, that the whole corporation of weavers in silk and woollen, would publish some proposals, (I wish they would do it to both Houses of Parliament) inviting persons of all degrees, and of both sexes, to wear the woollen and silk manufactures of our own country; entering into solemn, mutual engagements, that the buyer shall have good, substantial, merchantable ware for his money; and at a certain rate, without the trouble of cheapening: So that, if I sent a child for a piece of stuff of a particular colour and fineness, I should be sure not to be deceived; or if I had reason to complain, the corporation should give me immediate satisfaction; and the name of the tradesman who did me the wrong, should be published; and warning given not to deal with him for the future; unless the matter plainly appeared to be a mistake: For, besides the trouble of going from shop to shop; an ignorant customer runs the hazard of being cheated in the price and goodness of what he buys; being forced to an unequal combat with a dexterous, and dishonest man, in his own calling. Thus our goods fall under a general disreputation; and the gentry call for English cloth, or silk, from an opinion they have (and often too justly by our own faults) that the goodness more than makes up for the difference of price.

Besides, it hath been the sottish and ruinous practice of us tradesmen, upon any great demand of goods, either at home or from abroad, to raise the prices immediately, and manufacture the said goods more slightly and fraudulently than before.

Of this foul and foolish proceeding, too many instances might be produced; and I cannot forbear mentioning one, whereby this poor kingdom hath received such a fatal blow in the only article of trade allowed us of any importance that nothing but the success of Wood's project, could outdo it. During the late plague in France, the Spaniards, who buy their linen cloths in that kingdom, not daring to venture thither for fear of infection; a very great demand was made here for that commodity, and exported to Spain: But, whether by the ignorance of the merchants, or dishonesty of the Northern weavers, or the collusion of both; the ware was so bad, and the price so excessive, that except some small quantity, which was sold below the prime cost, the greatest part was returned back: And I have been told by very intelligent persons, that if we had been fair dealers, the whole current of the linen trade to Spain would have taken its course from hence.

If any punishment were to be inflicted on numbers of men; surely there could none be thought too great for such a race of traitors, and enemies to God and their country; who for the prospect of a little present gain, do not only ruin themselves, (for that alone would be an example to the rest, and a blessing to the nation) but sell their souls to hell, and their country to destruction; And, if the plague could have been confined only to these who were partakers in the guilt, had it travelled hither from Marseilles, those wretches would have died with less title to pity, than a highwayman going to the gallows.

But, it happens very unluckily, that, for some time past, all endeavours or proposals from private persons, to advance the public service; however honestly and innocently designed, have been called *flying in the King's face:* And this, to my knowledge, hath been the style of some persons, whose ancestors, (I mean those among them who had any) and themselves, have been flying in princes' faces these fourscore years; and from their own inclinations would do so still, if their interest did not lead them rather to fly in the face of a kingdom; which hath given them wings to enable them for such a flight.

Thus, about four years ago, when a discourse was published, endeavouring to persuade our people to wear their own woollen manufactures,[8] full of the most dutiful expressions to the King, and without the least party hint; it was termed "flying in the King's face;" the printer was prosecuted in the manner we all remember; (and, I hope, it will somewhere be remembered further) the jury kept eleven hours, and sent back nine times, till they were under the necessity of leaving the prisoner to the mercy of the court, by a special verdict. The judge on the bench invoking God for his witness, when he asserted, that the author's design was to bring in the Pretender.[9]

[Footnote 8: This was Swift's pamphlet entitled, "A Proposal for the Universal Use of Irish Manufactures." [T.S.]]

[Footnote 9: The action and language of Justice Whitshed. [T.S.]]

And thus also, my own poor endeavours to prevent the ruin of my country, by the admission of Wood's coin, was called by the same persons, "flying in the King's face;" which I directly deny: For I cannot allow that vile representation of the royal countenance in William Wood's adulterate copper, to be his Sacred Majesty's face; or if it were, my flying was not against the impression, but the baseness of the metal; because I well remembered; that the image which Nebuchadnezzar "commanded to be set up, for all men to fall down and worship it," was not of *copper*, but pure *gold*. And I am heartily sorry, we have so few royal images of that metal among us; the sight whereof, although it could hardly increase our veneration for His Majesty, which is already so great; yet would very much enliven it with a mixture of comfort and satisfaction.

Alexander the Great, would suffer no statuary, except Phidias, to carve his image in stone or metal. How must he have treated such an operator as Wood, who goes about with sackfuls of dross; odiously misrepresenting his Prince's countenance; and would force them, by thousands, upon every one of us, at above six times the value.

But, notwithstanding all that hath been objected by William Wood himself; together with his favourers, abettors, supporters, either public or private; by those who connive at his project, or discourage and discountenance his opposers, for fear of lessening their favour, or hazarding their employments; by those who endeavour to damp the spirit of the people raised against this coin; or check the honest zeal of such as by their writings, or discourses, do all they can to keep it up: Those softeners, sweeteners, compounders; and expedient-mongers, who shake their heads so strongly, that we can hear their pockets jingle; I did never imagine, that, in detecting the practices of such enemies to the kingdom, I was "flying in the King's face"; or thought they were better representers of His Majesty, than that very coin, for which they are secret or open advocates.

If I were allowed to recite only those wishes of the nation, which may be in our power to attain; I think they might be summed up in these few following.

First, That an end might be put to our apprehensions of Wood's halfpence, and to any danger of the like destructive scheme for the future.

Secondly; That halfpence might be coined in this kingdom, by a public mint, with due limitations.

Thirdly, That the sense of both Houses of Parliament, at least of the House of Commons, were declared by some unanimous and hearty votes, against wearing any silk or woollen manufactures, imported from abroad, as likewise against wearing Indian silks or calicoes, which are forbidden under the highest penalties in England: And it behoves us, to take example from so wise a nation; because we are under a greater necessity to do so, since we are not allowed to export any woollen manufactures of our own; which is the principal branch of foreign trade in England.

Fourthly, That some effectual methods may be taken to civilize the poorer sort of our natives, in all those parts of this kingdom where the Irish abound; by introducing among them our language and customs; for want of which they live in the utmost ignorance, barbarity and poverty; giving themselves wholly up to idleness, nastiness, and thievery, to the very great and just reproach of too many landlords. And, if I had in me the least spirit of a projector, I would engage that this might be effected in a few years, at a very inconsiderable charge.[10]

[Footnote 10: Since this hint was suggested, several useful seminaries have been instituted, under the name of "Charter Working Schools," in Ireland, supported by the royal benefaction of a thousand pounds a year, by a tax on hawkers and pedlars, and by voluntary subscriptions. The schools are for the education of boys and girls born of Popish parents; in most of them, the children manufacture their own clothing, and the boys are employed in matters relative to husbandry. [F.]

These Charter Schools, founded by Marsh, Bishop of Clogher, and adopted by Primate Boulter in 1733, were intended "to rescue the souls of thousands of poor children from the dangers of Popish superstition and idolatry, and their bodies from the miseries of idleness and beggary." In reality the scheme was one by which it was hoped to prevent the growth of Catholicism. The conditions and methods of instruction were positively cruel, since the children were actually withheld from any communication with their parents. Mr. Lecky deals with the subject fully in the first volume of his "Ireland in the Eighteenth Century," Froude gives the scheme his praise and admiration, but at the time of its institution it was the cause of "an intensity of bitterness hardly equalled by any portion of the penal code. Parents would rather do anything than send their children into such prisons where, at last, they would receive an education which, to their minds, must lead them to forfeit their soul's salvation." [T.S.]]

Fifthly, That due encouragement should be given to agriculture; and a stop put to that pernicious practice of graziers; engrossing vast quantities of land, sometimes at great distance; whereby the country is extremely depopulated.

Sixthly, That the defects in those acts for planting forest trees, might be fully supplied, since they have hitherto been wholly ineffectual; except about the demesnes of a few gentlemen; and even there, in general, very unskilfully made, and thriving accordingly. Neither hath there yet been due care taken to preserve what is planted, or to enclose grounds; not one hedge, in a hundred, coming to maturity, for want of skill and industry. The neglect of copsing woods cut down, hath likewise been of very ill consequences. And if men were restrained from that unlimited liberty of cutting down their own woods before the proper time, as they are in some other countries; it would be a mighty benefit to the kingdom. For, I believe, there is not another example in Europe, of such a prodigious quantity of excellent timber cut down, in so short a time, with so little advantage to the country, either in shipping or building.

I may add, that absurd practice of cutting turf, without any regularity; whereby great quantities of restorable land are made utterly desperate, many thousands of cattle destroyed, the turf more difficult to come at, and carry home, and less fit for burning; the air made unwholesome by stagnating pools and marshes; and the very sight of such places offensive to those who ride by. Neither should that odious custom be allowed, of cutting scraws, (as they call them) which is flaying off the green surface of the ground, to cover their cabins; or make up their ditches; sometimes in shallow soils, where all is gravel within a few inches; and sometimes in low ground, with a thin greensward, and sloughy underneath; which last turns all into bog, by this mismanagement. And, I have heard from very skilful country-men, that by these two practices in turf and scraws, the kingdom loseth some hundreds of acres of profitable land every year; besides the irreparable loss of many skirts of bogs, which have a green coat of grass, and yet are mangled for turf; and, besides the want of canals, by regular cutting, which would not only be a great convenience for bringing their turf home at an easy rate; but likewise render even the larger bogs more dry and safe, for summer pasture.

These, and some other speculations of the like kind, I had intended to publish in a particular discourse against this session of

Parliament; because, in some periods of my life, I had opportunity and curiosity to observe, from what causes those great errors, in every branch of country management, have arisen; of which I have now ventured to relate but few, out of very many; whereof some, perhaps, would not be mentioned without giving offence; which I have endeavoured, by all possible means, to avoid. And, for the same reason, I chose to add here, the little I thought proper to say on this subject.

But, as to the lands of those who are perpetual absentees, I do not see any probability of their being ever improved. In former times, their tenants sat at easy rents; but for some years past, they have been, generally speaking, more terribly racked by the dexterity of merciless agents from England, than even those held under the severest landlords here. I was assured upon the place, by great numbers of credible people, that a prodigious estate in the county of Cork, being let upon leases for lives, and great fines paid; the rent was so high, that the tenants begged leave to surrender their leases, and were content to lose their fines.

The cultivating and improvement of land, is certainly a subject worthy of the highest enquiry in any country, but especially in ours; where we are so strangely limited in every branch of trade, that can be of advantage to us; and utterly deprived of those, which are of the greatest importance; whereof I defy the most learned man in Europe, to produce me an example from any other kingdom in the world: For, we are denied the benefits which God and nature intended to us; as manifestly appears by our happy situation for commerce, and the great number of our excellent ports. So that, I think, little is left us, beside the cultivating our own soil, encouraging agriculture, and making great plantations of trees, that we might not be under the necessity of sending for corn and bark from England, and timber from other countries. This would increase the number of our inhabitants, and help to consume our natural products, as well as manufactures at home. And I shall never forget what I once ventured to say to a great man in England; "That few politicians, with all their schemes, are half so useful members of a commonwealth, as an honest farmer; who, by skilfully draining, fencing, manuring, and planting, hath increased the intrinsic value of a piece of land; and thereby done a perpetual service to his country;" which it is a great controversy, whether any of the former ever did, since the creation of the world; but no controversy at all, that ninety-nine in a hundred, have done abundance of mischief.

APPENDIXES

APPENDIX I

ADDRESSES TO THE KING[1]

"To the King's most Excellent MAJESTY: *The humble* ADDRESS *of the* Knights, Citizens *and* Burgesses, *in Parliament assembled.*

"MOST GRACIOUS SOVEREIGN,

It is with the utmost Concern, that We, Your Majesty's most dutiful subjects, the Commons of IRELAND in Parliament assembled, find ourselves indispensably obliged, to represent to Your Majesty, our unanimous Opinion: That the importing and uttering of *Copper Farthings* and *Halfpence* by virtue of the Patent lately granted to *William Wood,* Esq.; under the Great Seal of *Great Britain,* will be highly prejudicial to Your Majesty's Revenue, destructive of the trade and commerce of this nation, and of the most dangerous consequence to the properties of the subject.

[Footnote 1: Addresses by the House of Commons and the House of Lords presented to the King in conformity with the resolutions passed by these Houses. See Introductory Note to the Drapier's First Letter. The texts of these addresses are taken from "Fraud Detected: or, the Hibernian Patriot," printed by George Faulkner in 1725. [T.S.]]

"We are fully convinced, from the tender regard Your Majesty has always expressed for our welfare and prosperity, that this Patent could not have been obtained, had not *William Wood* and his accomplices, greatly misrepresented the state of this nation to Your Majesty, it having appeared to us, by Examinations taken in the most solemn manner, that though the terms thereof had been strictly complied with, there would have been a loss to this nation of at least 150 *per Cent.* by means of the said coinage, and a much greater in the manner the said *Half-pence* have been coined.

"We likewise beg leave to inform Your Majesty, That the said *William Wood* has been guilty of a most notorious fraud and deceit in coining the said *Half-pence,* having, under colour of the powers granted unto him, imported and endeavoured to utter great quantities of different impressions, and of much less weight than was required by the said Patent.

"Your faithful *Commons* have found, by experience, That the granting the power or privilege of coining *Money*, or *Tokens* to pass for *Money* to private persons, has been highly detrimental to your loyal subjects; and being apprehensive, that the vesting such power in any body politic or corporate, or any private person or persons whatsoever, will be always of dangerous Consequence to this Kingdom, are encouraged, by the repeated assurances Your Majesty hath given us of Your Royal Favour and Protection, humbly to entreat Your Majesty, That whenever you shall hereafter think it necessary to coin any *Farthings* or *Half-pence,* the same may be made as near the intrinsic value as possible, and that whatever profit shall accrue thereby, may be applied to the public service.

"And we do further humbly beseech Your Majesty, That you will be graciously pleased to give such direction, as you, in your great wisdom, shall think proper, to prevent the fatal effects of uttering any *Farthings* or *Half-pence* pursuant to the said Patent.

"As this enquiry has proceeded entirely from our love to our country, so we cannot omit this opportunity of repeating our unanimous resolution, to stand by and support Your Majesty to the utmost of our power, against all Your enemies, both at home and abroad; and of assuring Your Majesty, that we will, upon every occasion, give Your Majesty, and the world, all possible demonstration of our zeal and inviolable duty and affection to Your Majesty's most sacred person and government, and to the succession, as established in Your Royal House."

"To the King's most Excellent MAJESTY. *The humble Address of the Lords*
Spiritual and Temporal of IRELAND, *in Parliament assembled, against*
Wm. Wood.

"May it please Your most Sacred Majesty, WE the Lords Spiritual and Temporal in Parliament assembled, are under the utmost concern to find, that our duty to Your Majesty and our Country, indispensably calls upon us to acquaint Your Majesty with the ill consequences, which will inevitably follow from a Patent for coining Half-pence and Farthings to be uttered in this Kingdom, obtained under the Great Seal of *Great Britain,* by one *William Wood* in a clandestine and unprecedented manner, and by a gross misrepresentation of the state of this Kingdom.

"We are most humbly of opinion, that the diminution of Your Majesty's revenue, the ruin of our trade, and the impoverishing of your people, must unavoidably attend this undertaking; and we beg leave to observe to Your Majesty, that from the most exact Enquiries and Computations we have been able to make, it appears to us, that the gain to *William Wood* will be excessive, and the loss to this Kingdom, by circulating this base coin, greater than this poor country is able to bear.

"With the greatest submission and deference to Your Majesty's wisdom, we beg we may offer it as our humble opinion. That the reserving the coining of *Half-pence* and *Farthings* to the *Crown* and *the not intrusting it* with any private person, body politic or corporate, will always be for Your Majesty's service, and the good of your people in *this Kingdom.*

"In confidence, Sir, of your paternal care of the welfare of *this* country, we beseech Your Majesty, that you will be pleased to extend that goodness and compassion to us, which has so eminently shewed itself to all your other subjects, who have the happiness to live under your protection and government; and that you will give such directions as may effectually free us from the terrible apprehensions we labour under from the *Patent* granted to *William Wood."*

The following was the King's reply to the above address:

"GEORGE R.

"His *Majesty is very much concerned to see, That His granting the Patent for coining* Half-pence *and* Farthings *agreeable to the Practice of his Royal Predecessors, has given so much uneasiness to the*
House of Lords: *And if there have been any abuses committed by the*
Patentee, *His Majesty will give the necessary Orders for enquiring into, and punishing those Abuses. And will do everything that is in His*
Power, for the Satisfaction of His People."

APPENDIX II

REPORT OF THE ASSAY ON WOOD'S COINAGE, MADE BY SIR ISAAC NEWTON, EDWARD SOUTHWELL, ESQ., AND THOMAS SCROOPE, ESQ.[1]

"_To the right honourable the Lords Commissioners of his Majesty's Treasury.

"May it please your Lordships_,

According to your Lordships' Order, the pix of the copper-money coined at Bristol by Mr. Wood for Ireland, has been opened and tried before us at his Majesty's Mint in the Tower; and by the Comptroller's account, to which Mr. Wood agreed, there hath been coined from Lady-day 1723 to March 28, 1724, in half-pence, fifty and five tons, five hundred and three quarters, and twelve ounces, and in farthings, three tons, seventeen hundred and two quarters, ten pounds, and eight ounces, *avoirdupois*, the whole coinage amounting to 59 tons, 3 cwt, 1 qr. 11 lbs. 4 ozs., and by the specimens of this coinage which have, from time to time, been taken from the several parcels coined and sealed up in papers, and put into the pix, we found that sixty half-pence weighed fourteen ounces, *Troy*, and eight pennyweight, which is about a quarter of an ounce above one pound *avoirdupois*; and that thirty farthings weighed three ounces, and three quarters of an ounce *Troy*, and forty-six grains, which is also above the weight required by his Patent. We found also that both half-pence and farthings when heated red hot, spread thin under the hammer without cracking, as your Lordships may see by the pieces now laid before your Lordships. But although the copper was very good, and the money, one piece with another, was full weight, yet the single pieces were not so equally coined in the weight as they should have been.

[Footnote 1: The copy of this Report as here printed is taken from the tract already quoted in previous notes, entitled, "A Defence of the Conduct of the People of Ireland in their unanimous Refusal of Mr. Wood's Copper-money ... Dublin: Printed for George Ewing, at the Angel and Bible in Dames-Street, MDCCXXIV." As already noted, the assayists had for trial only those coins which were coined between March, 1723, and March, 1724, and these coins were neither imported into Ireland nor attempted to be uttered there. As Wood asked for the assay, he no doubt knew what he was about. But even as it stands, the Report was not very favourable to him. The author of the tract named above enters minutely into this point, and for a further inquiry the reader is referred to pages 15 to 19 of his publication. [T.S.]]

"We found also that thirty and two old half-pence coined for Ireland in the reigns of King Charles 2d., King James 2d., and King William 3d. and Queen Mary, and produced by Mr. Wood, weighed six ounces and eight pennyweight *Troy*, that is, one hundred and three grains and a half apiece one with another. They were much worn, and if about six or seven grains be allowed to each of them one with another for loss of their weight by wearing, the copper-money coined for England, in the reign of King William being already as much lightened by wearing, they might at first weigh about half a pound *avoirdupois*; whereas only thirty of those coined by Mr. Wood are to be of that. They were also made of bad copper, two of those coined in the reign of King Charles II. wasted much in the fire, and then spread thin under the hammer, but not so well without cracking as those of Mr. Wood. Two of those coined in the reign of King James II. wasted much more in the fire, and were not malleable when red hot. Two of those coined in the reign of King William and Queen Mary wasted still more in the fire, and turned to an unmalleable substance like a cinder, as your Lordships may see the pieces now laid before you.

"By the assays we reckon the copper of Mr. Wood's halfpence and farthings to be of the same goodness and value with the copper of which the copper money is coined in the King's Mint for England; or worth in the market about twelve or thirteen pence per pound weight *avoirdupois*; and the copper of which the half-pence were coined for Ireland in the reigns of King Charles, King James, and King William, to be much inferior in value, the mixture being unknown, and not bearing the fire for converting it to any other use until it be refined.

"The half-pence and farthings in the pix coined by Mr. Wood had on one side the head of the King, with this inscription GEORGIUS DEI GRATIA REX: And on the other side, a woman sitting with a harp by her left side, and above her the inscription HIBERNIA with the date. The half-pence coined in the reigns of King Charles, King James, and King William, had on one side the head of King Charles, King James, or King William and Queen Mary, and on the reverse a harp crowned.

"All which facts we most humbly represent to your Lordships. April 27, 1724."

APPENDIX III

TOM PUNSIBI'S DREAM[1]

> [Greek: "A ghar proseidon nukthi taeoe phasmata
> Disson oneiron, tauta moi——
> Ehi men pephaenen esthlha, dus telesphora,
> Eid echthra, tois echthroisin empalin methes
> Kai mae me plete te paront ei tines
> Doloisi beleueoin ekbalein, ephaes."]

Soph, Elec. [644-649].

Since the heat of this business, which has of late so much and so justly concerned this kingdom, is at last, in a great measure over, we may venture to abate something of our former zeal and vigour in handling it, and looking upon it as an enemy almost overthrown, consult more our own amusement than its prejudice, in attacking it in light excursory skirmishes. Thus much I thought fit to observe, lest the world should be too apt to make an obvious pun upon me; when beginning to dream upon this occasion, I presented it with the wild nocturnal rovings of an unguided imagination, on a subject of so great importance, as the final welfare or ruin of a whole nation.

[Footnote 1: The following tract, written probably by Thomas Sheridan, Swift's humorous friend, is interesting as affording an example of the lighter kind of literature brought into existence by this agitation. It may be that Swift had a hand in its composition. The text is taken from a copy of the original broadside in the South Kensington Collection. It was published during the height of the controversy. [T.S.]]

But so it was, that upon reading one of the Drapier's letters, I fell asleep, and had the following dream:

The first object that struck me was a woman of exquisite beauty, and a most majestic air, seated on a throne, whom by the figure of a lion beneath her feet, and of Neptune who stood by her, and paid her the most respectful homage, I easily knew to be the Genius of England; at some distance from her, (though not at so great an one as seemed to be desired,) I observed a matron clothed in robes so tattered and torn, that they had not only very nigh lost their original air of royalty and magnificence, but even exposed her to the inclemency of the weather in several places, which with many other afflictions had so affected her, that her natural beauty was almost effaced, and her strength and spirits very nigh lost. She hung over a harp with which, if she sometimes endeavoured to sooth her melancholy, she had still the misfortune to find it more or less out of tune, particularly, when as I perceived at last, it was strung with a sort of wire of so base composition, that neither she nor I could make anything of it. I took particular notice, that, when moved by a just sense of her wrongs, she could at any time raise her head, she fixed her eyes so stedfastly on her neighbour, sometimes with an humble and entreating, at others, with a more bold and resentful regard, that I could not help (however improbable it should seem from her generous august appearance) in a great measure to attribute her misfortunes to her; but this I shall submit to the judgment of the world.

I should now at last mention the name, were not these circumstances too unhappily singular to make that any way necessary.

As I was taken up with many melancholy reflections on this moving object, I was on a sudden interrupted by a little sort of an uproar, which, upon turning my eyes towards it, I found arose from a crowd of people behind her throne; the cause it seems was this:

There was, I perceived, among them the god of merchandise, with his sandals, mostly of brass, but not without a small proportion of gold and silver, and his wings chiefly of the two latter metals, but allayed with a little of the former; with those he used to trudge up and down to furnish them with necessaries; with these he'd take a flight to other countries, but not so dexterously or to so good purpose as in other places of his office, not so much for want of encouragement among 'em here, as on account of the haughty jealousy of their neighbours, who, it seems dreading in them a rival, took care to clip his wings and circumscribe his flights; the former, more especially, being, by these and other means so much worn, he performed his office but lamely, which gave occasion to some who had their own private interest more at heart, than that of the public, to patch up some of the places that were worn, with a metal of the same nature indeed, but so slight and base, that though at first it might serve to carry him on their errands, it soon failed, and by degrees grew entirely useless; insomuch, that he would rather be retarded than promoted in his business, and this occasioned the above disturbances among his dependents, who thereupon turned their eyes towards their mistress (for by this time she will I presume be better known by that, than the more homely and sociable name of neighbour) and not daring of late to say or do anything without her approbation, made several humble applications to her, beseeching that she would continue them that liberty of refitting these implements themselves, which she had been formerly pleased graciously to allow 'em; but these, however reasonable, were all rejected, whereupon I observed a certain person (a mean ill-looking fellow) from among a great number of people that stood behind the genius of England, who, during the whole affair had kept his eyes intently fixed on his neighbours, watching all their motions, like a hawk hovering over his quarry, and with just the same design: Him, I say, I observed to turn off hastily, and make towards the throne, where being arrived, after some preparations requisite, he preferred a petition, setting forth the wants and necessities, (but taking care to make 'em appear at least four times greater than they really were) of his neighbours, or as he might have more truly and honestly said his own, both which, for the latter, though not expressed, he chiefly intended, but modestly or rather knavishly left to be understood, he begged the royal licence to redress, by supplying those defects which were the occasion of 'em. This humble suppliant I observed both before and after this petition, seemed to employ his utmost industry and art, to insinuate himself into the good graces of two persons that stood on each side the throne;[2]the one on the right was a lady of large make and swarthy complexion; the other, a man, that seemed to be between fifty and sixty, who had an air of deep designing thought: These two he managed with a great deal of art; for the lady he employed all the little arts that win her sex, particularly, I observed, that he frequently took hold of her hand, as in raptures, to kiss it, in such a manner as made me suspect she did not always draw it back empty; but this he did so slily, that it was not easy for anybody to be certain of it: The man on the other hand, he plied his own way with politics, remonstrating to him the several things he had before the throne; which however, as might be presumed from his manner of attending to them, seemed to make little impression; but when he came to lay before him the great advantages that might accrue from thence to their mistress, and consequently to him, he heard him with the utmost eagerness and satisfaction; at last, having plainly told him, that he himself should be a considerable gainer by it, and thereupon, that every thing that came to his hands of that nature should be at his service: As a sort of token or earnest he kissed his hand in the same manner he had the lady's, and so retired; by these and the like means he soon brought over both parties to him, who, with a whisper or two, procured him the royal licence; whereupon he immediately fell to making up a metal, if it deserved the name, of a very strange composition, wherewith he purposed to refit the implements of that useful deity, but in such manner, that for the base metal he put into them, he would take care to draw away from them an infinitely more than proportionable quantity of gold and silver, and thereby render him almost incapable of taking flight to foreign countries; nay, at last perhaps utterly so, when under pretence of their not being completed, he should filch in more of his metal, and filch away more of theirs.

[Footnote 2: The Duchess of Kendal and Sir Robert Walpole. [S.]]

These things being therefore prepared, he sends 'em over to his neighbours, and there endeavoured to get them admitted by fair words and promises, being too sensible that they were not of themselves the most willing to accept of his favour, and indeed he was not deceived; for they being advertised of his designs, had taken the alarm, and had almost to a man united in one common faction against him. This generous ardour had first taken hold of the most active and important part, and if I may be allowed to call it, the heart of this body, from thence was on one side by a quick passage, and in its more refined parts, communicated through the blood to the contemplative, and reasoning, the head, which it inspired with noble thoughts and resolutions; and on the other, to the inferior extremities, which were thereby rendered more expedite and readier to obey the dictates of the head in a rougher method of opposition, from each of which extremities being carried back to its fountain, it was returned to them from thence, and so backwards and forwards, till the circulation and union were confirmed and completed, the sordid unnatural, offensive parts being in the meantime thrown off as dregs of nature, and nuisances of human society; but of these in so well-tempered a constitution, there were but few; however, when there were any to be found, though they had been of the most exalted nature, and bore most noble offices in this body, by any corruption became so, they shared the common fate, with this only difference, that they were rejected with greater scorn and contempt on account of their former dignity, as was found in one notorious instance; but on the other hand, among all the parts that were serviceable to the constitution on this occasion, there was not one more so, than a certain one whose name indeed is not openly known, but whose good offices and usefulness are too great ever to be forgotten; for it by its nice diligence and skill selected out things of the most noble and exquisite nature, by infusing and dispersing them to enliven and invigorate the whole body, which how effectually they did, our bold projector sadly experienced. For finding all his endeavours to pass his ware upon them, disappointed, he withdrew; but his patron on the other side being informed of what had passed, fell into a most terrible passion, and threatened, they say, I know not what, of making to swallow and ramming down throats; but while they were in deep conference together, methought all on a sudden a trap-door dropped, and down fell our projector; this unexpected accident did on many accounts not a little alarm the throne, and gave it but too great occasion to reflect a little on what had been doing, as what a mean ordinary fellow it had intrusted with the care of an affair of so great consequence that though their neighbours' refusal might possibly have put him to such straits as might be the great occasion of this disgrace, yet that very refusal could not be so universal and resolute without some reason, which could arise from nothing else but the unseasonableness or unworthiness of his offers, or both, and he, consequently, must deserve as much to suffer as they did; not for the better information, therefore in these surmises some of the neighbours were consulted, who confirming them, things seemed to bear a good face, and be in a very fair way of clearing up. When I awoke, I cannot say whether more pleased at the present posture of affairs, when I recollected how indifferent an one they had lately been in, or anxious when upon considering that they were not yet firm and settled, I was led to reflect in general on the uncertainty of events, and in particular, on the small reason the persons in hand can have to promise themselves prosperous ones, especially when they are depending in that part of the world.

Dublin, printed in the year 1724-5.

APPENDIX IV

A LETTER FROM A FRIEND TO THE RIGHT HONOURABLE ———[1]

Ceteri, quanto quis servitio promptior, opibus et honoribus extollerentur: Invalido legum auxilio, quae vi, ambitu, postremo pecunia turbabantur.—*Tacit. An.*

To THE RIGHT HONOURABLE ———

I fear your lordship in your wonted zeal for the interest of your country will think this paper very unseasonable; but I am very confident not more than one man in this kingdom will be of your lordship's judgment.

[Footnote 1: The two following severe letters are directly addressed to Lord Chief Justice Whitshed, and were generally circulated. They probably underwent Swift's correction, though they have too much of a legal cast to have been written by the Dean himself.... They were, perhaps, composed by Mr. Robert Lindsay, distinguished by Swift in his letter to Lord Midleton, as an eminent lawyer, as well as a man of virtue and learning, whose legal advice he used during the whole controversy. [S.]

The present letters are taken from copies of the original broadsides in the South Kensington collection. [T.S.]]

In matters of law your opinion has from our first acquaintance entirely guided me, and the things you have assured me I might depend upon as law, have few of them escaped my memory, though I have had but little conversation with you since you first appeared in Parliament and moved the House to resolve, That it is the indispensable duty of the judges of this kingdom to go through their circuits; nor have I had any since you fell sick and was made solicitor-general.

I have often heard your lordship affirm, and therefore I do affirm it, That the great ends for which grand juries were instituted, were the support of the government, the safety of every man's life and fortune, it being necessary some should be trusted to inquire after all disturbers of the peace, that they might be prosecuted and brought to condign punishment; and it is no less needful for every man's quiet and safety, that the trust of such inquisitions should be put into the hands of persons of understanding and integrity, that will suffer no man to be falsely accused or defamed; nor the lives of any to be put in jeopardy, by the malicious conspiracies of great or small, or the perjuries of any profligate wretches.

So material a part of our constitution are grand juries, so much does the security of every subject depend upon them, that though anciently the sheriff was by express law, chosen annually by the people of the county, and trusted with the power of the county, yet the law left not the election of grand juries to the will of the sheriff, but has described their qualifications, which if they have, and the sheriff return them, no man, nay no judge, can object to their being sworn, much less may they to their serving when sworn: And to prevent the discretionary power (a new-fashioned term) of these judges over juries, you used to say was made the statute of the 11th of Hen. 4.

Pardon me my lord if I venture to affirm, That a dissolving power is a breach of that law, or at least an evasion, as every citizen in Dublin in Sir Constantine Phipps's time perfectly understood, that disapproving the aldermen lawfully returned to the Privy-council was in effect assuming the power of choosing and returning——But your lordship and I know dissolving and disapproving are different terms.

I always understood from your Lordship the trust and power of grand juries is or ought to be accounted amongst the greatest and of most concern, next to the legislative: The honour, reputations, fortunes and lives of every man being subject to their censure; the kings of England have an undoubted power of dissolving parliaments, but dissolving 'till one was returned to their or their ministers' liking, has never been thought very righteous, and Heaven be praised never very successful.

I am entirely of your lordship's opinion, the oath of a grand juryman is not always sufficiently considered by the jurors, which is as follows.

"You shall diligently enquire, and true presentment make of all such articles, matters and things as shall be given you in charge; And of all other matters and things as shall come to your own knowledge, touching this present service. The King's counsel your fellows' and your own you shall keep secret," &c.—And from some other men's behaviour, I fear oaths are not always as sacredly observed as they ought to be: "The King's counsel, your fellows' and your *own* you shall keep secret"—Though our grandmothers my lord might have thought there was a dispensing power in the Pope, you and I profess no power upon earth can dispense with this oath, so that to force a man to discover the counsel he is sworn to keep, is to force him into direct perjury.

Suppose upon information taken before your Lordship of a rape committed, a bill of indictment were sent to a grand jury, and the grand jury return *ignoramus* on it, application is made to the Court to recommend it to them to reconsider it, and they return as before *ignoramus*—Suppose a judge with more than decent passion should ask them their reasons (which is their counsel) for so doing, nay should be so particular as to demand of them whether they thought the woman a whore. Must not all the world conclude somebody had forgot the oath of a grand juryman? Yes sure, or his own, or worse.—But suppose they should ask a juror a question might criminate himself? My Lord, you know I put not bare possibilities, it is generally believed these things have been done within an oak of this town—And if I am rightly informed, the restraint a juror is under by his oath, is so well understood, that a certain person desired the clerk of the Crown to change the form of it by adding this exception: "unless by leave or order of the Court."

These things, my Lord, would seem strange in Westminster-hall, and would be severely noted in St. Stephen's Chapel. The honour of the Crown would be thought a very false as well as weak plea for such proceedings there, as indeed it is an infamous one everywhere, for 'tis a scandal upon a king, if he is represented in a court of justice, as if he were partially concerned or rather inclined to desire, that a party should be found guilty, than that he should be declared innocent.

The King's interest and honour is more concerned in the protection of the innocent, than in the punishment of the guilty, as in all the immediate actions of his Majesty we find that maxim pursued, a maxim can never run a prince into excesses. We do not only find those princes represented in history under odious characters, who have basely betrayed the innocent, but such as by their spies and informers were too inquisitive after the guilty, whereas none was ever blamed for clemency, or for being too gentle interpreters of the law. Though Trajan was an excellent prince, endowed with all heroical virtues; yet the most eloquent writers, and his best friends, found nothing more to be praised in his government, than that in his time, all men might think what they pleased, and every man speak what he thought, this I say, that if any amongst us by violent measures, and a dictatorial behaviour have raised jealousies in the minds of His Majesty's faithful subjects, the blame may lie at their door.

I know it has been said for His Majesty's service, grand juries may be forced to discover their counsels: But you will confess a king can do nothing against law, nor will any honest man judge that for his service, which is not warranted by law. If a constant uninterrupted usage, can give the force of a law, then the grand jurymen are bound by law, as well as by their oaths, to keep the King's, their fellows' and their own counsel secret. Bracton and Britton in their several generations bear witness, that it was then practised; and greater proof of it needs not be sought, than the disputes that appear by the law-books to have been amongst the ancient lawyers, Whether it was treason or felony for a grand juryman to discover their counsels—The trust of grand juries was in those days thought so sacred, and their secrecy of so great concern to the kingdom, that whosoever should break their oaths, was by all thought worthy to die, only some would have them suffer as traitors, others as felons.

If a king's commands should come to the judges of a court of justice or to a jury, desiring them to vary from the direction of the law, (which it is criminal to say, and no man ought to be believed therein) they are bound by their oaths not to regard them. The statute of 2 of E. 3. 8. and 20 E. 3. I. are express; and the substance of these and other statutes is inserted into the oaths taken by every judge; and if they be under the most solemn and sacred tie in the execution of justice to hold for nothing the commands of the King under the great seal, then surely political views and schemes, the pleasure or displeasure of a minister, in the like case ought to be less than nothing.

It is a strange doctrine that men must sacrifice the law to secure their properties, if the law is to be fashioned for every occasion, if grand jurymen contrary to their oaths must discover their fellows' and their own counsels, and betray the trust the law has reposed in them, if they must subject the reasons of their verdicts to the censure of the judges, whom the law did never design to trust with the liberty, property, or good name of their fellow-subjects. No man can say he has any security for his life or fortune, and they who do not themselves, may however see their best friends and nearest relations suffer the utmost violences and oppressions.

Which leads me to say a few words of the petit jury, not forgetting Mr. Walters. I am assured by an eminent lawyer, that the power and office of a petit jury is judicial, that they only are the judges from whose sentence the indicted are to expect life or death. Upon their integrity and understanding the lives of all that are brought in judgment do ultimately depend; from their verdict there lies no appeal, by finding guilty or not guilty. They do complicately resolve both law and fact. As it hath been the law, so it hath always been the custom and practice of these juries (except as before) upon all general issues, pleaded in cases civil as well as criminal, to judge both of the law and fact. So it is said in the report of the Lord Chief Justice Vaughan in Bushell's case, That these juries determine the law in all matters where issue is joined and tried, in the principal case whether the issue be about trespass or debt, or disseizin in assizes, or a tort or any such like, unless they should please to give a special verdict with an implicate faith in the judgment of the Court, to which none can oblige them against their wills.

It is certain we may hope to see the trust of a grand juryman best discharged when gentlemen of the best fortunes and understandings attend that service, but it is as certain we must never expect to see such men on juries, if for differing with a judge in opinion, when they only are the lawful judges, they are liable to be treated like villains, like perjurers, and enemies to their king and country; I say my lord such behaviour to juries will make all gentlemen avoid that duty, and instead of men of interest, of reputation and abilities, our lives, our fortunes, and our reputations must depend upon the basest and meanest of the people.

I know it is commonly said, *boni judicis est ampliare juridictionem*. But I take that to be better advice which was given by the Lord Chancellor Bacon upon swearing a judge; That he would take care to contain the jurisdiction of the court within the ancient mere-stones without removing the mark.

I intend to pay my respects to your lordship once every month 'till the meeting of the Parliament, when our betters may consider of these matters, and therefore will not trouble you with any more on this subject at present. But conclude, most heartily praying——

That from depending upon the will of a judge, who may be corrupted or swayed by his own passions, interests, or the impulse of such as support him and may advance him to greater honours, the God of mercy and of justice deliver this nation.

    I am, my lord,
Your lordship's most obedient humble servant,
                N.N.
Dec. the First 1724.
    Dublin: Printed in the Year 1724.

A SECOND LETTER FROM A FRIEND TO THE RIGHT HONOURABLE
———

My Lord,

I think the best service men employed by His Majesty can do for him and this country, is to shew such prudence and temper in their behaviours as may convince every man they are not intrusted with any power but what is necessary and will always be exercised for the advantage and security of His Majesty's subjects.

For my own part I hold it the duty of every man though he has not the honour of serving His Majesty in public employment, not only, not to misrepresent the actions of his servants, but in matters of small concern, to wink at their follies and mistakes; I know the Jacobites and Papists our irreconcilable enemies are too watchful to lay hold of every occasion to misrepresent His Majesty and turn the faults of ambitious and self-interested servants upon the best of kings.

I hear some men say, that in my last to your lordship, there appears more of the satirist, than becomes a man engaged merely in the defence of liberty and justice; But I am satisfied I can with charity affirm, they are either such as have no knowledge of the several steps [that] have been taken to bring this poor country into ruin and disgrace, or they are of the number of those who have had a share in the actings and contrivances against it; for my lord, he must rather be an insensible stoic than an angry cynic, who can survey the measures of some men without horror and indignation—To see men act as if they had never taken an oath of fidelity to their king, whose interest is inseparable from that of his people, but had sworn to support the ruinous projects of abandoned men (of whatever faction) must rouse the most lethargic, if honest, soul.

I who have always professed myself a Whig do confess it has mine.

I beg leave in this place to explain what I intended in my last by the words, "unless by leave or order of the court," lest whilst I plead for justice I should do an injury to your lordship.

I do declare I never heard that story of your lordship, and I hope no man did believe it of you. My intention by that hint to remember you of Judge U—p—n and a certain assizes held at Wicklow, as I believe your lordship understood it, and as I now desire all the world may.

Having learned from your lordship and other lawyers of undoubted abilities, that no judge ought by threats or circumvention to make a grand-juryman discover the king's counsel his fellows' or his own I should not at present say anything in support of that position. But that I find a most ridiculous and false explanation seem to mislead some men in that point: Say they, by the word counsel is understood, such bills as are before the grand jury and the evidence the prosecutors for the crown have to support the charge against the subject—Lest that being known the party indictable may fly from justice, or he may procure false witnesses to discredit the evidence for the king, or he may by bribes and other indirect measures take off the witnesses for the crown.

I confess *I* take that to be the meaning of the word counsel, but I am certain that is not *all* that is meant by it, that is what must be understood when it is called the king's counsel, *id est*, the counsel or reasons for which the king by his servants, his attorney-general or coroner, has drawn and sent to the grand jury a charge against a subject.

But the counsel of a juror is a different thing, it is the evidence, the motives and reasons that induce him or his fellow-jurors to say *billa vera* or *ignoramus*, and the opinion he or they happen to be of when the question is put by the foreman for finding or not finding: This counsel every man is sworn to keep secret, that so their opinion and advice may not be of prejudice to them hereafter, That as they are sworn to act without favour or affection, so may they also act without FEAR. Whereas, were it otherwise the spirit of revenge is so universal, there are but few cases wherein a juror could act with safety to himself; either the prosecuted, as where the bill is found, or the prosecutor, where it is returned *ignoramus*, may contrive to defame the jurors who differ from them in opinion: As I am told has happened to some very honest citizens who are represented to be Jacobites since their opinions were know to be against ——. And sometimes revenge or ambition may prompt men to carry it further, as in the case of Mr. Wilmer, who in King Charles 2d's time was very severely handled for being one of an *ignoramus* jury.—— 'Tis not necessary to say whom he disobliged by being so.——But if I remember right his case was this.

He was a merchant, (and as I said, an *ignoramus* juryman) had covenanted with a servant boy to serve him in the West Indies, and accordingly sent him beyond sea: Upon suggestion and affidavit by which any person might have it, a writ *de homine replegiando* was granted against Mr. Wilmer; the sheriffs would have returned on the writ the agreement and the boy's consent, but the court (in the case of this Wilmer) Easter 34, Cha. 2. [*i.e.*, Charles the Second] in B.R. ruled they must return *replegiari fecimus* or *elongavit*, that is, they had replevy'd the boy, or that Wilmer had carried him away where they could not find him, in which last case Mr. Wilmer, though an innocent person must have gone to gaol until he brought the boy into court or he must have been outlawed—Shower's Rep. 2 Part.

I do not say this that I think the same thing will be practised again, or anything like it, though I know that very homely proverb, "More ways of killing a dog than hanging him."—But I instance it to shew, the counsels of every grand juryman should be kept secret, that he may act freely and without apprehensions of resentment from the prosecuted or prosecutor.

My resolution when I writ to you last, was, not to have said anything in this concerning the power of dissolving or dispensing, but as I have been forced to say something of the dispensing, for the same reason I must of the dissolving power.—A power undoubtedly in effect including that of returning, which makes me wish two men of great interest in this kingdom, differing in every other thing, had not undertaken to defend it, or they had better reasons for it than I have yet heard.

'Tis said, "This power is in the court as a right of resistance is in the people, as the people have a power superior to the prerogative of the prince, though no written or express law for it; so of necessity though no statute directs it, and it may seem to overturn the greatest security men have for their liberties, yet the court has a power of dissolving grand juries, if they refuse to find or present as the court shall direct."

Pray let us consider how well this concludes.

The people may do anything in defence of their lives, their religion and liberties, and consequently resistance is lawful, therefore an inferior court a *bene placito* judge may——Monstrous absurdity.

Another, I am sorry I can't say more modest argument to support it is this.—

"Considering," say they, "grand juries, it is but reasonable a discretionary power of dissolving them should be lodged in the judges."

By the words "considering grand juries," I must understand considering their understandings, their fortunes or their integrity, for from a want of one or more of those qualifications must arise the reason of such a discretionary power in the judges.

Though I shall not urge it as far as I could, I will venture to say the argument is at least as strong the other way—considering the judges.—

First as to their understandings, it must be confessed the benches are infinitely superior to the lower professors of the law: Yet surely it can't give offence to say the gentlemen of the several counties have understandings sufficient to discharge the duty of grand jurymen—If want of fortune be an objection to grand jurymen, *a pari ratione*, it is an objection to some other men.—Besides, that the fact is not true, for in their circuits, no judge goes into any county where he does not meet at least a dozen gentlemen returned upon every grand jury, every one of whom have better estates than he himself has—And these not during pleasure, which last consideration, saves me the trouble of shewing the weakness of the objection in the third qualification.

"Ay. But it was a necessary expedient to keep out Wood's brass."

Are the properties of the commons of this kingdom better secured by the knight-errantry of that day? In the name of common sense, what are we to believe? Has the undaunted spirit, the tremendous voice of ――― frightened Wood and his accomplices from any further attempts? Or rather has not the ready compliance of ――― encouraged them to further trials? The officers and attendants of his court may tremble when he frowns, but who else regards it more than they do one of Wood's farthings.

"There is no comparison," says another, "between the affair of Sir W. Scroggs and this of ―――. Sir W. discharged a grand jury because they were about to present the Duke of York for being a Papist, but ――― discharged the grand jury for not presenting a paper he recommended to them to present as scandalous, (and in which, I say, he was a party reflected on.)"

I agree there is a mighty difference, but whom does it make for?

A grand jury of a hundred (part of a county) take upon them to present a no less considerable person than the king's brother and heir presumptive of the crown, the chief-justice thinks this a matter of too much moment for men of such sort to meddle in, but a matter more proper for the consideration of Parliament: I would not be understood to condemn the jury; I think they acted as became honest Englishmen and lovers of their country; But I say if judges could in any case be allowed to proceed by rules of policy, surely here was a sufficient excuse. However the commons impeached him.

The determinations of ignorant or wicked judges as they are precedents of little weight, so they are but of little danger, and therefore it will become the commons at all times to animadvert most carefully upon the actions of the most knowing men in that profession.

I say, my lord, *at all times*, because I hear former merit is pleaded to screen this action from any inquiry.

I am sensible much is due to the man who has always preferred the public interest to his private advantages as ———— has done. When a man has signalized himself, when he has suffered for that principle, he deserves universal respect. Yet men should act agreeably to the motive of that respect, and not ruin the liberty of their country to shew their gratitude, and so, my lord, where a man has the least pretence to that character, I think 'tis best to pass over small offences, but never such as will entail danger and dishonour upon us and our posterity.

The Romans, my lord, when a question was in the senate, whether they should ransom fifteen thousand citizens who had merited much by their former victories, but losing one battle were taken prisoners; were determined by the advice of that noble Roman Attilius Regulus not to redeem them as men unworthy their further care, though probably it was their misfortunes not their faults lost that day.

Flagitio additis
Damnum: neque amissos colores
Luna refert medicata fuco

He thought they were not worthy to be trusted again:——

To shew them pity, in his mind, would betray the Romans to perpetual danger: *Et exemplo trahenti*

Perniciem veniens in aevum,
Si non periret immiserabilis
Captiva pubes

I hear some precedents have been lately found out to justify that memorable action; but if precedents must control reason and justice, if a man may swear he will keep his counsels secret, and yet by precedents may be forced to divulge them, I would advise gentlemen very seriously to consider, the danger we are in; and examine what precedents there are on each side of the question, for my part I think the commons of England are not a worse precedent than the judges of England.

Besides it must be remembered that precedents in some cases will not excuse a judge, even where they are according to the undoubted law of the land, as for instance,

Suppose a man says what is true, not knowing it to be true, though it be logically a truth as it is distinguished, yet it is morally false; and so, suppose a judge give judgment according to law, not knowing it to be so, as if he did not know the reason of it at that time, but bethought himself of a reason or precedent for it afterwards, though the judgment be legal and according to precedent, yet the pronouncing of it is unjust; and the judge shall be condemned in the opinions of all men: As happened to the Lord Chief Justice Popham a person of great learning and parts, who upon the trial of Sir Walter Raleigh; when Sir Walter objected to reading or giving in evidence, Lord Cobham's affidavit, taken in his absence, without producing the lord face to face, the lord being then forthcoming: The chief justice overruled the objection, and was of opinion it should be given in evidence against Sir Walter, and summing up the evidence to the jury the chief justice said, "Just then it came into his mind why the accuser should not come face to face to the prisoner, because, &c." Now if any judge has since found precedents, or has since picked up the opinion of lawyers, I fear he will come within the case I have put.

I foresee, if ever this question happens to be debated, *you know where*, gentlemen will be divided; Some will be desirous to do their country justice and free us from all future danger of this kind; Others upon motives not quite so laudable, will strive to screen, and with others private friendship will prevail: But I would recommend to your friends, who really love their country, to consider the several circumstances concurring in your lordship which probably may not in your successor: Let them suppose a person were to fill your place, from whose manifest ignorance in the law, we may reasonably conclude, his only merit is an inveteracy and hatred to this country. I say how could your best friends excuse themselves, if in regard to your lordship they should suffer such a precedent to be handed down to such a man unobserved or uncensured?

Invenit etiam aemulos infaelix nequitia—Ambitious men have not always been deterred by the unhappy fate of their predecessors, *Quid si floreat vigeatque?* But what lengths will they run if injustice and corruption shall ride triumphant?

Had somebody received a reprimand upon his knees in a proper place, for treating a printer's jury like men convict of perjury, forcing them to find a special verdict, I dare to say he had not been quite so hardy as to have discharged the grand jury or treated them in the manner he did, because they had not an implicit faith in the court; nor had he dared not to receive a presentment made by the second grand jury against Wood's farthings upon pretence it was informal, which I mention because the worthy Drapier has mistaken the fact.

Some of your lordship's screens I hear advise you to shew great humility and contrition for what's past, as the only means to appease the just indignation all sorts of men have conceived against you.——Were I well secured you will not recommend this letter to the next grand jury to be presented, I could give you more *seasonable advice*, but happen as it may I will venture to give you a little.

Fawning and cajoling will have but little effect on those who have had the honour of your acquaintance these ten years past, for Caligula who used to hide his head if he heard the thunder, would piss upon the statues of the gods when he thought the danger over—A better expedient is this,——

Tell men the Drapier is a Tory and a Jacobite.—That he writ "The Conduct of the Allies."—That he writ not his letters with a design to keep out Wood's halfpence, but to bring in the Pretender; persuade them if you can, the dispute is no longer about the power of judges over juries, nor how much the liberty of the subject is endangered by dissolving them at pleasure, but that it is now become mere Whig and Tory, a dispute between His Majesty's friends and the Jacobites, and 'twere better to see a thousand grand juries discharged than the Tories carry a question though in the right.— *Haec vulnera pro libertate publica excepi, hunc oculum pro vobis impendi.* Try this cant, pin a cloth over your eyes, look very dismal, and cry, "I was turned out of employment, when the Drapier was rewarded with a Deanery," I say, my lord, if you can once bring matters thus to bear, I have not the least doubt you may escape without censure.

To your lordship's zeal and industry without doubt is owing, that the Papists and the Tories have not delivered this kingdom over to the Pretender, so Caesar conquered Pompey that *Legum auctor et eversor,* and 'twas but just the liberty and laws of Rome should afterwards depend upon his will and pleasure.——The Drapier in his letter to Lord Molesworth has made a fair offer, "Secure his country from Wood's coinage," then condemn all he has writ and said as false and scandalous, when your lordship does as much I must confess it will be somewhat difficult to discover the impostor.

Thus to keep my word with your lordship, I have much against my inclinations writ this, which shall be my last upon the ungrateful subject.—If I have leisure, and find a safe opportunity of giving it to the printer, my next shall explain what has long duped the true Whigs of this kingdom. I mean *honesty in the "worst of times."*

Though your lordship object to my last, that what I writ was taken out of Lord Coke, Lord Somers, Sir Will. Jones, or the writings of some other great men, yet I will venture to end this with the sentiments of Philip de Comines upon some thorough-going courtiers.

"If a sixpenny tax is to be raised, they cry by all means it ought to be double. If the prince is offended with any man, they are directly for hanging him. In other instances, they maintain the same character. Above all things they advise their king to make himself terrible, as they themselves are proud, fierce, and overbearing, in hopes to be dreaded by that means, as if authority and place were their inheritance."

    I am,
      My Lord,
        Your Lordship's most
          obedient and most
            humble servant.
              N.N.

Jan. 4, 1724-5.

APPENDIX V

THE PRESENTMENT OF THE GRAND JURY OF THE COUNTY OF THE CITY OF DUBLIN.[1]

Whereas several great quantities of base metal coined, commonly called *Wood's halfpence,* have been brought into the port of Dublin, and lodged in several houses of this city, with an intention to make them pass clandestinely, among His Majesty's subjects of this kingdom; notwithstanding the addresses of both houses of parliament and the privy-council, and the declarations of most of the corporations of this city against the said coin; And whereas His Majesty hath been graciously pleased to leave his loyal subjects of this kingdom at liberty to take or refuse the said halfpence.

[Footnote 1: Chief Justice Whitshed, after browbeating the Grand Jury that threw out the Bill against Harding for printing the fourth Drapier's letter, discharged it, and called another Grand Jury. The second Grand Jury not only repeated the verdict of the first, but issued the following expression of its opinion on the matter of Wood and his patent. [T.S.]]

We the Grand Jury of the county of the city of Dublin, this Michaelmas term, 1724, having entirely at heart His Majesty's interest and the welfare of our country, and being thoroughly sensible of the great discouragement which trade hath suffered by the apprehensions of the said coin, whereof we have already felt the dismal effects, and that the currency thereof will inevitably tend to the great diminution of His Majesty's revenue, and the ruin of us and our posterity: do present all such persons as have attempted, or shall endeavour by fraud or otherwise, to impose the said halfpence upon us, contrary to His Majesty's most gracious intentions, as enemies to His Majesty's government, and to the safety, peace and welfare of all His Majesty's subjects of this kingdom, whose affections have been so eminently distinguished by their zeal to his illustrious family, before his happy accession to the throne, and by their continued loyalty ever since.

As we do with all just gratitude acknowledge the services of all such patriots, as have been eminently zealous for the interest of His Majesty, and this country, in detecting the fraudulent impositions of the said Wood, and preventing the passing his base coin: So we do at the same time declare our abhorrence and detestation of all reflections on His Majesty, and his government, and that we are ready with our lives and fortunes to defend his most Sacred Majesty against the Pretender and all His Majesty's open and secret enemies both at home and abroad: Given under our hands at the Grand Jury Chamber this 28th, November, 1724.[2]

George	Forbes,	David	Tew,
William	Empson,	Thomas	How,
Nathaniel	Pearson,	John	Jones,
Joseph	Nuttall,	James	Brown,
William	Aston,	Charles	Lyndon,
Stearn	Tighe,	Jerom	Bredin,
Richard	Walker,	John	Sican,
Edmond	French,	Anthony	Brunton,
John	Vereilles,	Thomas	Gaven,
Philip	Pearson,	Daniel	Elwood,
Thomas	Robins,	John	Brunet.
Richard Dawson,			

[Footnote 2: On August 20th, 1724, the Grand Jury, and the other inhabitants of the Liberty of the Dean and Chapter of St. Patrick's waited on the Dean, and read him the following Declaration, desiring him to give orders for its publication:

"The Declaration of the Grand-Jury, and the rest of the inhabitants of the Liberty of the Dean and Chapter of St. Patrick's, Dublin.

"We, the Grand-Jury, and other inhabitants of the Liberty of the Dean and Chapter of St. Patrick's, Dublin, whose names are underwritten, do unanimously declare and determine, that we never will receive or pay any of the half-pence or farthings already coined, or that shall hereafter be coined, by one William Wood, being not obliged by law to receive the same; because we are thoroughly convinced by the Addresses of both Houses of Parliament, as well as by that of his Majesty's most honourable Privy-Council, and by the universal opinion of the whole kingdom, that the currency of the said half-pence and farthings would soon deprive us of all our gold and silver, and therefore be of the most destructive consequence to the trade and welfare of the nation." [T. S.]]

APPENDIX VI

PROCLAMATION AGAINST THE DRAPIER.

"*Oct. 27th,* 1724.

"A proclamation for discovering ye Author of ye Pamphlet intituled A letter to ye whole people of Ireland, by M.B. Drapier, author of the Letter to the Shop-keepers, etc.

£300 Reward

BY THE LORD-LIEUTENANT AND COUNCIL OF IRELAND.

A Proclamation.

"CONTENT:

"Whereas a wicked and malicious pamphlet, intituled A Letter to the whole people of Ireland, by M.B. Drapier, author of the Letter to the Shop-keepers, etc., printed by John Harding, in Molesworth's Court, in Fishamble Street, Dublin, in which are contained several seditious and scandalous paragraphs highly reflecting upon his Majesty and his Ministers, tending to alienate the affections of his good subjects of England and Ireland from each other, and to promote sedition among the people, hath been lately printed and published in this kingdom: We, the Lord-Lieutenant and Council do hereby publish and declare that, in order to discover the author of the said seditious pamphlet, we will give the necessary orders for the payment of three hundred pounds sterling, to such person or persons as shall within the specified six months from this date hereof, discover the author of the said pamphlet, so as he be apprehended and convicted thereby.

"Given at the council chamber in Dublin, this twenty-seventh day of October, one thousand seven hundred and twenty-four.

"(Signed) Midleton *Cancer*. Shannon; Donnerail; G. Fforbes; H. Meath;
Santry; Tyrawly; Fferrars; William Conolly; Ralph Gore; William Whitshed; B. Hale; Gust. Hume; Ben Parry; James Tynte; R. Tighe; T. Clutterbuck.

"God Save the King."

APPENDIX VII

It is very interesting and even curious to note, that the signatories to the public expression of their attitude towards Wood and his patent, as shown by the Proclamation, should have almost all of them signed another document, in their capacities of Privy Councillors, which addressed his Majesty *against* Wood and the patent. So far as I can learn, Monck Mason seems to have been the first historian to discover it; nor do I find the fact mentioned by any of Swift's later biographers.

"It was rumoured in Swift's time," says Monck Mason, "but not actually known to him" (see Drapier's Sixth Letter), "that the Irish Privy Council had addressed his Majesty against Mr. Wood's coin. Having inspected the papers of the Council office, I shall lay before the reader the particulars of this event, which were never promulgated, probably, because they had not the desired effect, the premier [Walpole] having determined, notwithstanding all opposition or advice, to persevere in his ill-judged project.

"On the 17th April, 1724, at a meeting of the Council, in which the Duke of Grafton himself presided, it was ordered, that it should be referred to a committee of the whole board, or of any seven or more, 'to consider what was proper to be done to allay and quiet the great fears of the people, occasioned by their apprehensions of William Wood's copper money becoming current among them,' On the 6th of May, the committee reported, that they had considered the matter referred to them, and were of opinion, that an address should be sent to his Majesty, of which they then presented a draught. It was again on the 19th, referred to a committee of the whole board to prepare a letter, which was accordingly done on the next day.—The report was as follows:

"'To the King's Most Excellent Majesty, the humble address of the Lords
Justices, and Privy-Council.

* * * * *

"'May it please your Majesty,

"'We, your Majesty's most dutiful and loyal subjects, the Lords Justices and Privy Council, most humbly beg leave, at this time, to give an instance of that duty, which, as upon all other occasions, so more especially upon such as are of the greatest moment and importance, we hold ourselves always bound to pay to your Majesty.

"'Your Majesty's great council, the High Court of Parliament, being now prorogued, we conceive ourselves bound, by the trust which your Majesty has been pleased to repose in us, and the oaths we have taken, with all humility to lay before your Majesty the present state of this your kingdom, with reference to a great evil that appears to threaten it, to which, if a speedy remedy be not applied, the unavoidable consequence, as we apprehend, will be, the ruin of multitudes of your Majesty's subjects, together with a great diminution of your revenue.

"'Though the fears of your Majesty's subjects of this kingdom, in relation to the coinage of copper half-pence and farthings, were, in a great measure, allayed by your Majesty's most gracious resolution to do every thing in your power for the satisfaction of your people, expressed in your Majesty's answer to the addresses of both Houses of Parliament; yet, the repeated intelligence from Great Britain, that William Wood has the assurance to persist in his endeavours to introduce his copper half-pence and farthings amongst us, has again alarmed your faithful subjects, to such a degree, as already to give a great check to our inland trade. If the letters patent granted to William Wood should, in all points, be exactly complied with, the loss to be sustained by taking his half-pence and farthings would be much greater than this poor kingdom is able to bear. But if he, or any other persons, should, for the value of gain, be tempted to coin and import even more than double the quantity he by his patent is allowed to do, your people here do not see how it is possible for your Majesty's chief governors of this your kingdom, to detect or hinder the cheat.

"'It is found by experience, that we have already a sufficient quantity of half-pence, to serve by way of exchange in the retailing trade, which is the only use of such sort of money, of which, therefore, we find ourselves to be in no want.

"'And since, by the letters patent granted to the same William Wood, no man is required or commanded to take the said half-pence or farthings, but the taking them is left at liberty to those who are willing so to do; we most humbly submit it to your royal wisdom and goodness, whether it may not be for your Majesty's service, and the great satisfaction and good of your subjects, and very much tend to the allaying and quieting of their fears, that your Majesty should cause your royal pleasure to be signified to the Commissioners, and other officers of your Majesty's revenue in this kingdom, that they neither receive those half-pence and farthings, nor give countenance or encouragement to the uttering or vending of them; or that some other speedy method may be taken to prevent their becoming current amongst us.'"

APPENDIX VIII

Searching among the pamphlets of the Halliday Collection at the Royal
Irish Academy, Dublin, I came across a tract of twelve pages, printed by
John Whaley of Dublin in 1723, with the following title:

"The Patentee's Computation of Ireland, in a Letter from the Author of the Whitehall Evening-Post concerning the making of Copper-Coin. As also the Case and Address of both Houses of Parliament together with His Majesty's Most Gracious Answer to the House of Lords Address."

The writer of this tract in defence of the patent maintained the following propositions:

(1) That the Kingdom of Ireland wants a Copper Coin.

(2) That the quantity of this coin will be no inconvenience to it.

(3) That it is better than ever the Kingdom had, and as good as (in all probability) they ever will or can have, and that the Patentee's profit is not extravagant, as commonly reported.

(4) That the Kingdom will lose nothing by this coin.

(5) That the public in Ireland will gain considerably by it, if they please.

(6) That the Kingdom will have £100,000 additional cash.

As he states his arguments, they are quite reasonable. On proposition three, if his figures are correct, he is especially convincing. He details the cost of manufacture thus:

                                    s. d.

Copper prepared for the coinage at his Majesty's
  Mint at the Tower of London, costs per pound
  weight 1 6

Coinage of one pound weight 3-1/2

Waste and charge of re-melting 1

Yearly payment to the Exchequer and Comptroller 1

Allowed to the purchaser for exchange, &c. 5

Total charge 2 4-1/2

"So that the patentee," he concludes, "makes a profit of only 1-1/2_d._ in the half crown or about 5%."

The tract, however, is more interesting for the reprint it gives of the twenty-eight articles stated by the people in objection to the patent and the coin. I give these articles in full:

IRELAND'S CASE HUMBLY PRESENTED TO THE HONOURABLE THE KNIGHTS, CITIZENS, AND BURGESSES IN PARLIAMENT ASSEMBLED

MOST HUMBLY SHEWETH,

Whereas your Honours finding the late Grant or Letters Patents obtained by Mr. William Wood, for making Three Hundred and Sixty Tun weight of copper half-pence for the Kingdom of Ireland, were to be manufactured in London &c. which money is now coining in Bristol, and that the said money was to weigh two shillings and sixpence in each pound weight, and that change was to be uttered or passed for all such as were pleased to take the same in this Kingdom.

That it's humbly conceived Your Honours on considering the following
Remarks, will find the permitting such change to pass, exceeding Injurious and Destructive to the Nation.

First. That the same will be a means to drain this Kingdom of all its Gold and Silver, and ten, fifteen, or twenty per cent abated, will most effectually do the same.

2d. That the making such money in England will give great room for counterfeiting that coin, as well in this Kingdom, as where it is made.

3d. That the Copper Mines of this Island which might be manufactured in the nation, is by management shipped off to England by some persons at, or about forty shillings per tun, by others at four pounds and six pounds per ton, which copper when smelted and refined is sold and sent back to this kingdom at two shillings and six pence per pound weight as aforesaid, which is two hundred and eighty pound sterl. per ton.

4th. That two shillings and sixpence per pound weight is making the said coin of very small value, the said coin ought not to weigh or exceed two shillings in each pound weight as the English Halfpence are.

5th. That all such money brought to this Nation manufactured, is to be entered at value, which value is in the Book of Rates, ten per cent duty and excise.

6th. That no security is given to this Nation to make such money in any one point, the same may be found defective in either, as to baseness of metal, workmanship or weight, or to give gold and silver for the same, when the subject was, or may be burthened therewith.

7th. That if such monies as aforesaid be permitted to pass in this nation, all persons that have gold or silver by them would not part therewith, but Brass money must be carried from House to House on Truckles, and in the county by carts and horses, with troops to guard them.

8th. That such money will raise the price of all commodities from abroad, probably to three or four hundred per cent.

9th. That linen, yarn, beef, butter, tallow, hides and all other commodities, will raise to that degree by being bought with half-pence, and workmen paid with brass money, that commissions from abroad will not reach them, therefore such goods must lie on hands and remain a drugg.

10th. That the excise of beer, ale, brandy, &c., and hearth-money will be paid in such coin, the same falling first into the hands of the poor and middling people.

11th. That if any trouble should happen in this nation, no army could be raised with such specie, but an enemy in all appearance would be admitted with their gold and silver, and which would drive the nation before them.

12th. The Courts of Law could not subsist, for all the suits there must be supported and maintained with ready money. Viz. Gold and Silver.

13th. That all the bankers must shut up their shops, no lodgment would be made except Halfpence, such as would lodge their money with them, would rather draw off and cause a run on them, fearing that their specie should be turned into the said brass and copper money.

14th. That such bills as are drawn to the country, viz. Cork, Limerick, Waterford, Kingsale, Deny, &c. The Exchange would be instead of a quarter per cent, twenty per cent and then paid in the said Brass specie, by means of its being brought on cars, carts, or waggons, and guards to attend the same.

15th. That all the rent in the Kingdom would be paid in half-pence; no man would give gold or silver, when he had brass money to pay the same.

16th. That no one can coin or manufacture such a quantity of halfpence or farthings for this Kingdom, out of the same, but either he must be ruined in the undertaking or the nation undone by his project, in taking such light money, by reason of ten per cent, duty, and probably this session be made twenty or thirty per cent duty, and the exchange nine or ten per cent. Ten per cent abated to circulate them. Ten per cent factorage, freight, gabberage, key-porters, &c. all which is forty per cent, charged on the same.

17th. That if the said Wood was obliged to make his light money not to exceed two shillings in the pound weight according to the English coin, he would give up such grant, for six pence in each pound weight is 25 per cent.

18th. That the said twenty-five per cent is 19,360_l._ sterl. on the said 360 ton of copper, loss to this nation, by being coined out of this Kingdom, besides 80,690_l._ of gold and silver sent out of the Kingdom for brass or copper money.

19th. That the copper mines of this Kingdom is believed to be the metal such copper is made of, which verifies the English saying, That Irish people are wild, that would part with 200,000_l._ sterl. of their gold and silver, for their own copper mines, which cost them not one pound sterl.

20th. That the said Wood's factors probably may send in fourteen years double the quantity of copper which is 720 ton, then this Kingdom loses 38,720_l._ sterl. and parts with 161,280_l._ sterl. of their gold and silver for almost nothing.

21st. If any great sum was to be raised by this nation, on any emergency extraordinary, to serve his Majesty and his Kingdom how would it be possible to do the same; copper half-pence would not stem the tide, no silver now to be had of value, then no gold to be seen.

22d. That England also must be a great loser by such money, by reason the said half-pence being from 20 to 40 grains lighter and less in value than their own, so that the same will not pass in that Kingdom scarce for farthings a piece, how then shall the vast quantities of goods be paid for, that are brought from that Kingdom here, a considerable part of this island must be broke and run away for want of silver and gold to pay them their debts.

23d. That if the said Wood should get all that money, what power would he regard, and what temptation would he be subject unto on that head, he is but a man, and one almost as little known or heard of, as any one subject the king has on this side the water.

24th. That the vast quantity of sea-coal brought from England here, would not be had for such money; the colliers will keep both their ships and coal at home, before they trade with such a nation, as had their treasure turned into brass money.

25th. That the Army must be paid with such money, none else to be had, they would lay down their arms and do no duty, what blood and confusion then would attend the same.

26th. That no people out of any other Kingdom would come into this country to dwell, either to plant or sow, where all their money must be brass.

27th. That the beautiful Quay and river of Dublin which is now lined and filled with ships in a most delightful order, would then be scattered to other harbours, as also the new Range, there and now a building, would be left, nothing but empty places all as doleful as the weeping river, deserted by her fleets and armies of merchants and traders.

28th. That the aforesaid scheme is to be viewed and considered by a King and Parliament, that will do themselves and their nation justice, who will with hearts and hands, stem that tide and current, as never to suffer so dutiful and loyal a people to be ruined and undone without relief.

APPENDIX IX

DESCRIPTIONS OF THE VARIOUS SPECIMENS OF WOOD'S COINS

The following descriptions of the various varieties of Wood's coins, taken from a note in Monck Mason's "History of St. Patrick's Cathedral" (ed. 1819, pp. xcvi-xcvii), may be interesting to the student. The two varieties of the coins given as illustrations in this volume are reproduced from specimens in the British Museum.

Monck Mason obtains his information from Simon's "Essay on Irish Coins," Dublin, 1749, 4to; Snelling's Supplement to Simon issued in 1767; and the edition of Simon's work reprinted in 1810.

With the exception of No. II. of this list all of Wood's coins had, on one side, "the king's head laureat, looking to the left, with this inscription, GEORGIUS, DEI GRATIA, REX. On the reverse is the figure of Ireland, represented by a woman sitting, beside her, a harp: the differences consist chiefly, in variations in the attitude of the figure, and in the date of the coin."

No. I. 1722.—Hibernia, with both her hands on the harp, which is placed on her right side; her figure is full front, but she looks towards the right; round her this inscription, HIBERNIA, 1722. (Simon, plate 7, Numb. 160)

No. II. 1722.—Hibernia is seated as in the last, but has her head turned to the left, on which side there is a rock; round her is inscribed, HIBERNIA; in the exergue, 1722; on the obverse the usual head, the inscription, GEORGIUS D.G. REX. (Snelling, plate 2, Numb. 24.)

No. III. 1722.—Hibernia, in profile, looking to the left, holding, in her right hand, a palm branch, resting her left on a harp; round it, HIBERNIA, 1722. (Simon, plate 7, Numb. 161.)

No. IV. 1723.—Hibernia, as in the last; round her, HIBERNIA, 1723. (Simon, plate 8, Numb. 169.)

It was some of this coin that was submitted to Sir Isaac Newton for assay.

No. V. 1724.—Hibernia, as in the last two, differing only in the date. (Mentioned by Simon, but no engraving given.)

No, VI. 1724.—Hibernia, seated as in the three preceding; round her,
HIBERNIA: in the exergue, 1724. (Snelling, plate 2, Numb. 26.)

Mason notes of this specimen: "Mr. Snelling does not specify, particularly, in what respect this coin differs from those which precede; his words are, 'different from any other, and very good work, especially the halfpenny, which is the finest and broadest piece of his money I ever saw, and belongs to Mr. Bartlet.' They do not, however, appear to have attained to circulation in Ireland. A few might, perhaps, have been struck off by the patentee, to distribute among his own, and the minister's friends."

No. VII.—Mr. Snelling mentions, "another halfpenny, which has Hibernia pointing up with one hand to a sun in the top of the piece"; but of this he has not given any engraving.

The End

Printed in Great Britain
by Amazon